Postcolonial Perspectives on the Cultures of Latin America and Lusophone Africa

Postcolonial Perspectives on the Cultures of Latin America and Lusophone Africa

Edited with an Introduction by Robin Fiddian

LIVERPOOL UNIVERSITY PRESS

First published 2000 by
LIVERPOOL UNIVERSITY PRESS
Liverpool L69 7ZU

©2000 Liverpool University Press

The right of Robin Fiddian
to be identified as the editor of this work
has been asserted by him in accordance with
the Copyright, Design and Patents Act, 1988

All rights reserved.
No part of this book may be reproduced,
stored in a retrieval system, or transmitted,
in any form or by any means,
electronic, mechanical, photocopying, recording, or otherwise,
without the prior written permission of the publishers.

British Library Cataloguing-in-Publication Data
A British Library CIP Record is available

ISBN 0-85323-566-X (hardback)
0-85323-576-7 (paperback)
Typeset in Minion
by BBR, Sheffield
Printed by Bell & Bain, Glasgow

Contents

Preface   vii

Introduction   1
Locating the Object, Mapping the Field: the Place of
the Cultures of Latin America and Lusophone Africa in
Postcolonial Studies   *Robin Fiddian*

Chapter One   27
On Metropolitan Readings of Latin American Cultures:
Ethical Questions of Postcolonial Critical Practice
Mark I. Millington

Chapter Two   51
Ig/noble Barbarians: Revisiting Latin American Modernisms
Else Vieira

Chapter Three   79
José Carlos Mariátegui: Culture and the Nation
Patricia D'Allemand

Chapter Four   103
Doing Time in Peru: the Poetics of Multitemporality as
Method for Cultural History   *William Rowe*

Chapter Five   119
America, Americanism and the Third World in the Work of
Leopoldo Zea   *Robin Fiddian*

Chapter Six 141
Fernando Ortiz's Transculturation: the Postcolonial
Intellectual and the Politics of Cultural Representation
Catherine Davies

Chapter Seven 169
Caribbean Masks: Frantz Fanon and Alejo Carpentier
Stephen Henighan

Chapter Eight 191
Colonial Crosswords: (In)voicing the Gap in Mia Couto
Maria Manuel Lisboa

Index 213

Preface

The eight essays collected in this volume are conceived as a set of interventions in a rapidly expanding and often contentious field of debate. The diverse objects of their attention represent the cultures of the former colonial territories that belonged to the historic empires of Spain and Portugal in Latin America and parts of Africa. The uniform designation of those areas as colonies would be uncontroversial, were it not for a polemical study of 1992/95 in which Jorge Klor de Alva denied the proposition that '(Latin) American experience' (sic) stretching over more than three centuries after Columbus's landfall in 1492 could be usefully described in terms of colonialism. Contesting that view, the essays that make up this volume assume that considerations to do with colonialism and colonialist discourse are indeed germane to Latin America and Portuguese-speaking Africa. Furthermore, they unite in considering the cultures of Latin America and Lusophone Africa through a set of critical paradigms, issues and perspectives which began to develop around the mid-1980s, largely outside the parameters of Latin American and Luso-Brazilian studies.

The apparent marginalization of these specialisms within the relatively new subject of postcolonial studies has often been noted and could easily be backed up by a quantitative survey of the few items that have made their way into landmark publications such as the readers compiled by Ashcroft, Griffith and Tiffin (1989 and 1995) and by Patrick Williams and Laura Chrisman (1993). Yet, from a number of viewpoints, that marginalization, attributable as it may be to the vagaries and partialities of academic taste, is unjustified and in need of interrogation. By the time those readers were being planned, Peter Hulme (in 1985 and 1986), Jean Franco (in 1988), and Mary Louise Pratt (in 1992) had all published major work on colonial discourse in the Americas which could have prevented some of the more glaring omissions and generalizations that blighted Edward Said's references to Latin America in *Culture and Imperialism* (1993). By the mid-1990s, studies by Hugo Achugar, Peter Hulme, Walter Mignolo, Nelly Richard and Roberto Schwarz showed both a commanding range of knowledge and a high degree of critical acumen concerning the relevance of postcolonial theory to Latin American cultures.

Simultaneously, the postcolonial literature of Lusophone Africa was already well established as a legitimate field of critical inquiry: an important collection of essays edited by Patrick Chabal, with a substantial introduction by him, located the postcolonial literatures of Angola, Mozambique and other nations in a variety of historical and geographical contexts ranging from the immediate—and already dismembered—environment of Lusophone Africa, to the broader continental setting of recently decolonized Anglophone and Francophone African nations, as well as to the wider global setting of the Caribbean and Latin America, including, of course, Brazil, which had undergone a relatively untraumatic separation from metropolitan Portuguese authority early in the previous century. While much less theoretical in its orientation than the work of Pratt, Mignolo and others mentioned above, the Chabal volume established serviceable coordinates for comparative considerations of decolonization, Negritude, the Black Atlantic and other postcolonial themes.

If this was the state of affairs with regard to scholarship, the recognized canon of postcolonial authors and foundational texts already included, alongside Césaire, Fanon, Sédar Senghor and Glissant *et al.*, essays by Roberto Fernández Retamar and Amílcar Cabral. Work by Césaire and Fanon had been circulating for some time in Spanish America, as well as in the Francophone Caribbean; the writings of Cabral were no less a part of the postcolonial canon, replete with cross-references to Sédar Senghor and others.

This situation was largely a consequence of the successive waves of decolonization affecting Africa, in particular, in the wake of the Second World War. Lusophone Africa in the 1960s and 1970s provided examples of colonial struggle which had immediate significance for contemporary intellectuals in Latin America, who were able to view the issues and processes of Third World decolonization through a lens fashioned in the crucible of the Cuban Revolution.

The convening of a symposium in Oxford, England on 30 May 1998 on the subject of 'Postcolonial Perspectives on the Cultures of Latin America and Lusophone Africa' afforded an opportunity for further exploration of a field that had therefore already been mapped in some detail. The programme of the symposium included papers on the foundational thinkers, José Carlos Mariátegui, César Vallejo and Leopoldo Zea—intellectuals whose interest in topics such as the decolonization of the mind, *mestizaje*, *indigenismo* and nation-building marks them out as landmark figures in our field. That complementary canon of Hispanophone writers was subsequently augmented by Fernando Ortiz in a paper commissioned expressly for this volume. Other papers given at the Oxford symposium concentrated on literary topics connected with Alejo Carpentier, Brazilian modernism, and the writings of the Mozambican, Mia Couto. That second category of contributions has also been expanded in the process of consolidating the present volume.

The Editor wishes to acknowledge the invaluable assistance of Robert Young and Claudia Pazos Alonso, both of Wadham College, Oxford, who helped organize the symposium of 30 May 1998. The Fellows' Secretary, Margaret Matthews, and various other members of Wadham College also assisted with the day's events. Financial support was forthcoming from the Interfaculty Committee for Latin American Studies, University of Oxford; the Modern Languages Faculty and the Spanish Fund subsidized the academic programme of the symposium. The Editor wishes to thank all those who participated on the day and who subsequently cooperated in the joint effort to produce a set of proceedings of the symposium for eventual publication. A final word of thanks goes to Mr John

Wainwright of the Taylor Institution Library, Oxford University, for his unfailing support of the research efforts of hispanists and Latin Americanists throughout the University.

INTRODUCTION

Locating the Object, Mapping the Field: the Place of the Cultures of Latin America and Lusophone Africa in Postcolonial Studies

Robin Fiddian
Wadham College, Oxford

The Americas

The place of America in the field of postcolonial studies is a matter of keen debate, the principal terms of which were rehearsed in three interrelated articles from the early and mid-1990s. The first of these was a polemical essay by anthropologist J. Jorge Klor de Alva, which was published originally in 1992 in *Colonial Latin American Review* and reappeared in a revised and expanded version in another publication three years later.[1] Confronting an increase in the number of applications of postcolonial theory to '(Latin) American experience' (sic), Klor de Alva asked rhetorically, 'is an error being committed when scholars apply tools and categories of analysis developed in the twentieth century for understanding British colonialism, especially in India and Africa, to make sense of the experiences of sixteenth to eighteenth century Latin America?' (264), and contended that '(Latin) American experience has been "colonized" after the fact' (241). Essentially, Klor de Alva's thesis was that the American experience of colonialism differed so radically from that of colonized peoples in territories such as India, Indonesia, South Africa and Algeria that neither the category of 'colonialism' nor those of 'decolonization' and 'postcolonialism' could be made to serve a 'useful' purpose in the interpretation of 'the complex political and cultural processes that engendered postcontact and postindependence American societies' (248).

Written clearly as a provocation, Klor de Alva's essay was not without quirkiness or partiality. For one thing, it rested on a clever preemptive strategy which entailed the prior calling into question of the concept of colonialism, or, at least, of a certain way of understanding colonialism, in order to disqualify the concepts of decolonization and postcolonialism that followed from it. Yet, in the process, Klor de Alva proposed a definition of postcoloniality as 'a form of contestatory/oppositional consciousness, emerging from either preexisting imperial, colonial, or ongoing subaltern conditions, which fosters processes aimed at revising the norms and practices of antecedent or still vital forms of domination' (245), that is virtually identical to standard characterizations of the postcolonial. An example can be found in Ania Loomba, who described a repertoire of interests including 'opposition to the legacy of colonial domination', forms of oppression based on hierarchical notions of race, class and gender, the situation of the subaltern in the colonial order, and other elements.[2] Furthermore, not only does Klor de Alva's model accord with the life-experience of peoples in areas such as Mexico and Peru, first, as objects of European colonial discourse and, later, as sites of contestation of colonial authority, but it also resonates with echoes of a continental tradition of Latin American anti-colonialist thought that stretches from at least as far back as Martí and Rodó, through Mariátegui and de Campos, to Galeano and Darcy Ribeiro,[3] offering sometimes a prefiguration, sometimes a mirror image, of the postcolonial repertoire and canon.

A second critical observation (and one that follows on from

the above) centres on the idiosyncrasies of the mental map of Latin America that Klor de Alva brings to the debate. The conspicuous bracket in '(Latin) America' is open to many interpretations. Could it be ironic, on not just one, but two counts? A reminder, first, that the label 'Latin America', though accepted as a description of the subcontinent by a wide range of native thinkers,[4] remains contaminated at root by its origins in mid-nineteenth-century Napoleonic imperial discourse? And, second, a deliberately disingenuous use of a term whose referential pretensions are no longer assumed to be valid, in an age that is sceptical of totalizing *récits*? Less speculatively, and as Walter Mignolo has observed,[5] the principal (and perhaps only) referent of Klor de Alva's bracketed '(Latin) America' is the society of Latinos living in the southern states of contemporary USA. Whatever the intentions behind Klor de Alva's visually-arresting phrase, it clearly excludes the Hispanic and Francophone Caribbean, whether insular or coastal, and as a result is both incomplete and curiously unrepresentative of the geopolitical and cultural entity that is conventionally denoted by the term 'Latin America'.

Arguably, the provocative intent of Klor de Alva's essay constitutes its greatest value, in that it throws into relief essential questions concerning possible relationships between postcolonial studies and the cultures of Latin America and—I would add here—Lusophone Africa. For the purposes of this introduction, Klor de Alva's essay can be seen to articulate both the temporal and geopolitical dimension, and the critical dimension of postcoloniality, as that condition has been defined in leading primers of postcolonial studies. These are items which formed the core of the original agenda of postcolonial theory and have fed into the continuing debate about metropolitan theory and its applicability to cultures that are deemed peripheral, ever since. Both dimensions are discussed by Peter Hulme and Walter Mignolo, in separate essays which take up the challenge posed by Klor de Alva's now widely-reprinted essay.

In 'Including America' (1995), Hulme observes that 'America—in a continental sense—barely features on the map [of postcolonial theory] at all', and puts forward a number of arguments for redrawing the boundaries that circumscribe the field.[6] Pointing out that 'One of the positive effects of the postcolonial debate has been to re-awaken interest in the different forms of colonialism and imperialism', Hulme suggests that 'it would seem a strange definition of colonialism that would not include in its purview the European settlements in America that began in 1492' (118). Hulme is fully aware of the dangers involved in the construction of monoliths. He wisely admits that 'Spanish colonialism in America was undoubtedly different from British colonialism in India', but, in an open allusion to Klor de Alva's article, reasons that 'to deny that one was colonialism at all takes away the ground that would facilitate understanding of the particular differences' (119).

One powerful justification for the inclusion of America is the rich tradition of postcolonial theory associated with the Caribbean, as exemplified by Frantz Fanon, C. L. R. James, Edouard Glissant, George Lamming and Roberto Fernández Retamar (119). In addition, Hulme imagines the consequences of 'lengthening the historical perspective through and against which the postcolonial field is constructed in order that it include the colonial experience of the whole of the American continent', and suggests that agreement on 1492 as a starting point for a revised historiography of colonial relations around the globe '[would] provide the United States with a nineteenth- and twentieth-century imperial and colonial history that helps in the understanding of its current stance' (120). In line with this hypothesis, the United States could be credited quite legitimately with a 'postcolonial' past from the time of its independence from the British crown, and be seen to enter a new phase of its history at a point (Hulme suggests 1898) when its conduct in and beyond the Caribbean demonstrates a determination to exercise hemispheric imperial power.

If Hulme's definition of 'postcolonial' as referring to 'a *process* of disengagement from the whole colonial syndrome' (120) rings true for mid-eighteenth-century Anglo-America, it arguably applies equally well to the *criollo* and *mestizo* societies of late eighteenth-century Spanish America. Also, and inevitably, it applies to Cuba post-1959, bringing that island into the same (political) frame as other territories that were experiencing decolonization at that moment in parts of Africa and Asia. Hulme does not draw this conclusion in his essay, but it is an inference that is borne out by several contemporary Latin American thinkers (Roberto Fernández Retamar is a case in point, Leopoldo Zea, another) who pictured their societies as participants in an ongoing process of decolonization a full century-and-a-half after formal severance of links with the Spanish empire (I discuss this point at some length below, in the chapter devoted to Leopoldo Zea).

The elastication of the temporal dimension(s) of postcoloniality which Hulme proposes helps to promote his argument in favour of the inclusion of America in the postcolonial field, and affects consequential descriptions of relations between one Latin American nation and another and between a given nation in Latin America (say, Cuba) and another situated at a considerable geographical distance from it (say, Angola); simultaneously, a loosening of temporal constraints allows the positing of a common postcolonial identity on the basis of a shared political experience such as decolonization. The temporal dimension is, however, only one tool or criterion that might be used to refine existing models of postcoloniality. Hulme stresses a second dimension of the 'post' in 'postcolonial', which he, along with others such as Loomba, refers to as the 'critical dimension' of that term. For, in addition to temporal criteria, a no less defining element of postcolonialism is an attitude of 'contestation of colonial domination and the legacies of colonialism',[7] illustrated in the work of Fanon, Sédar Senghor, Cabral, and all other major figures of the postcolonial pantheon. Citing *Peau noir, masques blancs* as a quintessential postcolonial text, Hulme emphasizes 'the efforts [of Fanon's text] to think through and beyond the colonial situation' ('Including America', 121), and opens up a vista on Latin American writing since Bolívar, which would necessarily fit the frame of the identikit picture of a postcolonial literature sketched with reference to Fanon in 'Including America'.

Hulme completes his essay with some very brief remarks on the application of postcolonial studies to a broadly defined American culture. Interestingly, he envisages a comparison of Domingo Sarmiento and C. L. R. James as complementary types of the 'postcolonial intellectual' marked by certain life-experiences and committed 'to creating a culture for a newly independent country'. He then imagines a broader field of comparative study, which coincidentally adumbrates some of the contents of this volume:

> As time passes, and we keep re-reading Fanon, perhaps the similarities between American countries in their postcolonial phases and African and Asian countries in theirs will come to seem at least as important as their differences. (122)

By way of conclusion, Hulme stresses the importance of thinking sameness and difference in a reconfigured postcolonial studies which would include America once and for all, alongside the other world territories that were colonized by Europe after 1492 and into the middle of the twentieth century.

A strategy of simultaneously thinking sameness and difference is also pursued by Walter Mignolo in an essay entitled 'La razón postcolonial: herencias coloniales y teorías postcoloniales' (1997).[8] Fashioned in part as a response to the Klor de Alva article, Mignolo's essay also follows on directly from his earlier 'Occidentalización, imperialismo, globalización: herencias coloniales y teorías postcoloniales' (1995).[9] There, Mignolo had divided the history of Western territorial expansion into three phases: 1) 'Westernization', beginning in 1492 and continuing into the early decades of the nineteenth century; 2) 'imperialism', which reached its height in the second half of the nineteenth century; and 3) 'globalization', a process that gets under way at the end of the Second World War and is characterized by the transnationalization of capital and the virtually unrestricted growth of communications technology. At the centre of his earlier analysis, Mignolo had viewed the work of Latin American intellectuals such as Enrique Dussel and Rodolfo Kusch as postcolonial discourses expressing resistance to Western modernity from a site of enunciation located on the periphery; according to Mignolo, it is this challenge to the discursive authority of the centre that distinguishes postcolonialism from postmodernism—the latter understood as critiquing Western modernity from within its 'hermeneutic space' (Mignolo 1995, 39).

'La razón postcolonial' elaborates on those ideas, drawing a conceptual map of postcolonialism in which Latin America occupies a clearly defined space within widely-drawn global parameters. Two sets of distinctions help to clarify relations between different geographies and time-frames and, consequentially, between Latin American postcolonial thinkers such as Mariátegui, Dussel and Zea, and the exponents of late twentieth-century postcolonial theory including Gayatri Spivak and Homi Bhabha. The first set of distinctions is that made by Anne McClintock and others, between breakaway settler colonies (e.g. the United States, South Africa and Australia) and colonies where deep settlement occurred (e.g. Algeria, Kenya and Vietnam); this distinction is maintained by Mignolo, who refers to the breakaway settler colonies as 'type a', and uses the labels 'type b' and 'type c' to draw a further distinction between 'colonias de profundo asentamiento antes de 1945' and 'colonias de profundo asentamiento después de 1945' (Mignolo 1997, 54). A second set of distinctions is that between postcolonial situations (or conditions) and postcolonial 'ratio', which itself comprises 1) *discourses* of postcoloniality, and 2) *theories* of postcoloniality. With the aid of this scheme, Mignolo is able to acknowledge differences in the historical experience of the three types of colony, especially in relation to decolonization (which was accompanied by greater violence in type c than in type a) and in regard to the punctual chronologies of the transition from colonial to postcolonial status (ranging from the middle of the eighteenth century in the case of the separation of Anglo-America from the British Crown, to a number of points in time in the quarter-century following the end of the Second World War, in Africa and Asia). Just as importantly, Mignolo is able to distinguish between different types of colonial legacy, which allows him to assert a common identity between the intellectual responses arising in types b and c (which he regards as properly *postcolonial*), as against those of type a (which he considers to be more strictly *postmodern*).

It is ultimately the nature of a community's response to the legacies of colonialism that determines the make-up of the postcolonial *ratio* announced in the title of Mignolo's essay. This concept is defined early on as 'un grupo diverso de prácticas teóricas que se manifiestan a raíz de las herencias coloniales, en la intersección de la historia moderna europea y las historias contramodernas coloniales' (52). On the subject of the temporal coordinates of postcolonial reason, Mignolo is quite explicit: 'La razón postcolonial precede y coexiste con las situaciones/condiciones postcoloniales'—a point he reinforces by restricting his focus to 'la configuración sociohistórica manifestada a través de los pueblos que ganan independencia o emancipación de los poderes imperiales y coloniales de Occidente (tales como Europa hasta 1945, o los Estados Unidos desde el comienzo del siglo XX)' (53).

Apart from some interesting remarks about the anti-metropolitan bias of North American philosophical pragmatism, the most pertinent aspect of Mignolo's analysis is the compatibility of his model of postcolonial reason with the political and cultural history of Latin America in the twentieth century. In a working generalization about 'las colonias de profundo asentamiento ... (tipo b)' after the Russian Revolution, Mignolo attests to the impact of that schismatic event in parts of Latin America and detects in the work of Mariátegui, and subsequently in that of Dussel, Zea and Edmundo O'Gorman, a set of concerns which he claims are the prototypes of what will eventually come to be known as 'postcolonial discourse'. The author usefully invokes the distinction, flagged previously, between *discourses* and *theories*, and separates the work of Said, Spivak and other thinkers from earlier work produced in actual postcolonial situations by the likes of Césaire and Fanon. A crucial advantage of Mignolo's meta-theoretical observation is that it allows for significant interplay between the 'discursos postcoloniales' of one movement and moment (for example, the anti-colonialist critique expressed by Zea in essays leading up to *América en la historia* of 1958) and more highly developed theoretical constructs which, while belonging chronologically to a later stage of the postcolonial process, are no less deeply implicated in the conditions and situations found in former colonies of both types b and c (57).

Crucially, criteria based on chronology are put further into abeyance in the remainder of Mignolo's essay, where he echoes the views of a range of postcolonial theorists and commentators who query 'a relatively binaristic, fixed and stable mapping of power relations between "colonizer/colonized" and "center/periphery"' and advocate instead a movement towards a more fluid and mobile picture of postcolonial situations.[10] According to this line of thinking, postcolonialism would replace the anti-colonial critique of Fanon, Cabral and others with a paradigm that favours ambivalence, slippage and transcultural interaction, all together representing a concerted assault on the binary logic of imperialism. The difficulties involved in such an exercise are addressed below in a number of the essays that make up this volume. For the time being, we may conclude by acknowledging the many-sided contribution made by Mignolo to a critical discourse that is concerned with explaining the place of Latin America in the complementary fields of postcoloniality and postcolonial studies.

Lusophone Africa

The place of Lusophone Africa in the postcolonial field is a circumstance which requires no authentication. From Cabo Verde off the north-west coast to Angola in the south and Mozambique on the eastern seaboard, a handful of African territories were united by a common history of colonization by the Portuguese and liberation from the Estado Novo regime in the 1970s. Lusophone Africa entered the mainstream of postcolonial discourse through individuals such as Amílcar Cabral and Agostinho Neto, and was sutured into a wider African context through the work of Léopold Sédar Senghor and others.[11] In the secondary literature devoted to colonialism and decolonization in the Luso-African territories, excerpts from speeches by Cabral are included in Part One of the Williams and Chrisman reader under the heading 'Theorising Colonized Cultures and Anti-Colonial Resistance' (*Colonial Discourse and Post-colonial Theory*, 53–65), and enjoy a justifiably prominent place in the postcolonial canon.[12]

These connections notwithstanding, it is wise to acknowledge the diversity of experience of colonialism in the five nation-states of Angola, Mozambique, Guinea-Bissau, Cabo Verde and Sao Tomé e Príncipe. Patrick Chabal rightly insists on this point in his informative Introduction to *The Post-Colonial Literature of Lusophone Africa*.[13] Amongst other things, Chabal emphasizes the distinctiveness of the islands of Cabo Verde and Sao Tomé e Príncipe in respect of the history of their settlement (the islands were settled by the Portuguese in the fifteenth century), the ethnic and racial mixture of their populations, the prevalence of a sense of identity based on a common Creole language, and the survival of an oral culture 'combining age-old African traditions and beliefs with customs and intellectual ways of the Europeans with whom they came into contact' (Chabal, 13–14). That picture contrasts sharply with the colonial experience in Mozambique and Angola, which also differ markedly one from the other. As described by Chabal, 'Angola and Mozambique were vast continental territories of diverse African ethnic groups with a history of uneven Portuguese presence and poor colonial integration' (14). Mozambique in particular was poorly integrated by the Portuguese; as a result of the leasing of the northern half of the country to largely foreign-owned concession companies, Mozambique 'evolved as a lopsided and divided colony' quite unlike the two islands. Its racial mix 'was also a more complex patchwork than in most other African colonies', and white Portuguese settlers exercised an unusual degree of control over most of the country's agricultural and industrial economy (15).

Sharing certain of the above features with its sister colony,

Angola differed from Mozambique in three fundamental ways. 'First, it was better integrated as a territory. Secondly, the nationalist movements split along a largely ethnic tripartite division. And thirdly, there was in the capital Luanda and some other cities a Creole community with a long history and a distinct culture' (17). Chabal elaborates on the ethnic, cultural and political specificities of the capital, Luanda, which was a city with a history of multiracial culture, strongly African in character, and at one time 'dominated by a handful of rich and powerful Creole *mestiço* families' (18–19); attesting to the arrival of a large number of Portuguese immigrants in the twentieth century, Chabal observes that Luanda retained its multiracial character 'through the colonial period and into independence' (19).

A similar picture of difference coexisting with sameness emerges when the Portuguese territories are viewed from a perspective situating them within the wider context of the African continent. On the one hand, their history as 'colonial creatures … in which the establishment of the state preceded the construction of the nation' (5) is typical of the continent as a whole, as is the negotiation between indigenous forms of cultural expression and the European traditions introduced through colonialism; questions of cultural imperialism (including the influence of the metropolitan literary canon and the role played by a dominant European language in establishing a 'mental colonialism' parallel to operations in the economic and political spheres) are as relevant to twentieth-century Nigeria as they are to Angola. On the other hand, the historic ties between the modern nation-state of Angola and Portugal stretch much farther back than those between Great Britain and its colonies in Africa, and illustrate a fundamental difference between the African colonialist projects of these two European powers. Furthermore, education and literacy are fields in which the Portuguese colonies lagged behind their African neighbours, hindered by the Salazar regime which intervened in the cultural as well as the political life of the colonies: under the Estado Novo, measures of censorship were applied which had no contemporary equivalent in the Anglophone territories of colonial Africa.

Beyond the geographical bounds of Africa, the Lusophone territories converged in meaningful ways with former colonies in other parts of the world, most notably in the Caribbean and Latin America. With regard to the Caribbean, the historic traffic of African slaves who began to be transported, along with their traditional cultural practices, to islands such as Hispaniola early in the sixteenth century, was reversed four hundred years later in the shipping of a symbolic cargo originating in the literary-cum-political movement of Négritude in Haiti and Martinique, and, from the mid-1960s, of a real cargo comprising ideological dogma, soldiers, and weapons sent by the Cuban Revolution to assist in the decolonization of Angola. The ever-alert Chabal adverts to similarities in cultural make-up between the states of Cabo Verde and Sao Tomé e Príncipe, on the one hand, and Caribbean islands, on the other, where Creole cultures grew out of the encounter between African and European elements. He also emphasizes the importance of black literature from the Caribbean (including verse by Nicolás Guillén) for the evolution of Portuguese-African writing around the mid-point of the twentieth century, while accepting that some writers were influenced less strongly than others.

Connections with Latin America situate Lusophone Africa within an even wider network of political and cultural relations. Chabal describes a general similarity in the evolution of African and Latin American states from colonial dependence to postcolonial nationhood. He remarks especially on the assimilation and appropriation of European languages throughout the Third World, where English, French, Portuguese and other languages of empire '[were] reshaped to serve [the] linguistic and cultural needs' of local cultures (6). He also attests to a traffic of political and intellectual ideas which reached Lusophone Africa, along a variety of routes, from Brazil, providing timely examples and stimuli to an ongoing process of political and mental emancipation.

Without denying the existence of historical, political, racial, institutional, cultural, geographical and other factors which set Lusophone Africa off from the rest of the formerly-colonized world, the place of its component nation-states in the postcolonial field should require no further elaboration. Thanks to the efforts of Chabal and others,[14] the postcolonial cultures of Lusophone Africa can be seen both in their respective specificities and within a framework which permits legitimate comparisons to be made with other cultures across a given period of time. The availability of a theoretical apparatus such as that of postcolonial studies is crucial to the examination of those cultures in terms of the commonality of interests that they share with other postcolonial societies.

Defining the agenda

Overall, the studies of Chabal, Mignolo, Hulme and Klor de Alva collectively spell out the major items on the agenda of any project which seeks to apply postcolonial perspectives to the literary cultures of Latin America and Lusophone Africa. Arranged in the most schematic form, that agenda comprises the following issues and concerns:

- The role of the postcolonial intellectual (whether he be Fernando Ortiz, Aimé Césaire, Amílcar Cabral or Edward Said);
- Nationalism, the struggle for emancipation, and the forging of a cultural identity whose primary radius is local and national yet may expand to encompass an entire region and beyond (viz the supranational formations imagined in Pan-Africanism and Pan-Americanism);
- Strategies for achieving 'mental emancipation' (or a decolonizing of the mind);
- Social class, political agency and economic power. Manifesting itself differently in different areas of Latin America (including the Caribbean) and Lusophone Africa, this heading is concerned especially with the roles played by *criollo* and, in some cases,

mestizo elites, in both colonial and postcolonial societies. Considerations of gender are also relevant here;[15]

- Concerns of race, colour and ethnicity. In the twin cases of Latin America and Lusophone Africa, this tangled complex of ideas involves the categories of hybridity and *mestizaje*,[16] which differ in crucial respects from the concept of *miscegenation* as used in connection with the British Empire, and *métissage* as used in connection with the French presence in Canada.[17] The concerns of race, colour and ethnicity alluded to under this heading crystallize in ideologies such as *indigenismo* (which, as Elizabeth Mudimbe-Boyi has observed, travelled from Spanish America into the Francophone setting of Haiti in the 1930s),[18] the theory of a 'raza cósmica' promoted by José Vasconcelos in mid-1920s Mexico, *Negritude* (identified particularly with Aimé Césaire of Martinique but also espoused by Sédar Senghor of Senegal and transmitted to parts of Lusophone Africa), and 'the dialectic of Caliban', advocated as a strategy of anti-colonial resistance most famously by Césaire but also explored by Roberto Fernández Retamar in 1973 (after Rodó, Arciniegas and others);[19]

- The clash between different cultural formations and traditions, resulting in new formations which are the products of 'syncretism' or, alternatively, 'creolization'.[20] 'Mestizaje cultural', 'transculturación' and 'supersyncretism'[21] are complementary terms in a varied and nuanced vocabulary to do with cultural interaction. Beyond these lexical differences, the essential concern is with *processes*, not *states*, of cultural transformation. Theorists such as Fernando Ortiz, Haroldo de Campos and Roberto Fernández Retamar highlight the potentially subversive implications of forms of translation, cannibalization, and other adaptations of Western cultural models in colonial and postcolonial settings;

- Divergent accounts of temporality which call into question dominant paradigms of historical progress and modernity.

Alejo Carpentier, Carlos Fuentes and Eduardo Galeano all criticize models of history and modernity which preserve the 'backward' and 'peripheral' status of colonized people (including, for example, Amerindian communities, which are perceived—for the purposes of this argument—as victims of neglect and continuing internal colonization);[22] and

- The competition between ideologies ranging from Marxism and 'Third Worldism' to Liberation Theory and a revised humanism. Tensions between nationalism, regionalism and universalism.

While less extensive than the repertoire of postcolonial studies, this agenda approximates to it quite substantially and permits three conclusions to be drawn here. The first conclusion is that Latin American countries such as Peru and Mexico in the early twentieth century, and Cuba post-1898 and, again, post-1959, display the prototypical conditions and issues of postcolonial experience which will come to preoccupy intellectuals such as Césaire, Fanon and Cabral at later stages in the history of colonial relations in the world at large. The second conclusion is that the cultures of Latin America (including those of Cuba, Haiti and other Caribbean locations), along with the cultures of Lusophone Africa in the half-century or so leading up to and following decolonization, share common ground with postcolonial cultures elsewhere and have a significant contribution to make to postcolonial studies; from a reverse perspective, those cultures stand to benefit, too, from the theoretical insights derived from the work of Edward Said, Homi Bhabha and others, so long as those insights are combined with a sensitivity to local conditions, imperatives and needs.

The third conclusion has to do, not so much with matters of substance, as with the procedural constraints that weigh on the present volume. It should be obvious that the teeming agenda presented above is too vast and intricate to be addressed comprehensively in a single publication. This much was acknowledged by the participants in the Oxford symposium of 30 May 1998, and continues to limit the pretensions of the final edited volume. So, while the essays gathered here range widely in geographical and conceptual scope, they do not pretend in any way to exhaust postcolonial aspects of the cultures of Latin America and Lusophone Africa. More modestly, the essays address a number of topics which their authors feel to be compatible with an approach grounded in postcolonial studies. Some of those essays focus on major Latin American intellectuals—Mariátegui, Ortiz, Zea, de Campos—who can be reread productively in the light of postcolonial studies; other essays address specific points in the above agenda, which the authors study with reference to a variety of literary works ranging from a selection of poems by César Vallejo to a handful of short stories by Mia Couto. If there is a single thread which can be said to unite the essays contained in this volume, it is an interest in mapping significant local detail of the cultures of Latin America and Lusophone Africa on to the broad canvas of intercontinental colonial and postcolonial experience,[23] all the while acknowledging the historical and geographical specificities of the materials selected for study.

The essays

The importance of 'reading *Otherwise*', on which Djelal Kadir insisted in an important publication of 1993,[24] is reflected in Mark Millington's timely essay, 'On Metropolitan Readings of Latin American Cultures: Ethical Questions of Postcolonial Critical Practice'. Millington is acutely aware of the history of disjunctions between North American and European discourses and the peripheral cultures (especially those of Latin America) which have been instrumental to their analyses, and he seeks to articulate a position in which the First World professional academic may resist both the chimera of cultural relativism and the easy option of 'unreflective transnational access'. The modifications introduced into classic Marxism by José Carlos Mariátegui in Peru and subsequently by the ideologues of the Cuban Revolution illustrate processes of transculturation which exemplify the periphery's capacity to resist universalizing pressures radiating from 'the centre', at the same time as they imply a continuing capacity to transform more recent theories and ideologies of postmodernism and postcolonialism. This power to resist, of course, does not relieve metropolitan critics of an ethical obligation. Our professional and personal investments in the cultures that we teach and examine, and the diverse forms of dependence and interdependence which we all now live, force on us a recognition of the 'between position' occupied by metropolitan academic readers of Latin America who, in translating one type of theory or another to the periphery, must remain forever conscious of our positions and our politics. Millington's scrupulous interrogation of personal obligations and institutional constraints brings him into dialogue with an impressive range of authors and works in the intersecting fields of postcolonial and Latin American studies, and illuminates the ground(s) on which that intersection can properly take place.

The insidious, lingering influence of Eurocentric and positivist binaries is the concern of Else Vieira in 'Ig/noble Barbarians: Revisiting Latin American Modernisms'. A survey of the history of the civilization/barbarism dichotomy in Latin American culture identifies the most significant metamorphoses that have occurred over recent decades, in essays by Carlos Fuentes, Roberto Fernández Retamar and Rafael Humberto Moreno-Durán. The positing of *imagination* as an alternative to *barbarism* is seen as both liberating and politically empowering, and valorized accordingly by the three writers named above. However, a re-appropriation of the binary in 1994 by the German critic, Karl Kohut, is redolent, for Vieira, of the colonizing and judgemental attitudes towards Latin America that were typical of Europe in the age of empire. Sensing a moral motivation and civilizing thrust in Kohut's work, she rejects his approach as literal-minded and recidivist. Her criticism is all the more justified, she feels, in view of the thoroughness with which the civilization/barbarism binary had been deftly dismantled by Latin American modernist intellectuals around the time of the centenary of political independence from Spain and Portugal. Taking examples from the literatures of Colombia and Brazil, Vieira attests to the inspired cleverness with which Guillermo Valencia and Mário de Andrade used translation to problematize positivist antinomies, including that of civilization *vs.* barbarism. Literary translation of Old World originals becomes, in their hands, an activity that is charged with political significance, seeking liberation from 'mental colonialism' through an act of the imagination.

Peru in the 1920s and 1930s is the home of a nationalist revolutionary project articulated around the pivotal figure of José Carlos Mariátegui. In Chapter Three of this volume, Patricia D'Allemand returns to Mariátegui's reflections on art and culture and relates them to a broader critique of conservative and bourgeois values in postcolonial Peru. Myth, imagination and the languages and formal experimentation of the avant garde constitute a challenge to the dominant aesthetic of the time, whose legitimacy is further undermined by a rereading of Peruvian literature which sets out to give expression to the majority of the population marginalized and silenced since the Conquest. Crucially, for D'Allemand, Mariátegui takes issue not only with recalcitrant hispanicist conceptions but also with readings based upon the ideologies of *mestizaje* and a hard-line *indigenismo*, which share a unitary view of the Peruvian literary process. That view is inimical to Mariátegui's ideal of a plurality capable of accommodating the traditional and the avant garde, the local and the cosmopolitan, in an inclusive popular model of cultural emancipation and renewal. D'Allemand, whose primary disciplinary allegiance is to Latin American cultural studies rather than to postcolonialism, recaptures vividly the complexity of Mariátegui's critical discourse, which can be seen as foreshadowing the later agenda of postcolonial studies in several key respects.

The cultural heterogeneity that was theorized by Mariátegui is elaborated on by William Rowe in 'Doing Time in Peru: the Poetics of Multitemporality as Method for Cultural History'. Here, the work of Cornejo Polar and García Canclini adumbrates an enquiry into the possibility of rethinking time substantively, against the historically fractured backdrop of colonial and postcolonial Peru. Noting the prevalence, in the dominant historiography, of a single, unilinear time, which is that of narrative modernity, Rowe postulates other temporalities which would refuse to adjust to the centralizing narratives of the modern, and finds instances of them in the poems of *Trilce* by César Vallejo. Vallejo's avant-garde experiments with language and composition embody a variety of discontinuous and multiple times which are radically subversive of standard notions of temporal uniformity and historical progress. Through the intricacies of their designs, Vallejo's poems engage the reader in a series of hermeneutic operations which serve potentially as a method for cultural history.

Of all the authors who have been referred to in the course of this Introduction, César Vallejo is virtually alone in not being mentioned by Leopoldo Zea, whose work demonstrates an encyclopaedic familiarity with whole chapters of the postcolonial canon. From Bolívar, Martí and Rodó to Mariátegui and Vasconcelos; from Césaire and Fanon to Sédar Senghor and other Black African intellectuals, the range of reference displayed in the Mexican veteran's work is astonishing and provides firm evidence of the historical convergence of the fields of postcolonialism and Latin American discourse. 'America, Americanism and the Third World in the Work of Leopoldo Zea' documents Zea's ties with the broadest conceivable framework of mid-twentieth-century political ideas and charts his intellectual evolution from the early 1940s to the mid-1990s. Commitment to the Cuban Revolution and a sustained interest in themes of 'mental emancipation', *indigenismo*, Negritude and *mestizaje* mark Zea out as one of Latin America's leading postcolonial intellectuals, who echoes the call of Martí, Neruda, Galeano and countless others for Latin American unity against neo-imperialist interference. What is particularly striking about Zea is the passion with which, in the 1960s and 1970s, he sought to inscribe Latin America in the global context of decolonization. In doing so, he kept faith with the geopolitical vision of the Cuban Revolution while also expressing solidarity with the postcolonial intellectuals of nascent nations in Africa and Asia, as well as with those of his native America.

An absolutely essential figure in the postcolonial debate is Fernando Ortiz of Cuba. Cited, amongst other places, in *Key Concepts in Post-colonial Studies* (233–34), Ortiz is the author of the theory of 'transculturation' through which he accounted for the various syncretisms operative in Afro-Cuban culture. Transculturation was conceived as a response and corrective to the US anthropological term 'acculturation', which implied a one-way, top-down model of relations between a privileged donor culture (that of metropolitan Great Britain or France, for example) and a recipient culture in a colonial setting, which stood to derive benefits from the transmission to it of the values of Western civilization. In Chapter Six of this volume, Catherine Davies underlines the signal importance of Ortiz's work to the discipline of ethnography and spells out its political significance as an instance of the subaltern playing a constitutive role in colonial discourse. Her essay, 'Fernando Ortiz's Transculturation: the Postcolonial Intellectual and the Politics of Cultural Representation', surveys the Cuban thinker's intellectual genealogy and his evolution, over a period of some forty years, from a colonialist mind-set to postcolonial contestation. Ortiz's location of the specificity of Cuban experience, vis-à-vis that of Spain, in the existence of a black culture which was as yet undocumented, was iconoclastic: it enabled Ortiz to put the spotlight on issues of race and colour and to envisage an autonomous, hybrid national culture. Davies examines this point—and several more—in the light of work produced in a large number of academic disciplines from anthropology and art history to postcolonial studies. Paying particular attention to connections between the Caribbean and Africa, she compares Ortiz to both Fanon and Cabral and opens up fascinating vistas which anticipate the contents of later chapters of this volume.

Still within the ambit of the Caribbean, Canadian author Stephen Henighan reads *El siglo de las luces* by Alejo Carpentier alongside *Peau noir, masques blancs* by Frantz Fanon, to whom Carpentier renders an oblique homage in his canonical novel of 1962. Fanon's documented mistrust of theory as a distorting mask imposed on the periphery by the agents of empire supplies Henighan with an emblematic image around which to explore the question of the usefulness and consequences of meshing postcolonial discourse with Latin American cultural production. 'Caribbean Masks: Frantz Fanon and Alejo Carpentier' shares the same suspicion about metropolitan ideologies that was harboured by the authors themselves, and unpicks the discursive fabric of an essay by Homi Bhabha which is found, at certain levels, to uphold the centrality of the very same Eurocentric assumptions that it purports to delegitimize elsewhere. Turning to the plot of *El siglo de las luces*, Henighan emphasizes its anticolonialist logic, which he compares with that of Fanon and his fellow-Martinican mentor, Aimé Césaire. In differential terms, Carpentier is seen to deal with the interrelated issues of race, colour and colonial status from a more intellectual perspective than Fanon, whose writings on those subjects throb with a visceral intensity. Carpentier also distinguishes himself as the author of a theory of Caribbean hybridization which takes its place—literally, in this volume—alongside Ortiz's theory of transculturation, as a locally-produced model of postcolonial difference and self-affirmation. At the end of an essay which had begun by presupposing difference and by expressing considerable scepticism about the conjunction of postcolonial studies with Latin American cultural discourse, Henighan suggests ways in which each of these discursive fields stands to benefit from a more rigorous knowledge of the other. In the specific cases of Fanon and Carpentier, this would involve illuminating the authors' respective historical predicaments and shedding light on the different postcolonial situations of the Caribbean island societies of which they were widely recognized and pivotal spokesmen.

The postcolonial literatures of Lusophone Africa are represented in our volume by Mia Couto, who is the subject of a probing analysis by Maria Manuel Lisboa. Couto's status as a white Mozambican writer, schooled in a European education system and yet situated at a crossroads of races and cultures, raises questions to do with the politics of representation in a postcolonial society which emerged from five hundred years of imperial and colonial occupation into a state of civil war that lasted a full twenty years and came to a stop only in 1994. 'Colonial Crosswords: (In)voicing the Gap in Mia Couto' moves towards an understanding of those larger questions through consideration of a clutch of stories from the volume *Vozes anoitecidas*, of which one, 'De como se vazou a vida de Ascolino do Perpétuo Socorro', receives particularly close attention. Featuring a mixed-race, *caneco* protagonist of Indo-Portuguese extraction now living in Mozambique, the story depicts the distorting effects of imperialism on colonial subjects who aspire to mimic their colonial masters and end up falling ridiculously short of the standards of heroism and nobility which had inspired the Portuguese imperial project of yesteryear. The eponymous Ascolino Fernandes displays a fractured identity which cannot be reconciled with the ideology of race and colour on which the social order rests. M. M. Lisboa interprets his fragile subject status through the prism of the now canonical insights of Homi Bhabha and points out Ascolino's fearful failure to exploit the stratagems of subversive mimicry which are so important a part of Bhabha's analysis of colonial subjectivity. Subsequently, Ascolino's linguistic subservience is a cue for interrogating the author's own deployment of the Portuguese language at a level of virtuosity which cannot be separated from considerations of communication and power. For Lisboa, Couto's masterful literary style papers over a gap between the sophisticated native reader/speaker of Portuguese and the problematical Mozambican reality which it is the literary author's calling to address. Echoing Gayatri Spivak, Lisboa wonders: 'Who is [Couto] addressing? Who is his intended audience? Who does he claim to speak for?', in a strategic series of questions which point up the undeniable importance of ethical and political dimensions of postcolonial writing and criticism.

At the same time as it enhances the linguistic and thematic range of the present volume, Lisboa's study performs two formal functions which are salutary for the collection as a whole. First, her trenchant questions about Couto's role as postcolonial writer hark back to Millington's concerns, in the opening essay, about the ethics and politics of metropolitan readings of postcolonial literatures. Structurally, this echo provides an instance of repetition-with-a-difference which, while embodying a logic of restatement and return, ultimately opens up the prospect of further, ever more searching consideration of issues dealt with in the present volume. Second, the clearly defined African focus of Lisboa's essay emphasizes the broad geographical and geo-cultural horizons of the field(s) examined here, in which the Lusophone cultures of Africa might subsequently be compared and contrasted with the cultures of Anglophone and Francophone Africa, as well as with those of the Caribbean and Latin America. Prefigured, to a certain extent, in the geographical sweep of the eight chapters of this volume, that ambitious project is, ultimately, the business of an ongoing postcolonial study which remains under a continuing obligation to respect the historical and geographical particularities of different peoples and cultures, while it seeks to establish grounds of similarity between colonial and postcolonial experiences in various locations around the globe.

Notes

1   J. Jorge Klor de Alva, 'Colonialism and Post Colonialism as (Latin) American Mirage', *Colonial Latin American Review*, I, 1–2 (1992), 3–23. A revised and expanded version of the essay appeared under the title 'The Postcolonization of the (Latin) American Experience: a Reconsideration of "Colonialism," "Postcolonialism," and "Mestizaje"', in *After Colonialism: Imperial Histories and Postcolonial Displacements*, ed. Gyan Prakash (Princeton: Princeton University Press, 1995), 241–75. References in parentheses in the body of this Introduction are to the latter publication.

2   Ania Loomba, *Colonialism/Postcolonialism* (London and New York: Routledge, 1998), 14.

3   The key Galeano text in this connection is *Contraseña* (Buenos Aires: Ediciones del Sol, 1985); see in particular the chapters entitled 'El

oficio de escribir' (103–16) and 'Diez errores y mentiras frecuentes sobre literatura y cultura en América Latina' (117–37). By Ribeiro, see *As Américas e a civilizaçao: processo de formação e causas do desenvolvimento desigual dos povos americanos* (Petrópolis: Vozes, 1977) and *O dilema da América Latina: estruturas de poder e forças insurgentes* (Petrópolis: Vozes, 1978).

4   On the continuing favour that the name 'Latinoamérica' finds amongst many of the continent's intellectuals, see Daniel Samper Pizano, 'En busca de un gentilicio: Latinoamérica gana, pierde Hispanoamérica', *El Tiempo, Lecturas dominicales* (Bogotá), 5 February 1989, 4–5. A historical overview of the appropriation of the concept of Latinity in the New World is provided by Arturo Ardao in *América latina y la latinidad* (Mexico City: UNAM, 1993); I am grateful to Sr Leopoldo Zea for bringing this important volume to my attention. A less enthusiastic voice in the debate about the name 'Latin America' is that of Germán Arciniegas in the title essay of *América Ladina* (a selection of work by Arciniegas compiled by Juan Gustavo Cobo Borda) (Mexico City: Fondo de Cultura Económica, 1993), 428–29.

5   Walter Mignolo, 'La razón postcolonial: herencias coloniales y teorías postcoloniales', in *Postmodernidad y postcolonialidad*, ed. Alfonso de Toro (Frankfurt am Main: Vervuert; Madrid: Iberoamericana, 1997), 51–70 (56).

6   Peter Hulme, 'Including America', *ARIEL: A Review of International English Literature*, XXVI, 1 (January 1995), 117–23 (118). Earlier work by Hulme in the field of colonial discourse includes his now classic *Colonial Encounters: Europe and the Native Caribbean 1492–1797* (London: Methuen, 1986).

7   Loomba, *Colonialism/Postcolonialism*, 12.

8   In *Postmodernidad y postcolonialidad*, ed. Alfonso de Toro, 51–70.

9   *Revista Iberoamericana*, nos 170–71, vol. LXI (1995), 27–40.

10 Ella Shohat, 'Notes on the Post-Colonial', *Social Text*, 31/32 (1992), 114–40 (108), cited by Mignolo, 'La razón postcolonial', 52.

11 Sédar Senghor acknowledges Cabral in 'A New Humanism of the Twentieth Century', *The Africa Reader: Independent Africa* (London: Vintage, Random Century, 1970), 179–92 (also reproduced in Patrick Williams and Laura Chrisman, *Colonial Discourse and Post-colonial*

Theory: A Reader [New York and London: Harvester Wheatsheaf, 1993], 27–35). Significantly, Sédar Senghor is also the author of *Lusitanidade e Negritude* (Lisboa: Academia das Ciencias de Lisboa, 1975)—a slim volume comprising the text of the author's formal address on being admitted as a corresponding member of the Portuguese Academy.

12 The Cabral speeches anthologized by Williams and Chrisman include, especially, 'National Liberation and Culture', translated from the French by Maureen Webster and originally published in *Maxwell Graduate School Occasional Papers*, nos 53–57 (Syracuse University, 1970); also to be found in *Return to the Source: Selected Speeches of Amilcar Cabral* (New York: Monthly Review Press, 1973), 39–56.

13 Patrick Chabal, *The Post-Colonial Literature of Lusophone Africa* (London: Hurst, 1996).

14 See also Phyllis Peres, *Transculturation and Resistance in Lusophone African Narrative* (Gainesville: University Press of Florida, 1997), which is a valuable study, despite the fact that its focus is restricted mainly to Angolan writers.

15 Jean Franco is the author of a trail-blazing essay, 'Beyond Ethnocentrism: Gender, Power and the Third World Intelligentsia', first published in *Marxism and the Interpretation of Culture*, ed. C. Nelson and I. Grossberg (Basingstoke: Macmillan, 1988), 503–09 and 512–15, and subsequently reproduced in Williams and Chrisman, *Colonial Discourse*, 359–69. Other important work on postcolonialism and feminism includes S. Suleri, 'Woman Skin Deep: Feminism and the Postcolonial Condition', *Critical Inquiry*, XVIII (1992), 756–69, and Anne McClintock, *Imperial Leather: Race, Gender and Sexuality in the Colonial Context* (London and New York: Routledge, 1995).

16 On hybridity and *mestizaje* in Latin America, see, in particular, Klor de Alva, 'The Postcolonization of the (Latin) American Experience', 248–54, where the author discusses some of the political uses to which those two concepts have been put.

17 Bill Ashcroft, Gareth Griffiths and Helen Tiffin, *Key Concepts in Post-Colonial Studies* (London: Routledge, 1998), 136–37. The entry should be read in conjunction with Amaryll Chanady, 'La hibridez como significación imaginaria', *Revista de crítica literaria latinoamericana*, 49 (1999), 265–79.

18   Elizabeth Mudimbe-Boyi, 'Indigenism Revisited', a paper delivered at a conference entitled 'Caribbean Theories: Culture, Identity, Nation', which was held in Claremont, California, 1–3 April 1999, under the aegis of the Intercollegiate Department of Black Studies of the Claremont Colleges.

19   Roberto Fernández Retamar, *Calibán* (Montevideo: Aquí Testimonio, 1973). An English translation is published under the title, 'Caliban, Notes towards a Discussion of Culture in Our America', *Massachusetts Review*, 15 (Winter–Spring 1974), 7–72. An earlier application of the Ariel–Caliban motif can be found in Germán Arciniegas, 'Entre Ariel y Calibán', in *El continente de siete colores* (Buenos Aires: Sudamericana, 1965), 592–634.

20   See the indispensable essay by Wilson Harris, 'Creoleness. The Crossroads of a Civilisation?', in *Caribbean Creolization: Reflections on the Cultural Dynamics of Language, Culture, and Identity*, ed. Kathleen M. Balutansky and Marie-Agnès Sourieu (Gainesville: University Press of Florida, 1998), 23–35.

21   Antonio Benítez Rojo uses the term 'supersyncretism' to refer to 'the complex syncretism of Caribbean cultural expressions', in *The Repeating Island: The Caribbean and the Postmodern Perspective*, 2nd edn, translated from the Spanish by James E. Maraniss (Durham and London: Duke University Press, 1996), 12 ff.

22   On Carpentier, see the essay by Stephen Henighan which is included below as Chapter Seven. An important publication by Fuentes is *Valiente mundo nuevo: épica, utopía y mito en la novela latinoamericana* (Madrid: Mondadori España, 1990), especially the Introduction. In connection with Galeano, there is a pioneering study by Diana Palaversich, 'Galeano: el postmodernismo y el postcolonialismo', *Indiana Journal of Hispanic Literatures*, I, 2 (1993), 11–22.

23   See, in this connection, Robert L. Tignor, 'Colonial Africa through the Lens of Colonial Latin America', in *Colonial Legacies. The Problem of Persistence in Latin American History*, ed. Jeremy Adelman (New York and London: Routledge, 1999), 29–49.

24   Djelal Kadir, *The Other Writing: Postcolonial Essays in Latin America's Writing Culture* (West Lafayette, Indiana: Purdue University Press, 1993).

CHAPTER ONE

On Metropolitan Readings of Latin American Cultures: Ethical Questions of Postcolonial Critical Practice

Mark I. Millington
University of Nottingham

> By bringing from distant lands our forms of life, our institutions, and our vision of the world and by striving to maintain all that in an environment sometimes unfavourable and hostile, we were exiles in our own land.   *Sérgio Buarque de Hollanda*
>
> ... there is always an estranging abstraction at work in the processes of exchange between the subaltern object of analysis and its commodifying discourse, in which disciplinary knowledge-formation is always contestable precisely because, by definition, it is not and can never be the knowledge of the Other as the Other would know herself or himself.
>   *Gareth Williams*

One

My subject is cultural relations and, in particular, relations on the global North/South axis. I am going to consider the multiple and challenging factors at play in the contemporary reading and analysis of Latin American cultures from positions within the metropolitan nations. The context for my approaching this subject is the postcolonial world in which such readings now necessarily take place, a world acutely conscious of the ethical and political dimensions of dealing with the Other. It is a context which has been explored intensively over the last ten years and in which there has developed a productive questioning of how the methods used in analysis in one context are exported to others, a process which may lead to the problematic reduction of the Other to the Same. My aim is to avoid such a reduction and yet to achieve a position in which metropolitan critical practice can be brought into ethical engagement with postcolonial Latin American cultures. The problems inherent in such cultural engagements are pithily encapsulated by the Cuban-American critic, Gustavo Pérez Firmat, who signals the acute sensitivity of Latin Americans to the 'contribution' of non-Latin Americans to their cultural debates:

> ... one of the most insidious types of colonialism is the onomastic or conceptual, the situation that arises when the originality or distinctiveness of the home-grown is explained and rationalized using foreign categories, as if we could grow the guavas but needed someone else to package the paste.[1]

As if to mitigate such divisions, the title of Pérez Firmat's book on Cuban literature includes the word 'translation' and it is no exaggeration to say that modern approaches to cultural relations are saturated by a variety of words built around the prefix 'trans': for example, transnational, transfer, transplantation and, crucially, transculturation and translation. What is suggested by these words may be the ideas of movement and interaction as if, in the contemporary world of globalization, there were a smooth flow of cultural artefacts and practices between even the most remote locations. However, such a suggestion of smooth flow and interaction would be problematic in its overlooking of friction and resistance and as questionable as absolute rejection of cultural dialogue based on the relativizing principle of national discreteness. What I wish to delineate here is a middle position which would overcome the comforts of cultural relativism but without lapsing into the ease of unreflective transnational access.

I therefore offer this discussion as a position paper, and that in two senses. First, I want to explore the nature of the place from which the metropolitan critic speaks—his or her locus of enunciation[2]—specifically in relation to Latin American cultures. My concern is how metropolitan critics draw maps of the Latin American cultural field, how they constitute their Latin American objects of study. Second, and in order to carry out that exploration, I want to review some of the major currents of thinking about the broad postcolonial context in which we live and work in order to see what tools are available for constructing an ethical critical practice. In advancing on both these fronts I shall use the word 'theory' to designate all the concepts or tools or devices used by cultural critics to draw their maps: in other words, there is no intention of limiting the reference of the word 'theory' to contemporary critical theory. In addition, I must emphasize that I shall be taking culture as the horizon of my exploration and not just literature. This emphasis indicates something of the current reality of Latin America and the fact that its literatures occupy a relatively small, elite segment of a much larger field. This emphasis on culture therefore reflects recent critical thinking about Latin America and its heterogeneous creative realities.

Two

The inevitable starting point for my analysis is the postcolonial context of contemporary critical work. In terms of the metropolis's relation with Latin America, this is a highly political field full of delicate ethical issues. As a first step, it is worth considering the prefix 'post' in the term 'postcolonial'. On the one hand, 'postcolonial' may designate temporal succession and, more positively, imply a break with the colonial and the emergence of what is 'not-colonial' or independent. On the other hand, 'postcolonial' may be taken to designate the aftermath of the colonial and imply the continuity of its legacy. In that sense, despite the fact that most of Latin America has been independent of Europe for around 170 years, given a colonial experience of over 300 years in some places, the mere ejection of Spanish or Portuguese authority does not eliminate the structures of the colonial presence. Moreover, it is clear that, in the nineteenth and twentieth centuries, Latin America moved into a neocolonial phase when Great Britain and then the United States simply replaced Spain and Portugal in dominating the region economically, politically and culturally.

Postcolonial studies draw on both of these views of the postcolonial and their complex relations, now stressing independence and separation, now continued constriction and imposition, now disjunctive coexistence. In adopting these angles, postcolonial studies have sought to develop an oppositional stance against colonial or neocolonial practices and in full awareness of the political and ethical pressures involved. In the academic sphere, such a stance means highlighting the potentially oppressive relation of metropolitan knowledge production and its institutions to the lifeworld and cultures of the periphery. In taking this approach, a spotlight is focused on the range and applicability of theoretical thinking constantly emerging from the metropolis and its pretension to universality. A pertinent question here (and one to which I shall return) is asked by James Clifford, namely, how theory and theorists travel from one location into another and whether they stay the same or are altered by their travelling.[3] One might even encapsulate the broad issues involved by extending an already strong metaphor and asking: what kind of passport metropolitan theory travels on; what kind of visa or residence permit it requires when it reaches its overseas destination; and, crucially, who issues the passport and the visa.

In this context, it is not surprising that postcolonial studies should be committed to the validation and promotion of ideas and knowledge from the peripheries, that commitment being in no small measure a function of the crisis of authority and legitimation in the metropolitan nations. The traditional assumption of universal authority made by the metropolitan nations and their knowledge industries is no longer convincing, and cultural forms and practices from other locations have complicated and problematized the capacity of the metropolis to speak ethically. The periphery's questions and resistance have subverted the metropolis's confidence in the universal validity of its categories and forced a new awareness of the specific circumstances out of which theory and cultural practices arise. The result has been that the postcolonial world is deeply uncertain and full of crosscurrents, with multiple forms of transculturation. Consequently, it is hard to conceive of a neutral position in the postcolonial world—it is too fractured by the burden of accumulated history and contemporary pressures.

It has therefore become inappropriate to consider the cultural, let alone the literary, as disconnected from the full range of recent political and economic change. The rush for modernization in Latin America after the 1930s seemed to take for granted that modernity was good and an essential next step for the region even though it was seen that modernization might follow one of two paths: that of First World capitalism or Second World socialism. Both seemed to offer possible models. After the crisis and disintegration of the Second World and the faltering and crisis of confidence of the First, neither bloc any longer holds together as a centre of authority for the Third World. Many parts of the periphery have become deeply sceptical of where they fit into the modernization process. Moreover, the fruits of that modernization in Latin America have been very mixed and the resulting internal fractures and imbalances hard to reconcile with any notion of rational, integrated development. What modernization has not achieved is any more autonomy for Latin America in its relation with the metropolitan economies; indeed it has simply reconfirmed the way in which the region is tied to a system controlled from elsewhere. The neoliberal policies of the last twenty years of the twentieth century only reinforced the process of external exploitation of Latin American resources and labour. Domination is no longer by metropolitan governments and the US military but by transnational institutions and corporations with huge financial power. The scepticism in Latin America bred by its understanding of this broad picture underpins postcolonial thinking.

Three

Within this broad and variegated context, my question is how an ethical and therefore questioning critical practice is to be evolved for working with Latin American cultures. Both Edward Said and James Clifford have considered this issue under the shorthand formula of 'travelling theory'.[4] The formula is helpful, although it does suggest that the journeys undertaken by theory are somehow without an agent, as if theory decided for itself to move from one location to another. An additional dimension is required, and that is the acknowledgement that theory is exported out of certain locations or, alternatively, imported from elsewhere *by* critics or historians. The importation/exportation metaphors are evidently more comprehensive than travel alone, particularly as they allow for the interests involved in each activity.[5]

What is important here is the idea of movement from one national and cultural context to another. The problem which both Said and Clifford pinpoint is that it is all too easy for metropolitan theory to impose frameworks elsewhere because of their apparently informative effects. The concern is that what is singled out as significant merely confirms metropolitan interests and authority. This charge has resounded around the postcolonial world. Indeed, the very concept of a postcolonial literature has been criticized as the invention of metropolitan institutions. Nelly Richard has succinctly articulated the problem from the Latin American perspective: 'How are we to make use of theoretical conceptualizations knowing they form part of the normative standards of the center but without yielding to its grammar of authority, without adhering to its hierarchy of cultural power?'[6] Complementing Richard's point of view, Roberto Schwarz has highlighted the way in which merely importing ideas from elsewhere can result in a discrepancy between understanding and local conditions:

> Ideas are in place when they represent abstractions of the process they refer to, and it is a fatal consequence of our cultural dependency that we are always interpreting our reality with conceptual systems created somewhere else, whose basis lies in other social processes. In this sense, libertarian ideologies themselves are often ideas out of place, and they only stop being so when they are reconstructed on the basis of local contradictions.[7]

Schwarz sees negative results not only in the unreflective importation and adoption of theoretical frameworks, but also in other kinds of cultural importation such as literary forms. In his important essay, 'The Importing of the Novel to Brazil', he is explicit about the effects produced by the introduction into Brazil in the nineteenth century of the European realist novel with its characteristic structures and narrative emphases which he sees as distorting and falsifying local realities.[8] Fundamentally, Schwarz's concern is with deculturation, with the denial of local cultural specificity by elites intent on acculturating to or slavishly imitating prestigious material from elsewhere. However, the question which both Richard and Schwarz have ultimately to address is whether the *mere use* of metropolitan theory or cultural forms *necessarily* produces assimilation. An alternative question would be whether there is any way in which that theory or those forms can be deployed which will produce different kinds of understanding (perhaps precisely) because they are not compromised by local interests; whether the different formulations made available by them might not produce new knowledge.

It might be helpful to probe the issue of how theory travels a little further since thus far I have only considered this process along a North/South axis. One might also ask whether there is a seamless passage of theory between metropolitan centres: between Europe and the United States, or between different locations within

Europe. Such a question does help to keep one alert to the internal differentiation between the metropolitan nations (which has its obvious counterpart in internal Latin American differentiation) and to make one wary of the unreflective and unnuanced adoption of terms like 'the West' or 'Eurocentrism' as if such blanket terms were defensible except for the purpose of polemics. But having insisted on such a refinement, it does remain clear that there is an important extra dimension which the North/South axis implies: given historical and current relations of power, authority and influence along that axis, the travelling of theory in that direction can be seen to be a rather risk-laden operation.

The problems involved in the travelling of theory will become clearer if the nature of the journeys undertaken is considered in a little more detail.[9] Said has argued very persuasively that theories travel through four phases before reaching their destinations and being put into practice. He describes cumulative processes of transfer, adoption, resistance and modification:

> Such movement into a new environment is never unimpeded. It necessarily involves processes of representation and institutionalization different from those at the point of origin. This complicates any account of the transplantation, transference, circulation, and commerce of theories and ideas ...
>
> First, there is a point of origin, or what seems like one, a set of initial circumstances in which the idea came to birth or entered discourse. Second, there is a distance transversed, a passage through the pressure of various contexts as the idea moves from an earlier point to another time and place where it will come into a new prominence. Third, there is a set of conditions—call them conditions of acceptance, resistances—which then confronts the transplanted theory or idea, making possible its introduction or toleration, however alien it might appear to be. Fourth, the now fully (or partly) accommodated idea is to some extent transformed by its new uses, its new position in a new time and place. (Said, 226–27)

This is an illuminating and subtle account, but seems to be politically too neutral, overlooking the pressures of the postcolonial context. The description needs to be rendered less linear and the disruptions and contentions aroused by the movement of theoretical ideas need to be more adequately represented. This problem is something that Clifford pinpoints when he argues that Said's four 'stages' 'read like an all-too-familiar story of immigration and acculturation. Such a linear path cannot do justice to the feedback loops, the ambivalent appropriations and resistances that characterize the travels of theories, and theorists, between places in the "First" and "Third" worlds' (Clifford, 'Notes on Travel and Theory', 184). The stress here on loops, ambivalence and resistances is salutary and helps to highlight the question of whether theoretical ideas can lay claim to universality: can any conceptual framework derived from one context act as a sort of passe-partout into others? As a partial and indirect answer, it is worth recalling the outcome of the borrowing by intellectuals in the early nineteenth century of liberal ideas about democracy and self-determination first elaborated and put into practice in France, Britain and the United States. As the turbulent history of Latin America in the nineteenth century amply demonstrates, merely importing ideas without local consensus is unlikely to produce positive results. Such importation of metropolitan ideas into nineteenth-century Latin America was a further step in a very long history. If one merely considers the subsequent theoretical tradition of the region and writing about it, there are numerous conspicuous imports: Marx, Freud, Spengler, Ortega, phenomenology, social anthropology, semiotics, Derrida, Foucault and Lacan, to name only a few. These imports and the reasons for them were varied and location-specific, though some were quite widely embraced. What needs to be underlined, however, is that, in the contemporary postcolonial context, perceptions of the impact of such importation have become particularly negative, though not always coherent. Carlos Alonso outlines one example of incoherence when assessing Latin American relations with modernity:

what could be said is that both literature and cultural discourse in Spanish America exist as a simultaneous rejection and affirmation of the modern. One might propose that literature and Spanish American cultural rhetoric describe the same movement between opposing poles, but starting from opposite ends: literature begins with an understanding of itself as engaged in a struggle with the modern and moves in ways that are inconsistent with its avowed rejection of modernity. By contrast, Spanish American cultural rhetoric proceeds from its identification with modernity to a surreptitious turning away from it.[10]

Four

What seems to underlie the debate around postcolonial studies and Latin America is a tension between the local and the universal, between the national and the global. Postcolonial studies themselves seem somewhat ambivalent about this tension, on occasion regretting the erosion of national integrity and identity and on others displaying scepticism about the narrowness and political agendas of cultural nationalism.

Distrust on the periphery of metropolitan universalizing has sometimes led to resistance in the form of emphasized nationalism—a movement towards exclusivism or isolationism. And the logic of this response is not difficult to appreciate. It is evident that resistance to the homogenization perceived in universalizing theory may most readily be based on the nation and its apparently identifiable frontiers. The nation may appear to provide an unproblematic criterion for inclusion and exclusion. One idea or perspective belongs and is legitimate, another does not and is not. Such decisions are based on assumptions about what a given nation is and what is part of the authorized culture within it. However, in Latin America, those assumptions need to be counterbalanced by attention to whose model of the nation is being employed. In the region it is no easy matter to pinpoint what any nation is, given the heterogeneity of races, the multiple layering of cultures, the transculturation of forms, and the simultaneous presence of utterly unconnected life practices (some unmodified since pre-Hispanic times at one extreme, others forged out of modern cultures with their roots in Europe or the United States at the other extreme). It is impossible to claim that cosmopolitan Rio de Janeiro or Mexico City is any more or less characteristic of what it is to be Brazilian or Mexican than the indigenous cultures of the Amazon or Chiapas. And it is evident that there is very little to unite these extremes. Hence it is problematic to reject the Other and rely on essentialist, defensive notions of the national based on an exclusive affirmation either of the indigenous or of some other cultural strand: in the first place, it wilfully denies common ground with cultural concerns from elsewhere and, in the second place, it runs the risk of setting up what has been called an 'inverse racism' or 'indigenist obscurantism'.[11] Furthermore, nationalism has not proved itself an effective tool against the infiltration of theories from elsewhere: in the economic, political and cultural spheres, independence can hardly be said to exist any more except for those few groups uncontacted in the depths of the Brazilian jungle. What we all now live are diverse forms of dependence and interdependence.

The fundamental worry with travelling theory as exported by metropolitan thinkers or as imported by peripheral elites is that it will contribute to an undifferentiated, globalized homogeneity. The concern of postcolonial studies is that local specificity ceases to have any significance. It has become harder and harder to tell where one culture ends and another begins, not just within the metropolis but globally. There is constant movement towards cultural forms which are not hybrid but 'unlocalized', virtually ubiquitous and apparently denationalized. Transformations in communications and economics have eroded distinctions between internal and external, as Clifford has put it: 'The world's societies are too systematically interconnected to permit any easy isolation of separate or independently functioning systems'.[12] This blurring of national distinctions applies very precisely to Latin America and to any attempt to define where its borders are located, and that is exemplified by the way in which the border of Mexico with the United States has become highly porous. Moreover, given the size of the permanent Latin American presence within the USA which preserves very varied cultural and linguistic identities, it is now a fact that the fourth or fifth largest Spanish-speaking nation in the world is *inside* a metropolitan nation.[13]

The crucial impetus towards a convergence of cultural and life forms derives from modernization and modernity, projects based on a model of industrial progress and expanding capitalism centred on the metropolis. In a peripheral region such as Latin America, the commitment by certain sectors to modernization and to some aspects of modernity[14] has necessarily meant the embracing of Europeanizing and North Americanizing processes. This reality is spelt out by Richard:

> All the models to be imitated and consumed (industrial and economic organization, political structures, social behaviour, artistic values) were based on European prototypes. The construction of history in terms of progress and linear temporality is doubly inappropriate when applied to Latin American experience because it cannot accommodate the discontinuities of a history marked by a multiplicity of pasts laid down like sediments in hybrid and fragmented memories.[15]

Such fears about the effects of modernization also affect peripheral views of cultural theory with pretensions to universality, which easily become contaminated by resentments from other areas—the economic and the political—over exploitative practices. One current within postcolonial thinking would link the very notion of universal cultural theory with ethnocentrism—most often Eurocentrism. However, while it is clear that theories are elaborated in specific times and places so that their reach and applicability require close attention, a dogmatic linkage between transplanted theory and imperialism is too simplistic to merit much serious attention. Nonetheless, putting pressure on the unreflective practice of transplanting theory is an important reminder of the ethical dimension of critical practice. It is one element in a strategy of negotiating a line through the sterile and all-too-easy polarization between universalism and nationalism.

Five

In an effort to increase engagement with the local, there has developed in the United States in the last few years a project headed by the Latin American Subaltern Studies Group, which is modelled on the work of the Subaltern Studies Group focused on India.[16] One of the central concerns of the Group is to question the paradigms of representation and the range of cultural experience employed in mainstream academic work. The aim is to recover those subjects subordinated and silenced by political and social systems within Latin America, systems which have been reinforced by academic practice. This move is a significant development in the field of Latin American studies and it has had considerable impact on thinking about the ways in which fields of study are constituted and explored. In part, the Group is responding to the long-term impact of state policies within Latin America and their effect on social and cultural realities; more specifically, it seeks to pay attention to those marginalized in the region by the first wave of modernization (between the 1930s and 1970s) and by the second, neoliberal wave (in the 1980s and 1990s) which accompanied the return to democracy in many countries. There are two challenges for the Group: one is to understand why the Subaltern Studies paradigm is attractive to scholars currently working in the United States and whether this is another version of what Gareth Williams has called into question as identity/solidarity-based forms of Latin Americanism;[17] the other is whether the Group can achieve access to the thinking and experience of the subaltern communities when these things are precisely what are passed over in silence by accepted practices whether within the academic field or within the social and political realities of Latin American nations:

> It is the recognition of this role of the subaltern, how it curves, alters, modifies our life strategies of learning, understanding, and research, that underlies the doubts besetting [the] traditional disciplinary and historiographic paradigms, paradigms that are themselves related to the social projects of national, regional, and international elites seeking to manage or control subject populations ... (Beverley *et al.*, 137)

In seeking to overcome traditional paradigms and their inherent blind spots, members of the Group have paid special attention to the testimonial texts emerging from the region. This choice of material and the ways in which it demands to be treated have started to challenge the disciplinary boundaries between literature, anthropology, history and politics in ways which have undoubtedly been energizing.

There are dangers here, however. It is clear that there is a risk of investing in the subaltern Other, in privileging the point of view of the Other simply because it is Other and subordinated. What can develop is a 'reverse Orientalism' arising out of feelings of guilt: the acutely sensitive metropolitan reader intent on achieving a decolonizing perspective can easily slip into a stance where critical judgement is suspended or distorted. The logic of postcolonial thinking may appear to be to confer ultimate ethical primacy on marginal subjects merely because they are marginal, something which Neil Larsen has called the 'cult of alterity' (Larsen, 181). This logic is something of which the Group's 'Founding Statement' shows awareness when it alludes to the danger of metropolitan academics speaking *for* the subaltern when there is good evidence of 'subaltern resistance to and insurgency against elite conceptualizations' (Beverley *et al.*, 146).[18]

Six

The location of the postcolonial debate (including the part of it centred on the subaltern) is significant. It is probably not by chance that what have been called the loci of enunciation in the debate are mainly in the North. Many of those who occupy these places are from the periphery and now working in the metropolis, although a number are from the metropolis itself. It is also notable that most of the debate about the postcolonial and the subaltern is in English. While Chile and Brazil have participated in this debate, other Latin American nations have shown much less interest. It is perhaps predictable then that it is the Anglo North which debates the postcolonial issues and the metropolitan academy which apparently seeks to extend its authority by showing its awareness of peripheral others. One might speculate that, whatever the role of intellectuals from the periphery in postcolonial discussions, the result is yet another twist in the metropolitan academy's search to preserve its authority and prestige. Paradoxically, to highlight the loss of prestige by attending to the Other is an effective way of maintaining the intellectual initiative. The debate may therefore turn out to be the reverse of a burst of transparent self-assessment. Such a sceptical reading would signal indirectly that the loci of enunciation are not static but that modes of analysis and self-justification evolve, although the *relative* positions of the cultures under discussion remain the same: authority does not shift, although the way in which it is retained may have to change.

Interestingly, a distinguished voice from the periphery in Brazil, Antônio Cândido, has argued for the inevitability of Latin America's involvement with and cultural dependency on the metropolis given the nature of the long history that relates them.[19] For him, Latin America has naturally participated in a cultural universe to which it historically belongs and in which it long accepted that the lead was taken elsewhere. He differentiates between economic and political dependency and cultural dependency, and he also insists that after the 1930s Latin America moved into a new relation of cultural interdependence with Europe, though he does not specify which cultures are involved in this interdependence. This is a striking argument and one which contains elements of truth given the colonial past, but it is an argument which hardly does justice to the cultural complexity of the region, assuming as it does that there is *a* culture of Latin America and that it is a cosmopolitan one. It seems not unlikely that Cândido would have had as much difficulty adequately understanding the cultures and languages of Amazonian Indians as any European. He signally fails to account for the economic and social position of those intellectuals who led the process of importing cultural and political ideas from the metropolis, and therefore he neither interrogates their motives nor appears to grasp the existence of internal colonialism. In essence, Cândido's effort to homogenize the relation between metropolitan and Latin American cultures is the inverse of the posture of unquestioningly valorizing the subaltern Other. But the problem is that neither practice begins to negotiate the complex play of similarity and difference in the relationship.

Perhaps more revealing from the Latin American perspective than some sort of seamless interaction with Europe or the United States are the moments of tension or crisis in which Latin America attempts to 'talk back' to the metropolis and bring its cultural ambivalences to the surface. Such talking back takes various forms. At one extreme it involves deep scepticism and a questioning of any ideas separated from their context of origin either for export or import into Latin America. This is a case put forcefully by Richard:

> As long as imported theories and cultural movements remain divorced from the opposition of forces which are the only means of lending specific importance and historical density to the signs produced in Latin American cultures, they act as little more than orthopaedic aides within the contexts of those cultures. Characteristically, this kind of production exhausts itself in mere formal repetitions or 'doctrinal mannerism'. It produces pseudo-theories which are disassociated from

the intellectual struggle in which the original concepts and interpretations had to fight for supremacy. They are now no more than fetishes in what has become a merely ornamental construction. (Richard, 'Postmodernism and Periphery', 465)

By contrast, Schwarz argues that outright rejection of modes of thinking from outside Latin America is no real alternative to slavish imitation if it presupposes that there is an authentic Latin America waiting to be recovered. By contrast, Schwarz works towards a more nuanced contestatory position of constructive engagement with travelling theory which would entail its local 'naturalization'.

A good example of such a 'naturalization' into Latin America is Marxism. Marxism has a long history in the region; indeed it is impossible to conceive of the history of ideas in Latin America without a detailed consideration of it.[20] Marxism arrived with immigrant labour towards the end of the nineteenth century and has remained an important strand in the intellectual and practical political arena ever since. But some of the leading Marxist thinkers in Latin America refused merely to copy the European tradition, paying particular attention to local conditions and criticizing the perceived blind spots of Marxism's lack of attention to the anti-imperialist struggle. Further, Latin American Marxists questioned the orthodox view of the stages by which a society would reach a truly socialist form. José Carlos Mariátegui is a notable voice amongst those reformulating Marxism for Latin America. Mariátegui rejected certain strands of the Marxism which he had encountered in Europe—scientism, progressivism and objectivism—and he saw the inadequacy of Marxist class analysis for the conditions in his contemporary Peru. In that respect he was intent on rescuing a sense of the specific national conditions of Peru and, rejecting an orthodox Marxist model, he insisted on the enormous importance of agrarian issues for the understanding of the country's problems such that the relatively small Peruvian proletariat could not be seen as the exclusive revolutionary subject (Sánchez Vázquez, 120–21). In addition, Mariátegui opened Marxism to other strands of thought including psychoanalysis in an attempt to broaden its reach. Later thinkers (both Latin American and metropolitan) also extended Marxist economic theory in order to account for the continuation of structures of dependency within the global economic order. Their objective was precisely to achieve a local and regional accuracy in their analyses and to produce a broader and enriched Marxism by reducing the Eurocentrism of the original.[21] A similar effect could be argued for the Cuban Revolution, although at the level of practical politics. One of the things demonstrated by Cuba was that socialist revolution could evolve along more than one pathway and indeed take place without the involvement of proletariat or party. Even when the socialist affiliation of the revolutionary government in Cuba was confirmed in the early 1960s, the Marxism of the Revolution took its own course which hardly corresponded with orthodox models (as the Soviet Union discovered). Even so, such a transculturated form did not necessarily betray the spirit of the original theory.

One might call all these strands of thinking and practice in Latin American Marxism 'mimesis with a difference', and they correspond to the process of transculturation outlined by Ortiz when he describes how two cultures come together and interact to generate new hybrid forms.[22] If at one level the processes of transculturation of Marxism which I have just described are concrete examples of Ortiz's theory in practice, at another, his theory itself has become an example of Latin America talking back to the metropolis. As Catherine Davies analyses at length below (see Chapter Six), Ortiz's aim in elaborating his argument was to move beyond the limits of thinking about cultural contact inherent in the ideas of deculturation and acculturation which he saw as dominant in Anglo-American anthropology in the 1930s. Ortiz's theory is alive to the interactive process of cultural encounters and it makes no a priori assumptions about the power of one nation (practising deculturation on another) or the deference of that other (acculturating itself to the first). Ortiz's theory itself has now recently travelled to the metropolis, having been adopted into certain texts theorizing cultural relations.[23] This travelling of a peripheral theory into metropolitan thought is positive at least to the extent that the intellectual production of the periphery is taken seriously. But the motives for and the context of that travelling and what happens on arrival must not be overlooked. Another example, that of intellectuals from the periphery working in the metropolitan academy, effectively makes the point about how changes in context can compromise practice. At first sight, the presence of such intellectuals seems to be an example of the periphery's 'talking back', of its contribution to decentring the centre, and their presence is a notable feature of postcolonial studies in various disciplines. Intellectuals from Asia, Africa and Latin America have come to occupy prominent positions in the academic establishment in Europe and the United States. But the key question is whether these academics can be viewed simply as the representatives of cultural anti-imperialism, talking back within the metropolis. They occupy a profoundly ambiguous 'between' position, apparently leading the critique of an oppressive tradition of theorizing and political and economic practice and yet institutionally compromised, often having received advanced training within the metropolis and performing completely orthodox academic roles with high levels of respectability. Their 'betweenness' is ambiguous because they simultaneously enjoy the authority deriving from being at the centre in major universities and the postcolonial authority deriving from not being from the centre. They are transculturated individuals who, for professional reasons, depend on addressing themselves largely to a metropolitan audience in a way which contributes to furthering the focus on the metropolis as centre of debate and innovation. In fact, one might argue that these displaced intellectuals occupy a position not dissimilar to other kinds of cultural imports from the periphery. Just as cultural commodities travel from the periphery to the metropolis, so do cultural critics, and neither kind of import easily maintains its purity.

Seven

Relations between Europe and Latin America have become more complex in recent years, with ever more crosscurrents and interchanges, which are extremely difficult to map.[24] Underlying them is a dynamic and uneven process of interdependence in which the local and the global engage, interact and clash. It seems to me that although the respective positions of the two blocks are beginning to be less monolithic, they are still conditioned by current global political and economic realities which have not seen a change in the fundamental balance of power and suffering in the world.[25] Nonetheless, in reading the Other, each block, North and South, now finds it harder not to read and re-encounter itself. As a reader of Latin America, the metropolitan cultural critic cannot presume to occupy either the same position as a local reader or a position outside or beyond cultural flows or political power. And indeed, that reality is evident in this essay since I start by talking about metropolitan readings of Latin American cultures but find the focus broadening to include internal Latin American perspectives. It is important to emphasize the degree to which professional metropolitan readers of Latin America occupy a kind of 'between position', transculturated out of the metropolis to some extent though still enjoying the privileges of being within it, though these are clearly not the same 'between and within' as those of the Latin American critic in the metropolis. Between and within: that ambivalence may signal that there is no uniquely justified or ethically viable location. Even to say as much as this would not have seemed necessary for a metropolitan critic fifteen years ago. But it is no longer possible to think rigidly in terms of two blocks or of the Latin American Other as a discrete given to be accounted for with whatever theoretical tools are to hand. Each party is now involved in dynamic transformation via conflict, friction, asymmetry, translation and dialogue, in constant negotiation and diplomacy, with acute attention to the potential incommensurability of the horizons of thinking and theorizing. And we should therefore note that even the re-reading of the self is not simply benign, since it undoubtedly preserves a layer of self-legitimation.

Such formulations as these avoid the deceptive neatness of polarization and relativism. Above all, they acknowledge the importance of and tension between reciprocity and inequality, with each party attempting to think through respective positions and their politics. They indicate that, while theories may travel either at the prompting of the metropolis or of the periphery, they have to be translated or negotiated. So theories will travel but the ethical imperative is that they do so in collaboration with an active critical consciousness, as Edward Said has stressed:

> The critical consciousness is awareness of the differences between situations, awareness too of the fact that no system or theory exhausts the situation out of which it emerges or to which it is transported. And, above all, critical consciousness is awareness of the resistances to theory, reactions to it elicited by those concrete experiences or interpretations with which it is in conflict. (242)

Notes

1   Gustavo Pérez Firmat, *The Cuban Condition: Translation and Identity in Modern Cuban Literature* (Cambridge: Cambridge University Press, 1989), 31.

2   See Walter D. Mignolo, 'La razón postcolonial: herencias coloniales y teorías postcoloniales', *Celehis: Revista del Centro de Letras Hispanoamericanas*, IV, 4–5 (1995), 265–90, and 'Afterword: Human Understanding and (Latin) American Interests—The Politics and Sensibilities of Geocultural Locations', *Poetics Today*, XVI, 1 (1995), 171–214.

3   James Clifford, 'Notes on Travel and Theory', *Inscriptions*, 5 (1989), 177–88.

4   In addition to Clifford's essay on travelling theory, see also the essay by Edward Said to which it was a response: 'Traveling Theory', in *The*

World, the Text and the Critic (Cambridge, MA: Harvard University Press, 1983), 226–47.

5   There are other metaphors connected with travelling which it is also illuminating to mention here. Travel invokes the idea of borders and crossings with their connotations of controls, visas and work or residence permits. Travel is also related to the idea of traffic which can operate in multiple directions, as well as suggesting the appearance of cross-traffic and oncoming traffic. And traffic conjures up the idea of trafficking, which hints at the less than ethical importing and dealing in contraband articles. All these metaphors (and no doubt other connected ones) effectively throw light on the complex interrelations and tensions in cultural contact.

6   Nelly Richard, 'The Latin American Problematic of Theoretical-Cultural Transference: Postmodern Appropriations and Counter-appropriations', *South Atlantic Quarterly*, XCII, 3 (1993), 453–59. Characteristically, Gayatri Spivak has put a similar point even more trenchantly when she delivers an indictment against 'the ferocious standardizing benevolence of most US and Western European human-scientific radicalism (recognition by assimilation)', in G. C. Spivak, 'Can the Subaltern Speak?', in *Marxism and the Interpretation of Culture*, ed. Cary Nelson and Lawrence Greenberg (Urbana and Chicago: University of Illinois Press, 1988), 271–313 (294).

7   Roberto Schwarz, *Misplaced Ideas: Essays on Brazilian Culture*, ed. John Gledson (London and New York: Verso, 1992), 39.

8   See Schwarz (1992), 41–77.

9   The range of what travels to Latin America is huge, embracing not only cultural, political and philosophical theories but scientific and economic models, manufacturing processes, fashion, etc. However, such a diversity should not detract attention from the fundamental question of whether the importing into Latin America of, say, post-structuralist theory is radically different in political terms from importing, say, Baseian statistics or techniques of automotive production. The question would be whether all these imports are adequately conceived of together under the broad rubric of colonialism or imperialism.

10 Carlos J. Alonso, 'The Burden of Modernity', *Modern Language Quarterly*, LVII, 2 (1996), 227–35 (232).

11   Neil Larsen, *Reading North by South: On Latin American Literature, Culture and Politics* (Minneapolis and London: University of Minnesota Press, 1995), 141.

12   James Clifford, 'On Collecting Art and Culture', in *Out There: Marginalization and Contemporary Cultures*, ed. Russell Ferguson *et al.* (New York: The New York Museum of Contemporary Art, and Cambridge, MA: MIT Press, 1990), 141–69 (152).

13   John Beverley, José Oviedo and Michael Aronna (eds), *The Postmodernism Debate in Latin America* (Durham and London: Duke University Press, 1995), 141. It is estimated that by 2010 there will be more Hispanics than Blacks in the United States, and that by 2050 there will be over 81 million Hispanics in the country (*The Independent on Sunday*, 22 September 1996).

14   It is evident that, for example, in its political culture, Latin America has only just begun to develop certain practices of modernity such as accountability and institutional political opposition.

15   Nelly Richard, 'Postmodernism and Periphery', in *Postmodernism: A Reader*, ed. and introduced by Thomas Docherty (New York, London etc.: Harvester Wheatsheaf, 1993), 463–70 (465).

16   See Latin American Subaltern Studies Group, 'Founding Statement', in Beverley *et al.*, 135–46.

17   Gareth Williams, 'Fantasies of Cultural Exchange in Latin American Subaltern Studies', in *The Real Thing: Testimonial Discourse and Latin America*, ed. Georg M. Gugelberger (Durham and London: Duke University Press, 1996), 225–53.

18   It is a striking aspect of the Subaltern Studies project that there is a considerable degree of travelling theory involved in it. The key concept of the subaltern derives from Gramsci and was adapted into the Indian context, from where it has travelled in its new form to the United States in order to be redeployed in Latin American studies.

19   Antônio Cândido, 'Literatura e subdesenvolvimento', in *América Latina em sua literatura*, ed. César Fernández Moreno (São Paulo: Editora Perspectiva, 1979), 343–62.

20   See Adolfo Sánchez Vázquez, 'Marxism in Latin America', *Philosophical Forum*, XX, 1–2 (1988–89), 114–28.

21 See Sánchez Vázquez, 115–18, for a full discussion of the Eurocentric limitations in early Marxism.

22 Fernando Ortiz, *Cuban Counterpoint: Tobacco and Sugar,* trans. Harriet de Onis, introduced by Fernando Coronil (Durham and London: Duke University Press, 1995). First edition in Spanish: 1940. First edition of English translation: 1947.

23 See Antonio Benítez-Rojo, *The Repeating Island: The Caribbean and the Postmodern Perspective* (Durham: Duke University Press, 1992); Mary Louise Pratt, *Imperial Eyes: Travel Writing and Transculturation* (London and New York: Routledge, 1992); and Fernando Coronil, 'Introduction', in Ortiz, *Cuban Counterpoint*, ix–lvi. The paradox in terms of Ortiz's theory having travelled to the metropolis is that he himself looked to 'bring' the leading European anthropologist of the day, Bronislaw Malinowski, to Latin America by inviting him to lend his authority to his theory by writing an approving introduction to the first edition.

24 Electronic communication may now have rendered any attempt at mapping the full range of relations and interchanges between Europe and Latin America futile.

25 See Anne McClintock, 'The Angel of Progress: Pitfalls of the Term Postcolonialism', in *Colonial Discourse and Postcolonial Theory: A Reader*, ed. Patrick Williams and Laura Chrisman (New York, London etc.: Harvester Wheatsheaf, 1993), 291–304.

CHAPTER TWO

Ig/noble Barbarians: Revisiting Latin American Modernisms

Else R. P. Vieira
Universidade Federal de Minas Gerais, Brazil

As a Brazilian, as a Latin American, and as a visitor to Europe both literally and critically, I cannot help being struck by the stubborn implications of irrepressible Eurocentrisms, by die-hard binaries and their sinister effects. As recently as 1994, from Germany, there re-echoed the platitude of *Imaginación y barbarie*,[1] a revisionist invitation for the would-be Latin Americanist to be reinstructed in the colonizing polarities of nineteenth-century positivisms, long debated but too often subject to reflex rather than reflection. Whether or not we ponder the contexts of Domingo Faustino Sarmiento's juxtaposition of 'civilización y barbarie' and subsequent variations on the theme, it will always be necessary to resist the teleologies lurking within the very terms of analysis. It is not as if writers both Latin American and Latin Americanist have not many times already dismantled, debunked and, since the 1970s, deconstructed such oppositions, as we shall see.

It is with some circumspection that I regard the possibility of representing Latin America. Speaking for the continent in an undifferentiated manner is an impossibility. Yet, as I interrogate the re-emergence, in our days, of the catechizing, reforming, civilizing and, for that matter, colonizing bias of the imagination and barbarism binary, I shall explore two avenues of Latin American enunciation of postcolonial subjectivities in Hispanic and Lusophone cultures, each of which problematizes such juxtapositions, well-known to Hispanists, less so to Latin Americanists. One trajectory, which is conceptual, broaches the historically shifting meanings of the civilization/barbarism dichotomy as studied and contextualized by Roberto Fernández Retamar and Rafael Humberto Moreno-Durán.[2] It thus makes conspicuous the colonizing and cyclical dimensions of the binary and its variants, recently re-appropriated as a civilizing mission with a moral motivation, by Karl Kohut. The other trajectory leads to Colombian and Brazilian modernisms of the early twentieth century, approached not in aesthetic terms but rather in the cultural dimensions raised, for example, by the Brazilian Aracy Amaral.[3] With a suggestive title, 'As Duas Américas Latinas ou Três, Fora do Tempo', she stresses the unevenness of Latin American modernisms. She further points out that in Europe, at the end of the century, Modernism implied an urban behaviour that exalted the city, the phenomenon of the crowd, of loneliness and, as a result, was associated with a Romantic sense of the new. Among the Latin Americans, there occurs a re-evaluation of the national in the light of the discovery of the internationalism of Paris as the centre of convergence of the intellectuals and artists of the time. Simultaneously, a change of behaviour arises from industrialization, the growth of urban populations, and the arrival of a mass of immigrants, whose traditions are quite different from those of the colonizers, or even from the African culture that had been a fundamental element of *mestizaje*, and also the labour force in mining and agriculture, in the first centuries of European occupation.

As I contextualize peripheral manifestations of modernism beyond merely aesthetic parameters, my objective is to foreground a postcolonial dimension, more specifically, that of a cultural project aimed at breaking with mental colonialism upon the centenary of political independence from Spain and Portugal respectively. This is also the moment when new forms of colonialism, such as American imperialism, were emerging. Angel Rama, *inter alia*, remarks that 'US imperialism had initiated its advance in a series of events that captured the attention of all of Latin America: the Spanish American war in Cuba, and Colombia's loss of Panama for the creation of an interoceanic canal by the United States, followed by US intervention in the Caribbean basin'.[4] Latin American modernist intellectuals will be seen to problematize the antinomous nature of civilization and barbarism, holding the mirror of so-called barbarism to would-be civilization, exposing the barbarian in the civilized, and vice versa. Different modes of translation, in this period, move away from linguistic parameters and, as a cultural phenomenon, take on political tones, thereby revealing points of confrontation and forces of instability. Arguing that the cultural phenomenon of translation in Latin America, frequently conveying political messages of decolonization from the nineteenth century onwards, has not been fully appreciated, I further emphasize that it is often associated with the aesthetic categories of irony and parody. This second trajectory thus exemplifies how, in Colombia, for instance, irony emerges as a strategy in the writing of the poet-translator Guillermo Valencia. His 'barbaric hands' mishandle European aesthetics of permanence, manipulating the logic of supplementation and change. In Brazil, too, Mário de Andrade's intralingual translation of the discourse of the Portuguese scribes and catechists in 'Carta pras Icamiabas' will be shown not only to parody the discovery, in the sixteenth century, of the 'Terra de Vera Cruz' (Brazil's first name), but also to problematize positivist antinomies and values.[5] In both writers and texts, translation emerges as a strong critique of many of the dichotomies so dear to the colonizing impulse, in our days matched by a nostalgic Eurocentric revitalization of the binary.

Enchainment: from barbarism to civilization, from imagination to barbarism

Roberto Fernández Retamar, in *Algunos usos de civilización y barbarie y otros ensayos*, begins his well-known meditation on the plurality of meanings of the civilization/barbarism binary, making the proviso that it is *not* with the terrible shadow of Sarmiento that he is establishing a dialogue (173).[6] He initially traces the use of the term 'barbarian' to classical antiquity. In Greek, it means simply 'foreigner', including the Romans. In the Greek concept of the barbarian, difference is not established through race but through culture, unlike that of the Romans, for whom barbarians were the Germanic peoples (176–77). He further points out that in the middle of the eighteenth century there emerges the other term of the dichotomy, 'civilization'; it is this polarization that, from the end of the same century, is projected upon the whole world by developing capitalist Europe; in contrast, the barbarians are the colonies or semicolonies of so-called civilization (180–82). Relying on Eduardo Galeano, Fernández Retamar stresses that the Europeans introduced an unprecedented rapaciousness over the non-white peoples, under the common banner of 'colour', thereby re-establishing the parameter of race. His quotation from Baran and Sweezy is eloquent, citing racial prejudice as the white man's attitude, originating with the European conquerors of the sixteenth century to justify the expoliation (182). Sarmiento, he argues, grafted the metropolitan formula on to the Latin American continent: not belonging to the race which promoted civilization was justification enough for a people's enslavement or decimation (185). Sarmiento defends the subjugation of the natives for their transformation into civilized people; for him, civilization means the interests of the Latin American and the expanding metropolitan bourgeoisie. With an implacable racism, Sarmiento stigmatizes natives and *mestizos*, further approaching the struggle between European civilization and the native's barbarism. Coextensive with his compliment to Buenos Aires as a continuation of Europe, he deplores the fusion of whites, blacks and natives which has resulted in a homogeneous group characterized by love for idleness and industrial incapacity (190–91). As Sarmiento defends European interests and the extermination of the natives, he concedes that this policy is, indeed, unfair; yet he claims that they are incapable of progress whereas the Caucasian race is more intelligent, more beautiful, and the most progressive on earth (quoted on 195). Sarmiento thus cherishes the civilizing project of extermination and the supplanting of many natives and *mestizos* by European immigration (196). In counterdistinction, Fernández Retamar argues, José Hernández in his poem *Martin Fierro* presents the barbarian project, as in the eighteenth century Jean Jacques Rousseau had pointed out the evils that civilization, understood as the only valid reality, had wrought upon humanity (199, 216–17).

Rafael Humberto Moreno-Durán, in *De la barbarie a la imaginación*, argues that the civilization/barbarism debate is implicit in all Latin American cultural discourses. In his reading, Sarmiento's thesis exemplifies, on the one hand, the aspirations of the bourgeoisie and, on the other hand, the positivist ideas and the principles of Order and Progress, ideologically framing the continent (21). In the face of the natives' barbarism and the Europeans' civilization, electing one of the terms was a necessity; this obligation also implied a doomed coexistence (22). Civilization is a rich alternative offered by Europe and the United States, whereas a series of primitive and violent realities were enough to make one ashamed in the eyes of the enlightened world (23). The polarization is also carried over to country/city, the former exemplifying barbarism and the latter the defence against the threat of barbarism. The city, in this case Buenos Aires, harbours the initiatives of progress and order and is an heir, via cosmopolitanism, to the richest European culture (25). The Mexican Carlos Fuentes, Moreno-Durán argues, is associated with the emergence of the urban novel in Latin America, recreating in his work all the elements extracted from the objective reality of the city, which Sarmiento saw as the only environment in which all civilization is possible; Fuentes posits *imagination* as an alternative to barbarism, superseding civilization in the debate (27–28, 31). Moreno-Durán quotes from Fuentes's essay *La nueva novela hispanoamericana* (1969) the view that '[t]odo es lenguaje en América Latina: el poder y la libertad, la dominación y la esperanza', and that 'si el lenguaje de la "barbarie" desea someternos al determinismo lineal del tiempo, el lenguaje de la imaginación desea romper esa fatalidad liberando los espacios simultáneos de lo real' (Fuentes in Moreno-Durán, 29). It is then that Fuentes proposes a change of the terms of the original thesis, no longer opposing civilization and barbarism; through language, civilization had reached such a point that all reality changes into imagination. Next, Moreno-Durán expands on the perception that the *indigenista* writers Ciro Alegría and Ezequiel Martínez Estrada categorically hold that civilization and barbarism are one and the same thing. Yet, for Sarmiento and all the positivist bourgeoisie of the nineteenth century who have been manipulated by colonialist pressures, the only interest was civilization as a channel of progress; imagination had no role (33). Rebellion in Latin America is thus directed against the very bases of dependency. Imagination allows them to exercise freedom of expression. Indeed, it is the only form of violence to which they ought to commit themselves (34).

Karl Kohut, editor of *Literatura colombiana hoy: imaginación y barbarie*, does not grasp at all the metaphorical dimensions of imagination as another source of energy and form of expression, let alone the value of such a form of expression for a continent whose history has entailed the disqualification of the voice either through the colonial enterprise or, more recently, through censorship. Perhaps unaware of the European violence done to Latin America by reducing it to silence, Kohut further takes imagination at face value and, in a moralizing tone, opposes it to the concreteness of violence in Colombia. The latter, it seems to me, for this German at least, does not invoke at all the Holocaust. In his prologue, Kohut stresses that the civilization/barbarism dichotomy has prospered in Latin American thinking and known several avatars. Playing with these variations, including the ones described by Moreno-Durán from barbarism to imagination, one afternoon in Bogotá, in a casual conversation with Germana Espinosa, there emerged the idea of inverting this juxtaposition and using it as a subtitle for the conference on the new Colombian literature which would be held at the Catholic University of Eichstätt. Kohut asks, in the Introduction, how imagination can possibly live with barbarism without being labelled guilty. The traditional literary answer to the violence in Colombia seemed to be committed literature: to denounce violence and analyse its causes is to open the way first for an awareness-building and then for an improvement. Kohut's argument is that the term *imagination*, as against barbarism, because of its playfulness, seems to divert attention from the painful reality of the country in an irresponsible manner. The term *barbarism*, he further argues, applied to the situation in Colombia in the last decades, was for many a dangerous euphemism because it dilutes the political dimension of the term into a vague, ahistorical concept. Violence, he supposes, is always political, a means of oppression by a ruling class anxious to maintain its power at any cost. In this sense, Colombia will be a country of violence *par excellence* and its literature would be one of violence (9). It lies beyond my scope to discuss the simplicity of such a cause and effect relationship, but I shall give a summary of the author's argument. Kohut warns that one cannot forget that *la violencia* defines a concrete period in the recent history of the country, or even of the literature that emerged from it. Violence itself has not disappeared from reality nor from literature; in fact, it is so difficult to eradicate that it seems that the word is no longer enough to designate the phenomenon. This may be a telling reason why a group of Colombian writers and intellectuals preferred to talk about barbarism when launching a manifesto on the occasion of a bloody incident that caused indignation in public opinion for a few days, until other atrocities condemned it to silence (10). In the manifesto, they talk of being threatened by barbarism and the impunity surrounding it. Barbarism, in Kohut's discourse, is not used euphemistically to avoid *violence*, but to signal, on the contrary, a more general reality. The term *violence* designates any aggressive act, which could be either verbal or a murder. He therefore interrogates how one can define a generalized violence or its conscious and systematic use for political reasons. Asserting that economic elements also account for Colombian violence, which has its roots in the struggle for political power, he thus makes the point that the temptation must be constant for an artist to close his or her eyes to this reality and envelop him or herself 'en el idilio con las letras' (11). He further points out that in a text written in 1992, and published a year later, Carlos Fuentes vindicates imagination against all the requirements of realism and the social engagement that dominated the intellectual debate in the1950s. 'Invirtiendo el proceso de la creación', Kohut borrows words from Gustavo Cobo Borda to express the view that the novels reviewed in the book are a way of knowing the Colombian reality of those years as 'una sociedad enferma' (16). Following the same line of thought, Kohut reads it as a society that has lost traditional values. These processes of the collective consciousness in Colombian society are manifested in the barbaric struggle for political and economic power, or in the desperate attempt to build a private life amidst omnipresent barbarism. On the vitality of Colombian literature, he again quotes Cobo Borda who defines it as 'una cultura sana en un país enfermo', further to highlight his argument that society's infirmity still remains a constant threat to literature (20).

It is not my business here to approach the particular problem of violence in Colombia, or to return to the old debate whether literature should mirror reality, or even whether committed literature will affect the problem of violence in the country. What I would point out are ways in which Kohut's discourse re-echoes those of the imperial enterprises of 500 years ago and strikes a Latin American ear as reminiscent of the colonizing bias of positivism. The shift from *De la barbarie a la imaginación* to *Imaginación y barbarie* not only recovers the antinomous structure but also strongly echoes Sarmiento's dichotomy that has barbarism as the second term. Equally problematic is the reawakening of the colonial discourses of the fifteenth and sixteenth centuries. In Kohut's argument, there is a desire for an entity that will resolve differences and chaos; in his metaphysics, the 'barbaric colony' sounds like a fall from an origin. Such a theological dimension is impregnated with the criterion of absence that, in the past, justified the European 'salvation' of America. The same criteria that informed the colonial enterprise of the fifteenth and sixteenth centuries re-emerge, this time in 1991, on the eve of the quincentenary of Columbus's arrival in the so-called New World. Such a criterion of absence, also described as the criterion of negation by Albert Memmi,[7] both informs and legitimizes, for example, the whole colonial enterprise of Portugal in Brazil, itself a product of Renaissance Europe. This criterion becomes apparent in the first document written by the chronicler of the voyages to the crown of Portugal. Pero Vaz de Caminha attributes difficult communication with the natives not to language barriers but to their barbarism, 'nom ouve mais fala, nem emtendimento com eles per ha berberia deles seer tamanha, que se nom emtemdia, nem ouvia ninguem'.[8] He further emphasizes that 'eles nom lavram, nem criam, nem haa quy boy, nem vaca, nem cabra, nem ovelha, nem galinha' (30); accordingly, 'ho milhor fruyto, que neela se pode fazer ... será salvar esta jemte; e esta deve seer a principal semente, que V.A. em ela deve lamçar' (34). Another feature of the letter is that the local 'inferior' population is even denied a name, and when it does receive one later, it is actually the misnomer *Indian*; 'they' and 'people', the mark of the plural that Memmi has referred to, deny the population individuality and identity. To save the indigenous, unnamed 'inferior' population, an unrequested salvation that bred an insolvent debt to the 'superior' culture becomes the colonialist policy. I shall return to Caminha's letter and its rereadings below.

The line of argument of the celebrated scribe of the maritime voyages is eloquent enough, albeit a euphemistic variant of Kohut's. For him, pre-babelic harmony remains, of course, as a theological hypothesis. Yet for those who inherit and inhabit the postcolonial condition, the very thought of oneness bears with it an accompanying legacy and heritage of totalitarian attempts to superimpose on hybrid and irreconcilable differences a violent hierarchy. And the histories of Latin America are riddled with such impositions, such demands and much extermination. For—let there be no doubt—the admission of unresolvable pluralities, the stance against civilizing unicity, is also a theologico-political enterprise. Kohut is evidence that it is not possible to think (from) outside the dormant formative traditions of one's discourses. Further still, he signals the clash of discourses that has informed many exchanges between Europe and Latin America ever since the foundational acts were cast in the fifteenth and sixteenth centuries in the form of imperishable signs, the well-known expression I borrow from Rama. Such an imposition has indeed opened the deconstruction of colonial relations.

It is certain dimensions of postcolonial manifestations in Latin American modernisms that I now pinpoint in order to broach their decolonizing project and specific dismantling of the civilization/barbarism binary through translation, a space where frontiers are blurred if not altogether abolished.

Signs of postcolonial turbulence in Modernism

In the specificity of Latin American modernisms, movements of artistic, intellectual and cultural renovation formulated critiques of colonialism and its consequences for the region. Writings defended nationalism and revised theories of racial whitening; the valuation of *mestizaje* and *indigenismo* were banners for the search and affirmation of a Latin American identity. There come to mind the *criollo* socialist *indigenista* José Carlos Mariátegui, in Peru, and the anti-imperialist ideas and the democratization of university teaching of Julio Antonio Mella, in Cuba.[9] In Brazil, an awareness of a persistent mental colonialism, even though the country had been politically freed from Portugal for a hundred years, led to theorizing on the question of external influences (to which I would add a-critical imitation of imports); the *Pau Brasil Manifesto* (Brazil Wood Manifesto) of 1924, according to Coutinho, raised the question of one-way historical relationships in terms of literary borrowings, whereas the *Verde Amarelo Manifesto* (alluding to the colours of the Brazilian flag) of 1926 argued for a straightforward literary nationalism; these movements were diverse but had in common an interest in Brazil and the wish to stress the national element (471).[10]

The emergence of an urban-industrial economy in Latin America in the early 1900s brought about changes in the socio-economic structure, whereas internal and external migration introduced a new social dynamics to the region (Prado, 12–15). The tension between internationalism and nationalism is the dominant strain of the period's literature. The desire to break with traditionalism led to the encounter with the several '-isms' of the European avant-garde. In fact, the attempts to modernize in the cultural sphere parallel the technological development enabled by industrial civilization. Irlemar Chiampi highlights another dimension of the colonial debate which adds to the sense of a turbulent modernization in Latin America:

> Oitenta anos depois da Independência, e ao mesmo tempo de acontecimentos traumáticos como a guerra hispano-cubano-norte-americana (1898) e a tomada do istmo do Panamá pelos Estados Unidos (1903), as repúblicas latino-americanas mostravam os sintomas de sua conturbada modernização. Às grandes cidades do passado barroco, do vice-reinado (México, Lima), somam-se as novas urbes portuárias, como Buenos Aires e Montevidéu, cuja fisionomia se altera com o inchamento populacional provocado pela imigração estrangeira e pelas migrações internas; novas formas de vida e de trabalho, com a afirmação das classes médias e a diversificação das classes populares, sinalizam a vertigem do progresso e a babelização urbana, muito estimuladas pelos países industrializados, em busca de novos mercados para seus produtos e matérias-primas para fabricá-los.[11]

Chiampi also notes Martí's and Rodó's intellectual views of the process:

> José Martí, o primeiro escritor a exercer efetivamente o papel de intelectual moderno na América Hispânica, registrou ... a percepção do novo conceito de tempo que desmembrava as mentes, com o empuxo do capitalismo e a modernização burguesa. Tempos, diz o poeta cubano, de 'reenquiciamiento y remolde', numa sorte de desconcerto e lucidez que terá notável eco no tom messiânico que outro grande intelectual modernista, o uruguaio José Enrique Rodó, assume diante da crise social, política e moral da América Hispânica dos oitocentos. (187)

Beatriz Sarlo, referring to the specific case of Buenos Aires, stresses that there remains, in a contradictory and hardly explicable way, the idea of a periphery and of a culturally tributary space, endowed with the character of a monstrous or inadequate formation with reference to Europe.[12] Ana Maria Belluzzo, in turn, highlights other features of this turbulent panorama that supposes a relationship between the American countries and the international centres as well as an internal unevenness between socioeconomic modernization and cultural modernism. Modernism thus presents itself as the awareness of a dilemma: 'como é possível estar na ponta do tempo e situar-se em países pré-industriais, com marcas da história colonial, recém-saídos do regime escravista?'[13] Still according to Belluzzo, the Anthropophagous Movement of the 1920s in Brazil overcomes the contradiction of dependent countries through the digestion and the incorporation of colonizing civilizations, whereas Mexican muralism stands as a project of social emancipation (24). In Colombia, Rafael Maya remarks, Modernism was like a second independence from Spain, at least in its origins. France, Germany, England had a greater influence on the making of a modernist aesthetics than did the Peninsula.[14]

The specific cultural redefinitions of the continent correlate with the Latin American avant-garde project of rediscovering America. In this play of identities, there are discussions of nation and race which go beyond the positivist interpretations of the previous century. Ideas come to the surface concerning the fusion of several cultures into one and redimensioning notions of copy and original. There emerges an alternative discourse, namely, one of translation, revising such simplistic dichotomies as civilization and barbarism. The archetypal example of Babel thus sites us in the context of deconstruction of mental colonialism through translation. *Trans*—a prefix that disrupts univocity and dichotomies.

Ig/noble Modernist barbarians translating

Derrida has approximated translation and the deconstruction of empire:

> Before the deconstruction of Babel, the great Semitic family was establishing its empire, which it wanted universal, and its tongue, which it also attempts to impose on the universe ... raising a tower, constructing a city, making a name for oneself in a universal tongue which would also be an idiom, and gathering a filiation ... Out of resentment against that unique name and lip of men, he [God] imposes his name, his name of father; and with this violent imposition he opens the deconstruction of the tower, as of the universal language.[15]

On the subject of translation and empire, I share Homi Bhabha's view of the different and the differential, the confrontation of the alien and the foreign in translation:

> In the restless drive for cultural translation, hybrid sites of meaning open up a cleavage in the language of culture which suggests that the similitude of the symbol as it plays across cultural sites must not obscure the fact that repetition of the *sign* is, in each specific social practice, both different and differential. It is in this sense that the enunciation of cultural difference emerges *in its proximity* ... [t]hrough that apprehension of difference [it becomes possible] to perform the act of cultural difference. In the act of translation the 'given' content becomes alien and estranged; and that, in its turn, leaves the language

of translation *Aufgabe*, always confronted by its double, the untranslatable—alien and foreign.[16]

Bhabha makes explicit use of the term 'cultural translation' with reference to strategies of empowerment of the postcolonial subject. In order to relate cultural translation to insurgent acts and the renewal of the past, he relies on Fanon's view of the importance of subordinated peoples asserting their indigenous cultural traditions and retrieving their repressed histories. Disjunctive temporalities, the foreignness of language, the ambivalence of cultural difference are some of the key terms that describe his view of cultural translation, one which desacralizes the transparent assumption of cultural supremacy (226–29). In Latin America, translation as a supplement and intralingual translation will be seen to be modalities of cultural translation which anticipate Bhabha's formulation; in its dismantling of binaries and mental colonialisms, translation found an eloquent moment in the 1920s. Cultural translation for Bhabha is blasphemy, as is the case he analyses of Rushdie's *The Satanic Verses*. In contrast, cultural translation in Latin America tends to depart from the dimension of blasphemy highlighted by Bhabha. Rather, as mentioned, in its association with irony and parody, the latter understood etymologically as a parallel canto, cultural translation in Latin America has been a privileged mode for the expression of postcolonial subjectivities.

Presenting a project of translation as supplement to the original, the Colombian poet-translator Guillermo Valencia brings to visibility historical difference while subverting through irony the dichotomy of the civilized and the barbarian. He makes his entrance into literature when Modernism was emerging in Spanish American letters and at a moment of intense intellectual activity, when the modernist revolution was already changing existing values. Literary translation blossomed in an environment that attempted an 'aggiornamento' of the local culture, beyond imitation of the foreign and towards assimilation, that ended up changing its own themes and techniques.[17] Valencia produced several translations and in

1929 published *Cathay*, a collection of Chinese poems which he had translated from *La Flute de Jade* of Franz Toussaint; he also translated Oscar Wilde, Victor Hugo, Paul Verlaine, Charles Baudelaire, Johann Wolfgang Goethe, Reiner Maria Rilke, Rabindranath Tagore and Machado de Assis, among others.

No metaphor, no matter how efficient, represents a plenitude, a satisfaction. Efficacy depends on fragmentation and discontinuities. It is in this light that I shall analyse Valencia's project of renewal of the past and his textualization of the encounter with the other in a third space where original and translation, disrupting dichotomies and one-way flows, are both donors and receivers of forms and meanings. In a sonnet that he wrote as a gift to Enrique U. White, another renowned Colombian translator, he offered his own version in Spanish of Keats's 'Ode on a Grecian Urn'.[18] He mentions that the urn, once in his possession, because of his 'barbarian clumsiness', broke into fragments which lay at his feet; with a 'gentle hand', he decides to reunite the pieces and send the restored urn to White:

A UNA URNA GRIEGA
(De John Keats)

ENVÍO
Al ingeniero Enrique Urban White

    La grácil urna que cincel ignoto
legó al futuro, con primor labrada,
el noble Keats dejó transfigurada
por su mano genial un exvoto.

    Vino hasta mí y en mi poder se ha roto
el ánfora gentil: despedazada,
yace a mis pies. Mi atónita mirada
nublan las amarguras del devoto.

    Qué hacer? Cuanto mi bárbara torpeza
hizo trizas, con mano diligente
busco, acomodo y ligo, pieza a pieza.

> Restaurada la urna floreciente,
> la calco en vil arcilla, con presteza,
> y te la envío cariñosamente.

Valencia's apparent subservience and acceptance of the colonizing epithet of 'barbarian' and its implications of unruly destructiveness only highlight the greater complexity of his project of permanence collateral with change, as distinct from Keats's own project of permanence in art.[19] It is a well-known fact that Keats describes in his poem one of the Greek urns in the British Museum; transposing a non-verbal sign to a verbal one, Keats transfigures 'a silent form', 'a bride of quietness' into 'rhyme to be heard'. A Greek urn is taken to the Museum, crystallizing time and transformation, keeping the other, in Keats's words, like an 'unravished bride'.[20] In fact, the theme of permanence in art is well-developed in Keats's poem: abstracted from a world of transformation and decadence, in which 'old generation shall this generation waste', the urn remains untouchable and untouched. Keats's very reading of the procession carved on the urn can be seen as a metaphor of continuity, which is further corroborated by expressions such as 'play on', 'forever' and, above all, 'Thou shalt remain' in the last stanza of the poem.

Noteworthy here is the exploration by the Brazilian theorist of translation, Haroldo de Campos, of the satanic dimensions of a project that unleashes the epistemological challenge of discontinuities and breaks with the tyranny of a preordained logos. In Valencia's sonnet, as supplement, the Greek urn that travelled 'unravished' from the classical past to the museum and thence to Keats's poem, travels via translation towards the future in Latin America, where, possessed and broken by the translator's hands, it is again reassembled and lives on, but transformed. Its continued existence in a different corporeality transcends the crystallization of history effected by the museum: it is also a pre-text for the autonomous creation of a sonnet that supplements the original. In fact, in the first stanza of Valencia's sonnet, the urn is described as having arrived in the future, that is, the translator begins exactly where

Keats's prediction had ended. Past and future merge as Valencia feeds on, and ironizes, Keats's theme that art outlives time and deterioration in order to theorize translation as continuation, through the reconstruction and renovation of the original. For Valencia, art represents permanence and change. Possessed by the Latin American hand, the properties of its closures were undone, fissures were created, spaces were open for it to be filled. Clumsy … or deft?

Another Latin American practice, that of intralingual translation, involving disruption of the authority of hegemonic discourses, has been crucial to giving a historical voice to the colonized. In this modality of cultural translation, elements are rearticulated but the same language remains. As attention is diverted from the linguistic component of translation, its historical and cultural dimensions only become more salient. The Argentine Jorge Luis Borges has been recognized as the initiator of intralingual translation to subvert hegemonic discourses. Such is the case with his Pierre Menard, a translation from Spanish into Spanish, in which he obliterates Cervantes and all the historical context of colonization and cultural domination.[21] Menard's ambition was to produce pages that would coincide in all the details with Cervantes's. For this purpose, he would subscribe to the project of duplication of seventeenth-century Europe—which would mean for him learning Spanish well, saving the Catholic faith, fighting the Moors or the Turks and so on (91). Ironically, the project of duplication is the least interesting, which leads to the decision of keeping the *Quixote* but obliterating Cervantes from the scene, which also meant the exclusion of the autobiographical foreword (91). In his alternative version, Menard would enter Cervantes's text through his own experiences and not through gypsies, conspirators, mystics, Philip the Second, *autos da fé* and the like (93). In an ambiguous gesture, Borges copies the original but obliterates the origin, supplementing it with his own history. Such a transgressive dimension of translation in Borges has been highlighted by Aníbal González: 'the new version must arise as if it were another, yet not altogether different work, "another, yet the same", as Borges says in one of his favourite phrases. For translation to work it must be transgressive; it must hold nothing sacred.'[22]

Borges's challenge regarding 'another, yet the same' has been taken up most recently by the critic and theorist of Latin American literature, Bernard McGuirk. Situating self-in-other/other-in-self not only in Judaic philosophical but also in myriad Latin American intellectual debates, McGuirk juxtaposes Levinasian or Derridean concepts of translation with the literary praxes of Borges himself and, say, the Brazilian João Guimarães Rosa, the Guatemalan Augusto Monterroso or, most tellingly, the Argentine Susana Thénon. He unveils the (post)colonial dimension of intralingual translation of her *Ova completa* [*Complete Eggs*] (1987) in his analysis of her treatment of the Malvinas/Falklands conflict in 'Poema con traducción simultánea Español–Español'. Thénon is shown to attack a cyclical colonizing aggression at the same time as undermining its illusory binarism of a past and present (1492/1982) which might make history emerge as mere linguistic repetition, banal (non-)quincentenary. Translation functions rather as an intensifier of violence, be it in the Church/State complicity of missal/missile or in her passage from the 'amen' of self-satisfied completion, inseparably theological and teleological, to 'omen' and a warning of resistance.[23]

Well before Borges and Thénon, however, the Brazilian Mário de Andrade, associated with the Antropófago Movement of the1920s, had explored the potential of intralingual translation to dismantle colonialism and its subsequent rereadings through the old positivist binaries. In 'Carta pras Icamiabas' (dated 30 May 1926), he transposes the sixteenth-century document written by the Portuguese scribe, Pero Vaz de Caminha, on 1 May 1500, into the cultural context of his own decade. This is when there was a re-evaluation of a persistent mental colonialism one hundred years after the political independence of Brazil. The political dimensions of intralingual translation as articulation of (post)colonial subjectivities become apparent through initial reference to another version of the letter which was published in 1865 by João Francisco Lisboa, in Brazil and subsequently in Lisbon in 1901. Lisboa's version foregrounds the language component, thus exemplifying the common philological understanding of intralingual translation as the modernizing of texts:

> Empregamos o termo 'traduzir', mesmo em relação à esta carta, por que está em um português tão antigo, e a ortografia é tal, que ao comum dos leitores não seria hoje fácil a sua inteligência, se não procurássemos remoçá-la, mediante a tradução que fizemos. Êste documento raríssimo, pôsto que já publicado em quatro diversas edições, só o temos visto, sob essa forma obsoleta e difícil, na *Corografia brasílica* do Padre Aires do Casal e em uma tradução de Fernão Denis.[24]

In contrast, intralingual translation as the articulation of political subjectivities unveils differences not only inside language but also inside discourses and histories. Language, in its superficial sameness, betrays, it becomes a daemonic double, unleashing confrontations and alternative readings. In fact, the inextricability of translation and parody becomes quite apparent in Latin American discourses on the subject. The Argentine Roberto Ferro, for example, has remarked that parody is the privileged mode through which Latin America has problematized power hierarchies manifested in the paradigm of centre/periphery and in the series model/copy, original/translation; it is a mode which dismantles the sacralizing presuppositions of protocols of anteriority and privileged model, undoing the one-way movement between metropolis and colony.[25] Another Argentine, Noé Jitrik, elaborates the specificity of parody in Latin America as one that modifies the reading of a text A through the apprehension of a text B, whether through recontextualization or through deformation; reference is made to the colonial context as he spells out procedures associable with parody, including translation:

> Deformaciones, apropiaciones, plagios y traducciones son, entonces, aparatos de escritura que si bien indicarían una

condición de sumisión, también—y esto es lo propio de la literatura colonial latino-americana—manifestarían un deseo de redimirse de ella mediante otros aparatos complementarios; por ejemplo, el distanciamento y la deformación.[26]

Such Latin specificity, Jitrik argues, implies another way of approaching parody as rendered in *para* ('by' in Greek) and *oidia* ('canto'); *parodia* thus means 'by the canto', 'co-extensive with the text in a broad sense' (13–14). The Brazilian Haroldo de Campos has also developed the concept of 'plagiotropy' in relation to translation, relating it to parody in the etymological meaning of 'parallel canto'.[27] Plagiotropy, for de Campos, who stresses the etymology of 'plagios' as 'oblique', 'transverse', means the translation of tradition. Semiotically speaking, it is an unlimited semiosis as found in Pierce and Eco, and again has to do with the etymological meaning of parody as 'parallel canto' to designate the non-linear transformation of texts throughout history (75–76). This etymological reactivation of parody had been elaborated by de Campos in 1973 in his *Morfologia do Macunaíma* and previously introduced in his *Oswald de Andrade: trechos escolhidos* (1967).[28] Bakhtin's dialogism and polyphony, as well as Kristeva's reformulation of them in intertextuality, are close to de Campos's (and, for that matter, also Jitrik's) etymological reading of parody, as de Campos demonstrates (*Deus e o diabo*, 73–74).

In her analysis of the novel *Macunaíma*, by Mário de Andrade, Eneida Maria de Souza notes that he makes a parody of the scene of colonization and catechism, which aimed to make the Indians white inside by forcing on them the white man's religion and customs. But the eponymous hero Macunaíma is metamorphosed into a white man outside, a caricature of the colonization project.[29] As such, he enters the world of progress of São Paulo, where he emerges as Macunaíma the Emperor. I would add that in the novel *Macunaíma* one finds a 'body-becomes-history' not only parodying the official chronicles of colonization but also writing a critique of the positivistic ideology of racial whitening. When Macunaíma is leaving his dwellings, he wakes up early to go to the estuary of the Rio Negro where he would like to leave his conscience. A new being is about to emerge. As he approaches São Paulo, as it was a very hot day, he and his brothers thought of bathing in a pond. What they did not know is that the pond contained holy water, an element of Christianity but also one of purification. When dark-skinned Macunaíma, the first to bathe, got out of the pond he was blond, blue-eyed and fair-complexioned, '*a água tinha lavado seu pretume*' (29–30). When his brother Jiguê took notice of the miracle, he dived into the water which, already stained by Macunaíma's blackness, gave Jiguê a bronze colour. Maanape, the second brother, was the last one to try but, as most of the water had been spilled, he could only wash away the blackness of the palms of his hands and the soles of his feet. Whitening becomes a precondition for Macunaíma to enter the world of civilization, from where he writes the 'Carta pras Icamiabas'. But what of his hybrid brother? What of the two-coloured one? Would the white soles and hands entitle him to belong to the race identified with civilization?

In what follows, I take up Roberto Schwarz's suggestion of exploring the elements of parody in 'Carta pras Icamiabas'; his claim is that 'in countries where culture is imported, parody is almost a natural form of criticism'.[30] In this trajectory, I shall also extemporize from the shift of point of view suggested by Silviano Santiago in a recent reading of Caminha's letter. Santiago stresses neither the sender of the letter, Caminha, nor its content but rather what the letter performs on behalf of the Portuguese monarch and what it fails to perform in relation to the greatest actors in the whole scenario of the discovery: the sailors. As the letter reaches its destination and the king takes possession of it, he simultaneously takes possession of the land and human beings described in it. The letter creates for history the event of the discovery of a country by a European one and the emergence of a Western nation-state called Brazil. The annexation of Brazil to the kingdom involves the sailors' discovery of the land and donation of it, the king's taking possession, and the Pope's sanctioning of the possession.

But what of reciprocity to the sailors who have been the active ones? The dream of a woman is the only reason remaining for the sailors' maritime voyages. And what of the natives who have been dispossessed and live outside European feudalism and mercantilism? On a land that does not require ploughing, the main seed that the King sows is the word of God that will bear the best fruit: the christianized barbarian.[31]

As I bring into focus the 'christianized barbarians' in 'Carta pras Icamiabas', my own reading coalesces with what Bhabha has theorized as the third space of enunciation, in which 'the transformational value of change lies in the rearticulation, or translation, of elements that are *neither the one ... nor the other ... but something else besides* which contests the terms and territories of both' (219). For Macunaíma uses and disabuses the reader of even the possibility of the usefulness of cause-and-effect arguments and positivist modes of discourse. The letter is written by Macunaíma, from the 'boa cidade de São Paulo—a maior do universo, no dizer de seus prolixos habitantes', in his capacity of Emperor of the Virgin Forests. Macunaíma, culturally hybrid, belonging and not belonging, establishes a linguistic and rhetorical complicity with Caminha. Yet he will do so foregrounding the spaces of transgression of binaries only hinted at by his precursor.

In Caminha's letter, a big rug marks off the boundary between the well- and over-dressed Portuguese Captain, wearing a big golden necklace, and the naked natives. The garment emerges as a symbol of culture and of the civilized in contrast with nakedness, interpreted as an absence of civilized features. At one point, a tired native fell asleep naked on the Captain's rug, breaking the boundaries between the civilized and the non-civilized, the superior and the inferior. The Captain immediately gave orders for him to be covered with a blanket; yet, his initiative, while performing a moralizing mission, makes the blanket a grotesque reminder of the act of transgression. The barbarian, lying between two layers of civilization—the rug and the blanket—weaves a link between the worlds of civilization and barbarism, dismantling the binarism. On another occasion, the

Portuguese, again as part of their civilizing mission as disseminators of faith and empire, are fixing the Cross, an element of Christianity heavy with connotations of sin and redemption. The natives come to help, and, once more unware that they are treading on forbidden ground, they dance naked. In a parallel move, the scribe himself transgresses the conventions of official discourse and, by way of repetition, brings out the erotic—there comes to mind the number of occasions in which he refers to the beautiful bodies of the Indians, with nothing to cover their shaven 'vergonhas'.

A movement from repressed to unrepressed desire transforms blankets into see-through fabrics and, more tellingly, 'vergonhas' into 'graças'. The ladies Macunaíma sees in São Paulo are, in part, reminiscent of the Captain—they are overdressed in scintillating jewels and adornments imported from all over the world. Yet, their very fine clothes hardly cover their 'graças', which links them with the naked natives. Repression is there and not there, the barbarian dwells in the civilized and the civilized in the barbarian as they move between the worlds of order and disorder. The ladies are polyglots, they are elegantly attired and reveal a fine taste for lobsters. But, at the same time, they are great money-grabbers. Moving between the cosmopolitan world and the marginality of prostitution, they are 'dóceis e facilmente trocáveis por pequeninas e voláteis folhas de papel a que o vulgo chamará dinheiro—o "curriculum vitae" da civilização', as Macunaíma says (98). It is via the unrepressed element in civilization, sexuality, that Macunaíma is inscribed into the mercantile world. The ladies 'brincam' and do so with great ability, not only for the sake of it but also in exchange for metal, champagne and lobsters (99). Yet, Macunaíma, maybe parodying the ideology of a Sarmiento who saw in importation of immigrants from Europe a way of advancing the cause of civilization, intends these ladies who had 'mestras da velha Europa', especially France, to be a model for the Icamiabas to learn love games. If imported from the city to the country, they would teach the Icamiabas 'um moderno e mais rendoso gênero de vida' (de Andrade, 103). He warns, though, that the risk is that such 'civilized women' might make use of beasts so as not to lose their bread-earning power (104). The animalistic features of civilization gain in definition as Macunaíma refers to São Paulo as the beautiful capital of the Latinness in which we live—one inhabited by 'a fauna urbana' (105).

São Paulo is the city that lives between order and disorder or where order thrives on disorder. Its organized inhabitants live and develop according to the positivistic dictum of the Brazilian flag, 'Ordem e Progesso', but for the wrong reasons. As the city is full of thieves, they have trained an impressive police that has the further duty of entertaining the maids; as the city had very good hospitals, it attracted the South American lepers; the balance of population is achieved through the microbes that decimate the inhabitants. Such an epitome of equilibrium—order and progress—Macunaíma predicts, will soon be a colony of England or the USA. Already conversant with the logic of mercantilism, he asks the Icamiabas for more beans to compensate for the price-drop in the cocoa market, thus enabling him to pay the money-grabbers. Ironically, the christianized barbarian closes the letter by sending his blessings to the Icamiabas.

Macunaíma and the São Paulo ladies do not inhabit either but rather both the territories of the civilized and the barbarian. Mario de Andrade, in fact, unlike the Argentine author of *Martin Fierro*, does not postulate barbarism as an alternative to civilization. What he highlights is the barbarian in the colonized and the civilized in the barbarian. Rather than the mutually exclusive terms of civilization and barbarism, the liminal space which he foregrounds subverts the possibility of oneness. This space further reveals the complex co-existence of a colonial legacy and the pressures of modernization—the very stuff of Latin American Modernism broached from a political and cultural perspective.

By way of conclusion, I return to the shadow of colonialism lurking behind Kohut's juxtaposition of imagination and barbarism, and again I ask whether it is possible to think from outside the dormant traditions of Eurocentric discourses and their assimilation in Latin America. In and out of the chain and enchantment of binaries, I have tried to show both the noble and the ignoble in the civilized and the barbarian alike—inseparably. And I re-echo Silviano Santiago's ever resonant but underheeded words in the debate on the postcolonial in Latin America, highlighting the concept of inbetweenness:

> Entre o sacrifício e o jogo, entre a prisão e a transgressão, entre a submissão ao código e a agressão, entre a obediência e a rebelião, entre a assimilação e a expressão,—ali, nesse lugar aparentemente vazio, seu templo e seu lugar de clandestinidade, ali, se realiza o ritual antropófago da literatura latino-americana.[32]

Notes

1 Karl Kohut, 'Introducción' to *Literatura colombiana hoy: imaginación y barbarie [Actas del Simposio 'Literatura Colombiana Hoy, Imaginación y Barbarie' del 5 al 8 de noviembre de 1991]*, ed. K. Kohut (Frankfurt am Main: Vervuert/Madrid: Iberoamericana, 1994), 9–24.

2 Roberto Fernández Retamar, *Algunos usos de civilización y barbarie y otros ensayos* (Buenos Aires: Editorial Contrapunto SRL, 1976); Rafael Humberto Moreno-Durán, *De la barbarie a la imaginación* (Barcelona: Tusquets, 1976).

3 Aracy Amaral, 'As Duas Américas Latinas ou Três, Fora do Tempo', in *Fundadores da modernidade*, ed. Irlemar Chiampi (São Paulo: Editora Ática, 1991), 174.

4 Angel Rama, *The Lettered City*, trans. and ed. John Charles Chasteen (Durham and London: Duke University Press, 1996), 76.

5 In Mário de Andrade, *Macunaíma: o herói sem nenhum caráter* (Belo Horizonte: Itatiaia, 1985), 94–111.

6 Page references given in parenthesis in the text mirror the linear progression of my summary of the contents of this essay by Fernández Retamar. I adopt the same practice in the subsequent paragraphs that are devoted to brief summaries of contributions by Moreno-Durán and Kohut.

7   Albert Memmi, *Retrato do colonizado precedido pelo retrato do colonizador*, trans. Roland Corbisier (Rio de Janeiro: Paz e Terra, 1977), 81.

8   All the references to Pero Vaz de Caminha's document are taken from *Corografia brasílica de Ayres de Casal: Facsimile da edição de 1817*, introduced by Caio Prado Junior (Rio de Janeiro: Imprensa Nacional, 1945), 12–34 (19).

9   Luiz Fernando Prado, *História contemporânea da América Latina 1930–1960* (Porto Alegre: Ed. da Universidade/UFRGS, 1996), 13–16.

10 Afrânio Coutinho, *A Literatura no Brasil*, vol. 3 (1) (Rio de Janeiro: Livraria São José, 1959), 67.

11 Irlemar Chiampi, 'A modernidade nas literaturas de língua espanhola', in *Fundadores da modernidade*, 180–88 (187).

12 Beatriz Sarlo, 'Modernidad y mezcla cultural: el caso de Buenos Aires', in *Modernidade: vanguardas artísticas na América Latina*, ed. Ana Maria de Moraes Belluzzo (São Paulo: Fundação Memorial América Latina: UNESP, 1990), 31–34 (32).

13 Ana Maria de M. Belluzzo, 'Apresentação', in *Modernidade: vanguardas artísticas na América Latina*, 9–12 (10).

14 Rafael Maya, *Los orígenes del modernismo en Colombia* (Bogotá: Impr. Nacional, 1961), 23.

15 Jacques Derrida, 'Des Tours de Babel', trans. Joseph Graham, in *Difference in Translation*, ed. with an introduction by Joseph Graham (Ithaca and London: Cornell University Press, 1985), 165–207 (166–69).

16 Homi K. Bhabha, *The Location of Culture* (London and New York: Routledge, 1994), 163–64.

17 Alan S. Trueblood, 'Wilde y Valencia: La Balada de la cárcel de Reading', in *Estudios: edición en homenaje a Guillermo Valencia 1873–1973*, ed. Hernán Torres (Cali: Carvajal y Cia, 1976), 139–96.

18 Guillermo Valencia, '"A una urna griega" (de John Keats) envío *Al ingeniero Enrique Urban White*', in *Obras poéticas completas* (Madrid: Aguilar, 1948), 844.

19 Frances R. Aparicio, in *Versiones, interpretaciones, creaciones: instancias de la traducción literaria en Hispanoamérica en el siglo veinte*

(Gaithersburg: Ediciones Hispamérica, 1991), 38 considers the sonnet as a metaphor for the process of poetic and linguistic decodification and recodification. En passant, she argues that its tone of modesty cannot be taken literally and alludes to the possibility that it can be a reflex of the colonial relation between Latin America and Europe. It is thus Valencia's articulation of subaltern subjectivities through the ironic handling of the civilization/barbarism binary on which I elaborate.

20 References to Keats's 'Ode on a Grecian urn' are from *The Poetical Works of John Keats*, ed. H. W. Garrod (Oxford: Oxford University Press, 1958).

21 First published in 1941. References here are to Jorge Luis Borges, 'Pierre Menard, Author of the Quixote', in *Collected Fictions*, trans. Andrew Hurley (Harmondsworth: Allen Lane/The Penguin Press, 1998), 88–95.

22 Aníbal González, 'Translation and Genealogy: *One Hundred Years of Solitude*', in *Gabriel García Márquez: New Readings*, ed. Bernard McGuirk and Richard Cardwell (Cambridge: Cambridge University Press, 1987), 65–80 (72).

23 Bernard McGuirk, 'Post-Back to the Suture: On the Un*seam*liness of Patriarchal Discourse in Susana Thénon's *Ova Completa*', in *Latin American Literature: Symptoms, Risks & Strategies of Post-Structuralist Criticism* (London and New York: Routledge, 1997), Chapter II.

24 Quoted in Manoel de Sousa Pinto, *Pero Vaz de Caminha e a carta do 'Achamento' do Brasil: lições proferidas em 5 e 7 de Maio de 1934* (Lisboa: Imprensa da Universidade, 1934), 32–33.

25 Roberto Ferro, 'Introducción', in *La parodia en la literatura latinoamericana*, ed. with an introduction by R. Ferro (Buenos Aires: Facultad de Fiolosofía y Letras–UBA, 1993), 7–12 (7).

26 Noé Jitrik, 'Rehabilitación de la parodia', in *La parodia en la literatura latinoamericana*, 13–32 (29).

27 Haroldo de Campos, *Deus e o Diabo no Fausto de Goethe* (São Paulo: Perspectiva, 1981), 74.

28 Haroldo de Campos, *Morfologia do Macunaíma* (São Paulo: Perspectiva, 1973) and Haroldo de Campos, *Oswald de Andrade—Trechos Escolhidos* (Rio de Janeiro: Agir, 1967).

29 Eneida Maria de Souza, *A pedra mágica do discurso: jogo e linguagem em Macunaíma* (Belo Horizonte: Editora UFMG, 1988).

30 Roberto Schwarz, 'Beware of Alien Ideologies: An Interview with *Movimento*', in *Misplaced Ideas: Essays on Brazilian Culture*, ed. with an introduction by John Gledson (London and New York: Verso, 1992), 33–40 (40).

31 Silviano Santiago, 'Destinos de uma carta' (conferência plenária), *Congresso 1498–1998: Raízes, Rotas e Reflexões* (Association of Hispanists of Great Britain and Ireland, Braga, Universidade do Minho, 7–11 September 1998).

32 Silviano Santiago, *Uma literatura nos trópicos: ensaios de dependência cultural* (São Paulo: Editora Perspectiva, 1978), 28.

CHAPTER THREE

José Carlos Mariátegui: Culture and the Nation

Patricia D'Allemand
Queen Mary and Westfield College,
University of London

Discussing Mariátegui's critical works in the context of a postcolonial approach to Spanish American and Lusophone cultures calls for a note of clarification. While the writings of the Peruvian undoubtedly constitute a major contribution to the dismantling of colonial perspectives within reflections on literature and culture in Latin America, I am nevertheless somewhat sceptical about the legitimacy—and indeed the productivity—of attempts to assimilate Mariátegui into postcolonial studies.[1] Amongst my concerns vis-à-vis this type of reading strategy are the danger of dehistoricization of Latin American discourses, the dilution of their particular traits and multiplicity of meanings, and the consequent loss of sight of local traditions of thought, as well as the silencing of local debates. What worries me is the tendency to homogenize critiques of colonialism and modernity that have emerged from within very distinct colonial histories and societies. I am not denying the usefulness of locating affinities between the objectives of postcolonialism on the one hand, and those of either the critical thought of the Latin American Left, or of the region's cultural criticism, on the other, but I am very wary of the effects of constructing new universalist theoretical approaches.[2] Such a construction and the imposition of such approaches upon Latin America bring with them, after all, the risk of erasing the very distinctiveness of those histories and societies, of possibly establishing single agendas, sometimes at the expense of local ones, and even of undermining the relevance of the thinkers of the region to contemporary debates on Latin American culture.[3] In the particular case of Mariátegui, whom I would place within this tradition of Latin American cultural criticism, I have a fear of new simplifications of the multifaceted nature of his critical writings, all too reminiscent of the reductionism to which they were subjected by a rather dominant orthodox Marxist tendency amongst his critics, a reductionism that will be examined in this essay.

There is an abundance of commentary on Mariátegui's work, yet relatively little attention has been paid to his aesthetic and cultural reflections. When these are examined, the focus of the analysis tends to concentrate on 'El proceso de la literatura', the last of his *Siete ensayos de interpretación de la realidad peruana*, an essay that covers only one aspect of his multiple enquiries into the processes of emancipation and renewal within the Latin American cultural sphere.[4] This narrow treatment of Mariátegui's work, derived perhaps from a tendency to divorce art and politics in the discourse of the Peruvian thinker, is evident even in one of his best critics, Antonio Cornejo Polar, whose important work on Andean *indigenismo* can be largely understood as a development of central aspects of 'El proceso …'. With a few exceptions such as Antonio Melis and Alberto Flores Galindo, Mariátegui's critics have not been disposed to engage in a positive reading of the unorthodox aspects of his writings, which have thereby been ignored or discounted as 'irrational' or 'idealist' deviations within his Marxism. This reticence on the part of Mariátegui's critics to approach what in fact constitutes one of the creative aspects of the Peruvian's Marxism has led to an incomplete reading of his proposals, which to a large extent distorts them. Such reluctance, on the other hand, is partly explained by the difficulties which have traditionally accompanied Marxist thought when accounting for the creative phenomenon, and, on a more general level, is a consequence of the dominance of the scientifist tendency within Latin American social sciences until a few years ago.[5] In many ways this narrow approach to Mariátegui's critical discourse has impoverished its capacity to intervene in the current cultural debate. My essay discusses the reasons for this selective reading of Mariátegui's critical project and proposes a reading that sets out to restore not only the complexity of his critical discourse but also its relevance to contemporary concerns within Latin American cultural criticism.

The selective treatment of Mariátegui's critical project can be understood to a certain extent in terms of the nationalist and anti-imperialist positions that have prevailed within intellectual production of the Latin American Left from the 1960s onwards. Within the region's cultural criticism, these positions have led to a privileging of literatures articulated to local traditional cultures, in opposition to and in preference to urban literatures which are a part of the internationalized circuits of culture. This bi-polarization of Latin American literature is actually a perspective more typical of contemporary criticism than of Mariátegui's proposals.

In synthesis, although the image of Mariátegui's discourse offered by critics may be valid, it is certainly incomplete; a good part of his reflections on questions of art and culture are not included. Such reflections do not merely constitute an appendix to his political discourse. In fact, contemporary Latin American criticism can find alternative ways of dealing with some of its central problems by referring to both Mariátegui's approach to the articulation of the two spheres without subordination of one to the other, and his treatment—derived from this approach—of the languages and formal experimentation of the avant-garde. Furthermore, an examination of the plurality of aesthetic projects which Mariátegui is able to handle is as useful for the current cultural debate as is an analysis of the ways in which his understanding of the national question brings him to vindicate Andean tradition and to retrieve it for modern Peruvian culture, without falling into sectarian or programmatic attitudes. The revolutionary and transforming potential of art is not the preserve of spaces articulated to traditional cultures; the innovation of Peruvian literature allows for a multiplicity of quests which does not exclude that of languages which are produced in the cities and become part of the internationalized circuits of culture. Finally, it would also be a great loss to the discipline to undervalue the importance of the very nature of Mariátegui's approach to literature, an approach which keeps him from falling into either aprioristic ideological positions or readings centred on the content of works of art to the exclusion of formal aspects. Mariátegui's enthusiasm for Martín Adán's work, for example, demonstrates his integral conception of art and his awareness that form, and not just ideological content, is an object of criticism. This aspect of his aesthetic discourse has been either neglected or, more often, undervalued as part of his 'idealist' or 'irrational' outlook. I would argue that, on the contrary, Mariátegui does not abandon a Marxist and historical perspective but instead constructs a critical discourse that articulates the literary, the historical, and the ideological. His project avoids both ahistorical aestheticism on the one hand, and ideological readings where formal processes are swamped by content, on the other.

Mariátegui's literary criticism is an important part of his nationalist revolutionary project. The debate on culture and artistic activity constitutes a central axis of his discourse and is an integral component of his project of general transformation of Peruvian society, as is so eloquently illustrated by the politico-cultural work undertaken by his journal, *Amauta*.[6] Basically, Mariátegui does not conceive of art as totally independent from politics, because for him politics is in fact 'la trama misma de la historia'.[7] Although it is true that for Mariátegui the 'mito de la Inteligencia pura'—the supposed autonomy of the intellectual in the face of political ideologies—is no more than the acceptance of the status quo, it is also true that he does not consider it possible to assimilate the work of the intellectual or artist to political discourses without some mediation.[8] Mariátegui states that no great artist can be apolitical.[9] This does not mean, however, that intellectual work is subordinated to political discourse. Referring to criticism, Mariátegui emphasizes the 'indivisibility' of the 'spirit' of man and the consequent 'coherence' between his intellectual work and his political thinking. But he is keen to add that this cannot imply his considering art or literature from 'puntos de vista extraestéticos'; on the contrary, he adds, 'mi concepción se unimisma, en la intimidad de mi conciencia, con mis concepciones morales, políticas y religiosas, y … sin dejar de ser concepción estrictamente estética, no puede operar independiente o diversamente'.[10]

But, on the other hand, Mariátegui writes that politics cannot be dictated to by art either: 'La ideología política de un artista no puede salir de las asambleas de estetas. Tiene que ser una ideología plena de vida, de emoción y de verdad. No una concepción artificial, literaria y falsa.'[11] This position is made clearer in his reading of the surrealist movement, which in his view '[r]econoce validez en el terreno social, político, económico, únicamente al movimiento marxista. No se le ocurre someter la política a las reglas y gustos del arte … Los suprarrealistas no ejercen su derecho al disparate, al subjetivismo absoluto, sino en el arte.'[12] So, in Mariátegui's discourse this 'derecho al disparate' and 'al subjetivismo absoluto' has nothing to do with the idea of 'art for art's sake'. Moreover, the notion of 'disparate', with its antirationalist function, was to play an important role in Mariátegui's criticism precisely in terms of the avant-garde's historical and subversive character regarding the forms, values and conceptions of the world, dominant in bourgeois aesthetics. Mariátegui champions the surrealists' formula which he synthesizes as 'Autonomía del arte, sí: pero, no clausura del arte' ('El balance del suprarrealismo', 47–48).

Art cannot function as a vehicle for escaping from reality. What interests Mariátegui about the surrealists is the subsequent relationship between the artist and the man, although this does not lead him to allow the logic that governs the political action of the man to swallow the logic that governs the practice of the aesthete. If the surrealists' project of subverting bourgeois culture is realized in their art through recourse to 'disparate', in their life their course of action is different, as described so graphically and humorously by Mariátegui:

> El artista que, en un momento dado, no cumple con el deber de arrojar al Sena a un *Flic* [emphasis in the original] de M. Tardieu, o de interrumpir con una interjección un discurso de Briand, es un pobre diablo.
>
> ('El balance del suprarrealismo', 48)

Mariátegui's interest in Adán's production of what the critic calls the 'anti-sonnet' demonstrates his emphasis on the importance of form and his belief that form can have an even greater subversive power than content.[13] At the same time, however, Mariátegui makes a distinction between formal and technical innovation: technical innovation alone cannot pose a challenge to the foundations of bourgeois art and culture. The true rupture has to happen at the very heart of both; this is why Mariátegui is so interested in those proposals within the avant-garde which erode the rationalist foundation of bourgeois aesthetics. He initially notes this in connection with Dadaism, a movement which he says 'arremete contra toda servidumbre del arte a la inteligencia ... [coincidiendo] con el tramonto del pensamiento racionalista'.[14] Years later, Mariátegui revises his perception of the scope of the movement, pointing out its limitations and judging it instead to be the precursor of surrealism. Without denying that the Dadaist movement was surrealism's point of departure, Mariátegui considers that surrealism surpasses it and pushes it towards an antirationalist undertaking which only then becomes truly radical.[15]

This Mariateguian perspective is not confined to his aesthetic conception but it is within the frame of a broader critique of the domain of bourgeois Reason and permeates his whole discourse. In Antonio Melis's opinion, any reading of Mariátegui's project which does not take this issue into account runs the risk of being a distortion, or at best overlooks central aspects of his work. Melis begins by questioning the ideological definition of Mariátegui's Marxism proposed by his critics. This definition describes it as a discourse laden with irrationalist elements attributed to his attachment to authors such as Nietzsche, Bergson, Freud, Unamuno, and especially Georges Sorel.[16] Melis believes that classifying Mariátegui as an idealist thinker involves overlooking certain historical junctures which influence his work as a political leader. These include his rejection of the Social Democrats' subjection to bourgeois rationality, and his polemic with their reformism, as well as their evolutionist and positivist conception of Marxism.[17] Furthermore, the appearance in the postwar period firstly of the Bolshevik phenomenon, and subsequently of the fascist response to it, had awakened a nostalgia among the 'vieja burocracia socialista y sindical' and the 'vieja guardia burguesa' for the peaceful coexistence of the years before the war.[18] However, Mariátegui believes that, as a result of the war, the bourgeoisie had had their 'mitos heróicos' shattered, with the consequent crisis of bourgeois articles of faith leading directly to the search for new 'myths' to drive the future forward.[19]

With justification, Melis insists on articulating any interpretation of Mariátegui's theory on 'myth'—a central component of his project—to his debate with social democracy, in order to avoid dehistoricizing it as most of his critics tend to do. In effect, they simply discard it as an irrationalist ideology [20] or identify it as one of the 'impure' aspects of Mariateguian Marxism. Instead, these critics could have concerned themselves with the pluralism of his ideological formation and with the examination of the relationship between his 'bases marxistas y leninistas y [su] atención hacia otras líneas de pensamiento' which could account for the 'tactical' foundations of his discourse and his contributions to Marxism in terms of his critique of the economistic positions within it.[21] Mariátegui's 'irrationalism' is re-evaluated by Melis in terms of a critique of the rationalism of bourgeois thought and an attempt to found a new concept of rationality: 'Mariátegui ... aboga por una razón creadora que esté a la altura del deber fundamental [del movimiento obrero] de modificar la realidad' (Melis, 'Medio siglo ...', 133–34). This proposal of Mariátegui's, upon which Melis makes no further comment, must be found in his discourse on myth, which I will refer to later on.

Melis extends this important hypothesis on Mariateguian political thought to his aesthetic conception, successfully throwing light on Mariátegui's critique of the aesthetic principles of realism. Melis states that the Peruvian's discourse on realism also shows evidence of 'la intuición de que el dogma del realismo significa, de hecho, la relación de continuidad entre estado burgués y estado proletario'.[22] There certainly appears to be a connection between this observation about Mariátegui's conception of realism, and his enthusiasm for surrealism's anti-rationalist methods, for the avant-garde's recourse to 'disparate', fantasy and imagination, and for its break with the principle of verisimilitude. This can be deduced from, for example, his article 'La realidad y la ficción' or his writings on Martín Adán.[23]

The type of treatment challenged by Melis tends in fact to resort to readings of 'influences', which do not take into account either the matrices or historical and cultural mediations which form part of any process of reception, appropriation and refunctionalization of discourses. Further, these readings overlook not only the operations involved in the selection of such discourses but also the fact that, rather than clinging to the importance or significance of a discourse within its original intellectual field, it is more important to determine the different function it assumes once it has been rearticulated and readapted to a new context. In the case of Mariátegui's appropriation of the Sorelian discourse on myth, this implies rethinking it with a view to retrieving its historical dimension, and underlining the specificities of Mariátegui's cultural context.

I should here make some observations on certain historico-cultural conditionings of the processes of intertextuality present in Mariátegui's work. First, within the attempt to relocate the Sorelian notion of myth in Mariátegui's writings, it is worth noting Oscar Terán's comment on Mariátegui's *colonidista* experience, which, given its decadentist sensibility, was to operate as one of the discursive matrices which would help to explain Mariátegui's inclination for the anti-'progress' and anti-intellectual ideology of Sorelism.[24] Secondly, I must mention Estuardo Núñez's observation, cited by Alberto Flores, on the relationship between Mariátegui and surrealism, as it sheds light on yet another core issue in Mariátegui's discourse, which also accounts for his interest in the Sorelian theory of myth. According to Estuardo Núñez, Mariátegui not only plays a fundamental role in the introduction of the surrealist movement in Peru, but he also finds '[un] parentesco entre un movimiento que reivindicaba la imaginación y la espontaneidad creativa, con un continente alejado del racionalismo y la ilustración, donde el sentimiento importaba más que lo racional'.[25] Thirdly, Melis emphasizes that Mariátegui's empathy with both Sorel and Bergson's voluntarist positions can be understood in the context of his witnessing the bankruptcy of European positivist social democracy and its incapacity to move the masses, which led him to reject the economism of the Marxism of the Second International and to re-evaluate the 'impulso ideal del movimiento obrero' over and above the passive acceptance of economic factors. His critique of European social democracy stimulates the emphasis of his analysis of the specific characteristics of Peruvian society, in particular the incipient nature of his country's proletariat and predominance of an indigenous or *mestizo* peasantry.[26]

Furthermore, Mariátegui's critique of economism and evolutionist attitudes is framed in the cultural atmosphere of his generation, which celebrates 'el poder de la subjetividad y la acción creadora de la conciencia … [y privilegia] la "voluntad heróica"'. José Aricó writes that, as a consequence, Mariátegui's 'idealist' perspective expresses 'el reconocimiento del valor creativo de la iniciativa política y la importancia excepcional del poder de la subjetividad para transformar la sociedad, o para desplazar las relaciones de fuerza más allá de las determinaciones "económicas" o de los mecanismos automáticos de la crisis'.[27] This category of myth in Mariátegui's discourse combines, as noted by Oscar Terán, a cultural and an economic content which allows Mariátegui to identify the particularity of the Peruvian agrarian problem—the fact that, for the Indians, the land has not only an economic value, but also a cultural one. This is the basis of Mariátegui's articulation of a socialist project to Andean cultural tradition.[28]

Finally in this context, I would like to refer to Flores Galindo's characterization of Mariátegui's work as that of:

> un periodista, un hombre en estrecho contacto con otros hombres, sumergido en la vida cotidiana, interesado más por el impacto de sus ideas, por la emoción que generaba en sus contemporáneos que por la certeza cartesiana de su pensamiento: de allí la tesis del marxismo como un mito—fuerza movilizadora, un elan, una agonía, un entusiasmo vital—de nuestro tiempo. (59)

Flores Galindo disqualifies any orthodox reading of Mariátegui's thought, because in Mariátegui there is no room for rationalist or doctrinal straitjackets. As William Rowe points out, the freedom of Mariátegui's thought for the integration and transformation, in a productive manner, of ideas and experiences from diverse cultural and intellectual traditions is possibly without equal. This liberty allows him to articulate myth and revolution, politico-religious Andean thought, and politico-secular Western thought.[29]

I have already indicated how myth plays a key role in Mariátegui's critique of bourgeois rationalism and how it is the basis of his counterhegemonic project. He believes that rationalism precipitated the crisis within the bourgeois order through its erosion of myth, of a 'metaphysical conception of life': 'La crisis de la civilización burguesa apareció evidente desde el instante en que esta civilización constató su carencia de un mito'.[30] The crisis began with the ageing of its 'renaissance liberal myth' and its incapacity to inspire people now as it did in its time: 'Nada más estéril que pretender reanimar un mito extinto' ('El hombre y el mito', 21–22). Myth in Mariátegui's work—whether he calls it religion, invention of the imagination, or utopia—corresponds to a historical project and has a transforming nature. The imagination for Mariátegui does not operate totally independently of historical circumstances; rather, historical circumstances dictate the limits of the imagination: 'El espíritu humano ... pugna por modificar lo que ve y lo que siente, no lo que ignora. Luego, sólo son válidas aquellas utopías que nacen de la entraña misma de la realidad.'[31] In conclusion, we should not lose sight of the fact that Mariátegui's reflections on myth constitute, as I have already stated, a quest for alternatives to a socialism conceived from a positivist perspective, a reshaping of the social democratic and bourgeois vision of politics, and an endeavour to formulate a revolutionary strategy anchored in national reality.[32] Myth, which appeals not to reason but to 'passion' and 'will', is more capable of moving people to action and the construction of a new order: 'La fuerza de los revolucionarios no está en su ciencia; está en su fé, en su pasión, en su voluntad ... Es la fuerza del Mito' ('El hombre y el mito', 22).

In 'La lucha final', Mariátegui insists that the creative power of the 'illiterate man' exceeds that of the intellectual, and that the former has a greater capacity to find 'su camino'.[33] And in Peru, that popular epic—the double project of social revolution and construction of the nation—would have, as has already been stressed, autochthonous roots. It would be articulated to indigenous culture, whose outlook, with its traditional connection to the land, would coincide with socialist goals.

The lack of myth experienced by bourgeois culture is also evident in bourgeois art: 'La literatura de la decadencia es una literatura sin absoluto'. Avant-garde art records the lack of myth and the need for it: 'El artista que más exasperadamente escéptico y nihilista se confiesa es, generalmente, el que tiene más desesperada necesidad de un mito' ('Arte, revolución y decadencia', 19). Moreover, the double process of rupture followed by the forging of new projects is directly related to Mariátegui's premise that the point of departure for a true aesthetic revolution is the break with the realist principle of bourgeois art: 'Liberados de esta traba, los artistas pueden lanzarse a la conquista de nuevos horizontes', in search of new myths which can rescue art from the crisis. 'La raiz de su mal [de la literatura moderna] no hay que buscarla en su exceso de ficción, sino en la falta de una gran ficción que pueda ser su mito y su estrella'.[34] Mariátegui's defence of fantasy and the imagination in art, as the principal vehicle to erode old realism, corresponds to his conviction that realism is, in fact, the best guarantee for a separation between art and reality.[35] In works which predate the incorporation of the national dimension into his aesthetic reflections, Mariátegui already sketches out a connection between myth and popular culture—that source of creative imagination with counter-hegemonic potential and the power to subvert the rationalist foundations of the bourgeois order.[36] This connection between myth and popular culture, however, did not really form an essential part of the critical writings in which an international perspective dominated; it would only be incorporated into his aesthetic parameters in his analysis of the question of national literature, especially in 'El proceso de la literatura'. Here he elaborates his proposal of articulation between national literature and popular culture which is of unquestionable importance for current criticism.

The national dimension of Mariátegui's aesthetic discourse would only be legitimized from a socialist point of view in his writings dating from 1925 onwards, in particular his article 'Nacionalismo y vanguardia en la literatura y en el arte', originally published in *Mundial*, Lima, 4 December 1925.[37] In 'Lo nacional y lo exótico' (October 1924), Mariátegui's view of nationalism within the discussion on Peruvian culture was that it served the conservative idea and assisted in the rejection of modernization and social transformations. For Mariátegui this nationalism was not only reactionary but also embodied an opportunistic attitude, since it only vetoed as foreign any progressive ideology, while unscrupulously appropriating any other which instead strengthened its position. Finally, nationalism distorted the notion of national reality in that it tried to deny its place within the Western sphere. The West provided the only cultural space which was left to Peru to construct its nationality, given the destruction of any autochthonous route by the Spanish Conquest.[38] However, in his post-1925 writings, as I have discussed elsewhere, Mariátegui shows a different understanding of the nationalist issue in his country's cultural debate.[39] While delegitimizing *hispanista* nationalism for its lack of popular content and its divorce from the traditions of the majority of the population, Mariátegui champions a nationalism which retrieves Andean history and culture. But what is central to a non-reductionist reading of Mariátegui is that he does not conceive of this nationalism as an alternative to the cosmopolitanism of the avant-gardes. In fact their cosmopolitanism may provide a way into the national.[40] Mariátegui foresees the transformation of Peruvian culture as the result of the united efforts of *indigenista* nationalism and avant-garde cosmopolitanism.

Mariátegui actually confirms, rather than explains, this bridge between cosmopolitanism and nationalism in the Latin American avant-garde. Nevertheless, there are various ideas in his article 'Nacionalismo y vanguardismo' which enable the tracing of the key to that explanation. It must be found in the articulation between cosmopolitanism and popular culture, which is never made explicit by Mariátegui. It must not be forgotten that Mariátegui justifies nationalism from a socialist perspective through his analysis of imperialism and the national independence movements in the colonial countries. For him, these movements always receive 'su impulso y su energía de la masa popular' ('Nacionalismo y vanguardismo', 74–75). The nationalism vindicated by Mariátegui is of a revolutionary and popular nature legitimized as a progressive phenomenon by its popular character. Producing a national literature entails incorporating popular culture into it, and this should not be done at the expense of the cosmopolitan education of the Peruvian or Latin American writer. Furthermore, producing a national literature does not mean adopting *indigenismo* as the only path towards it.

In his polemic with Luis Alberto Sánchez on the subject of *indigenismo*, Mariátegui clarifies that, far from being a programme, *indigenismo* is above all an open debate, a part of the cultural innovation of Peru. And he adds emphatically that rather than 'imponer un criterio', he wishes to 'contribuir a su formación'.[41] This attitude accords with his efforts towards the hegemonization of the innovative forces within both the political and cultural spheres. Even if it would take a leading role in the demolition of the Aristocratic Republic, *indigenismo* is not intended to monopolize the national scene.

A rereading that wants to do justice to the density of Mariátegui's critical thought must acknowledge that 'El proceso de la literatura' cannot constitute a paradigm and synthesis of his critical discourse, given that this essay does not display the critic's attention to the multiple forms of innovation he finds in the literature of his time. In order to fully appreciate Mariátegui's approach, we must look at the whole body of his work and read 'El proceso …' as part of that whole. In the last of his *Siete ensayos*, Mariátegui proposes a rereading of the development of Peruvian literature which challenges the traditional and monolithically Hispanist vision of oligarchical discourse dominant until then in Peruvian criticism, a paradigm of which is the work of Riva Agüero (*Siete ensayos*, 349). Against that view he proposes, from a nationalist perspective and with a dualist conception of the cultural composition of Peruvian society, a literary process which seeks to give expression to the majority of the population, marginalized and silenced since the Conquest.[42] For Mariátegui, Peruvian literature cannot be studied 'con el método válido para las literaturas orgánicamente nacionales, nacidas y crecidas sin la intervención de una conquista' (*Siete ensayos*, 236), and this implies in the first place the unresolved conflict between Andean and Spanish cultures.

As pointed out by Cornejo Polar, this approach to Peruvian literature constitutes a radical break in relation to previous readings of it, from recalcitrant hispanicist conceptions, to those based upon the ideology of *mestizaje*, to hardline *indigenista* proposals. These all share a unitary view of the Peruvian literary process, while Mariátegui's questions that very unity and highlights precisely its multiplicity and conflictive nature, characteristics derived from the composition of a society whose plurality stems from 'la invasión y conquista del Perú autóctono por una raza extranjera que no ha conseguido fusionarse con la raza indígena, ni eliminarla, ni absorberla'.[43] In questioning the legitimacy of the notion of unity and in promoting instead that of plurality, Cornejo reminds us, Mariátegui not only throws light on the ways in which both the literary process and its corpus had until then been mutilated, but he opens the road for a retrieval of all the 'sistemas literarios no eruditos producidos en el Perú'.[44] This will be in fact one of the Mariateguian perspectives which will fertilize one of the most important contributions to Latin American cultural criticism of the last 25 years, that is Cornejo Polar's own discourse on the heterogeneity of Andean literatures.[45] Consistency in the dismantling of ideals of unity to the benefit of the rendering of plurality will actually also prove to be one of the most difficult tasks for Latin American criticism, which, in its attempt to challenge homogeneous and elitist views of the literatures of the region, will fall into new homogenizations based on the privileging of literary systems articulated to rural popular culture traditionally undervalued or even excluded from national literary histories.[46]

It is only fair to point out that Cornejo's appraisal of Mariátegui's discourse overlooks the fact that ideals of unity and integration are not alien to Mariátegui's perspective. Cornejo is right in highlighting the category of plurality as a fundamental dimension of his interpretation of Peruvian society, culture and literature of the period. However, as a possibility projected towards the future, that longed-for goal of unity is evident at various points in his writings; in 'Pasadismo y futurismo', Mariátegui tells us, 'El pasado ... dispersa ... los elementos de la nacionalidad, tan mal combinados, tan mal concertados todavía. El pasado nos enemista. Al porvenir le toca darnos unidad' (24). In 'Réplica a Luis Alberto Sánchez', he states that he has 'constatado la dualidad nacida de la conquista para afirmar la necesidad histórica de resolverla', and then adds that 'No es mi ideal el Perú colonial ni el Perú incaico sino el Perú integral'.[47] The roots of this difficulty can probably safely be located in the nostalgia amongst Latin America's intelligentsia for the completion of the process of national unification unsuccessfully undertaken by the region's nineteenth-century political elites, a nostalgia present even in the most radical critics of the liberal project in Latin America.

Returning to Mariátegui's discourse, it is clear that against a literature without a nation and without popular content, Mariátegui seeks to set a literature which is capable of eradicating colonial thought and of acting as a foundation for a truly national literature. Mariátegui's critical endeavour is interwoven with a political one, in that he is simultaneously proposing a social project as an alternative to the prevailing regime. *Indigenismo*—the consciousness of a 'new Peru'—would in fact prepare the way for social revolution.[48]

The strategy which governs the writing of Mariátegui's 'El proceso de la literatura' can partly be attributed to the need to break the conservative hegemony of national literary history as well as to the political pressures acting on Mariátegui. In Cornejo Polar's accurate opinion, in 'El proceso ...' Mariátegui is basically interested in 'las relaciones de las clases sociales con el tipo de literatura que producen, con la crítica que generan sobre su propia literatura y sobre la que corresponde a otros estratos y con el modo cómo—literatura y crítica, productos obviamente ideológicos—se inscriben dentro de diversos y contradictorios proyectos sociales'.[49] This essay of Mariátegui's, however, should be considered as just another aspect within the whole of his aesthetic reflections, rather than as the definitive text of his critical proposal. Our understanding of his views on the relationship between the popular-national model and aesthetics, and his ideas on *indigenismo* and its place within the Peruvian literary process should take into account these observations, as should our understanding of the potential tension within his critical discourse, between on the one hand his thoughts on realism and on the other its role within the *indigenista* movement, a theme that would in fact never be developed by Mariátegui.

In his prosecution ('proceso') of 'national' literature and his unfavourable verdict, Mariátegui departs from the lucid premise that the mediocrity of Peruvian literature and its incapacity to endure is due to the absence of links to popular tradition and its insistence on remaining in the orbit of Spanish literature (*Siete ensayos*, 244–45). Furthermore, for Mariátegui, the failure to produce a national literature stems from the very failure to incorporate popular imagination. A prime example for Mariátegui will be provided by Argentinean literature with its capacity to articulate popular (national) and cosmopolitan elements. Just as there should be no contradiction between cosmopolitanism and nationalism, there should not be a contradiction between *indigenismo* and the avant-garde. As has been mentioned, for Mariátegui *indigenismo* bridges political and cultural avant-gardes and artistic and popular imagery. Mariátegui may assign *indigenismo* a key role in the project of renewal of Peruvian culture, but he does not intend it to monopolize such a project, or indeed the literary sphere (*Siete ensayos*, 334–35). We only need to remind ourselves of his defence of the 'disparate puro' discussed earlier to have an idea of the multiplicity of languages he is able to handle.

Cultural criticism in Latin America is indebted to Mariátegui in more ways than one. His reflections on the production of art and literature in a society fractured by social and racial conflict and inequality, born of a history of Conquest and violent imposition of an alien cultural apparatus over the native one, are an obvious point of departure. In this vein, Mariátegui's interpretation of *indigenismo* would in fact lay the foundations for the most important study of this subject produced within contemporary Peruvian criticism— Cornejo Polar's writings on Andean *indigenismo*. Less frequently discussed, and certainly grossly undervalued aspects of his works, are his considerations on art and politics, the articulations between artistic and social imagination, and more specifically, his concern with the problems of form specific to literary activity. These problems, incidentally, constituted the subject matter of the Russian formalists' theorizations. Today the discipline has yet to credit Mariátegui for a conception of art which emphasizes its anticipatory, prefigurative and subversive capacity, taking it beyond mere reflection or representation. As I have pointed out on another occasion,[50] Mariátegui's conception of the relationship between art and society is much more complex than that of art as reflection offered by Lukacsian aesthetics. While Lukacs's reading of the avant-gardes totally misses their counterhegemonic potential, Mariátegui's grants them their capacity to search for alternative projects.

Latin American criticism has its own history of reductionism in this area—notably in connection with the terms in which it has tended to deal with the articulation between aesthetics and cultural nationalism, with the consequent tendency to oversimplify and polarize the literary traditions of the region. This is a risk that Mariátegui, as has been noted, seems capable of avoiding through his refusal to dogmatically reduce the notion of national identity or to exclude cosmopolitan languages or to set them up in opposition to local traditions, as has been the trend amongst some of the most important recent rereadings of the Latin American literary process.[51]

Notes

1   Neil Larsen amongst others has already convincingly questioned such processes of assimilation, in 'Indigenismo y lo "poscolonial": Mariátegui frente a la actual coyuntura teórica', *Revista Iberoamericana*, LXII, 176–77 (1996), 863–73.

2   For an account of cultural criticism in the region, see Patricia D'Allemand, *Latin American Cultural Criticism: Re-Interpreting a Continent* (Lewiston, Queenston and Lampeter: Edwin Mellen Press, 2000). The present essay is an abbreviated and revised version of a chapter in that book.

3   A challenging discussion of these issues is provided by Hugo Achugar, 'Leones, cazadores e historiadores: a propósito de las políticas de la memoria y del conocimiento', *Revista Iberoamericana*, LXIII, 180 (1997), 379–87.

4   For a discussion of Mariátegui's critical discourse, see Xavier Abril *et al.*, *Mariátegui y la literatura* (Lima: Editora Amauta, 1980); Adalbert Dessau, 'Literatura y sociedad en las obras de José Carlos Mariátegui', in Antonio Melis *et al.*, *Tres estudios* (Lima: Biblioteca Amauta, 1971), 51–109; Alberto Flores Galindo, *La agonía de Mariátegui: la polémica con la Komintern* (Lima: Desco, 1980), Chapter 3; Elizabeth Garrels, 'Mariátegui, La edad de piedra y el nacionalismo literario', *Escritura*, 1 (1976), 115–28; Neil Larsen, '*Indigenismo* y lo "poscolonial"', 863–73; Antonio Melis, 'Mariátegui: primer marxista de América', in *Tres estudios*, 11–49. Melis is also the author of 'Estética, crítica literaria y política cultural en la obra de José Carlos Mariátegui, apuntes', *Textual*, 6 (1973), 66–69, 'El debate sobre Mariátegui: resultados y problemas', *Revista de crítica literaria latinoamericana*, 4 (1976), 123–32, 'La lucha en el frente cultural', in *Mariátegui en Italia*, ed. Bruno Podestà (Lima: Editora Amauta, 1981), 127–42; and 'Medio siglo de vida de José Carlos Mariátegui', in Xavier Abril *et al.*, *Mariátegui y la literatura*, 125–34. See, finally, Mabel Moraña, *Literatura y cultura nacional en Hispanoamérica (1919–1940)* (Minneapolis: University of Minnesota, 1984), Chapter 5; Yerko Moretic, *José Carlos Mariátegui* (Santiago de Chile: Universidad Técnica del Estado, 1970), Chapters 3 and 4; and Francisco Posada, *Los orígenes del pensamiento marxista en Latinoamérica: política y cultura en José Carlos Mariátegui* (Madrid: Editorial Ciencia Nueva, 1968), Chapter 3, and Posada, 'Estética y marxismo en José Carlos Mariátegui', *Buelna*, 4–5 (1980), 73–86 (previously published in *Textual*, 5–6 [1972], 24–31).

5   Jean Franco refers to this issue and the difficulties of finding a new critical language, in her commentary on Néstor García Canclini's book, *Culturas híbridas: estrategias para entrar y salir de la modernidad.* See 'Border Patrol', *Travesía*, 1, 2 (1992), 134–42.

6   For Mariátegui, the struggle for socialism constituted a long-term project which involved not only the political development of the masses, but also patient work within the cultural sphere. His conception of the journal *Amauta* must be seen within this framework. He founded it in 1926 with the double purpose of serving as an organ of expression for the various progressive forces within Peruvian society in the 1920s and stimulating a process of innovation which he intended eventually to lead in order that it might oppose the dominant culture en bloc.

7   José Carlos Mariátegui, 'Arte, revolución y decadencia', in *El artista y la época* (Lima: Biblioteca Amauta, 1959), 18–22 (20).

8   'El proceso a la literatura francesa contemporánea', in *Defensa del marxismo*, 4th edn (Lima: Biblioteca Amauta, 1973), 117–26 (121).

9   'Aspectos viejos y nuevos del futurismo', in *El artista y la época*, 56–59 (58).

10 'El proceso de la literatura', in *Siete ensayos de interpretación de la realidad peruana*, 47th edn (Lima: Biblioteca Amauta, 1985), 229–350 (230–31).

11 'Aspectos viejos y nuevos del futurismo', in *El artista y la época*, 58.

12 'El balance del suprarrealismo', in *El artista y la época*, 45–52 (47).

13 'El anti-soneto', in *Peruanicemos al Perú* (Lima: Biblioteca Amauta, 1970), 156–57.

14 'El expresionismo y el dadaismo', in *El artista y la época*, 64–69 (69).

15 'El grupo suprarrealista y Clarté', in *El artista y la época*, 42–45 (43).

16 See mainly the following works by Robert Paris: 'El marxismo de Mariátegui', in *Mariátegui y los orígenes del marxismo latinoamericano* (Mexico: Siglo XXI, 1978), 119–44 and, in the same volume, 'Mariátegui: un "Sorelismo" ambiguo', 155–61; 'La formación ideológica de Mariátegui', in *Mariátegui en Italia*, 79–114; and *La formación ideológica de José Carlos Mariátegui* (Mexico: Siglo XXI, 1981).

17 Antonio Melis, 'El debate sobre Mariátegui: resultados y problemas', 124.

18 Mariátegui, 'La emoción de nuestro tiempo: dos concepciones de la vida', in *El alma matinal y otras estaciones de hoy*, 4th edn (Lima: Biblioteca Amauta, 1959), 12–18 (16).

19 'El hombre y el mito', in *El alma matinal y otras estaciones de hoy*, 18–23 (18–19).

20 See Melis, 'Medio siglo de vida de José Carlos Mariátegui', in Xavier Abril *et al.*, *Mariátegui y la literatura*, 133.

21 Melis, 'El debate sobre Mariátegui: resultados y problemas', 126, 129 and 130.

22 Melis, 'Medio siglo de vida de José Carlos Mariátegui', 133. On the Mariateguian discourse on realism, see Melis's articles, 'Estética,

crítica literaria y política cultural en la obra de José Carlos Mariátegui, apuntes' and 'La lucha en el frente cultural'. Also, by Francisco Posada, see Chapter 3 of his study, *Los orígenes del pensamiento marxista en Latinoamérica: política y cultura en José Carlos Mariátegui*. In contrast to Melis, Posada finds Mariateguian hypotheses on realism to be 'insufficient' and frequently points out Mariátegui's 'incapacity' to 'understand theoretical problems', etc. However, we would suggest that Posada's method suffers from an interpretation in terms of 'influences' and from a continual attempt to assimilate Mariátegui to the classic texts of Marxist aesthetics, which leads him to dehistoricize his discourse and to lose sight of the scope of Mariátegui's critical contribution. On the same theme, see also Yerko Moretic, *José Carlos Mariátegui*, who reads Mariátegui's discourse on realism from the point of view of Marxist aesthetics and then refers it to the current debate on realism. Finally, although Mabel Moraña equivocally defines Mariátegui's proposal on bourgeois realism and the anti-rationalist methods of surrealism as 'realism', she does offer a more useful analysis, stressing the proposal's creative function over a simply reproductive function (see her *Literatura y cultura nacional en Hispanoamérica [1919–1940]*, 88–91).

23 See 'La realidad y la ficción', in *El artista y la época*, 22–25; and in *Peruanicemos al Perú*, 'La casa de cartón de Martín Adán', 150–54, 'Defensa del disparate puro', 155, and 'El anti-soneto', 156–57.

24 Terán, 'Los escritos juveniles de Mariátegui', *Buelna*, 4–5 (1980), 18–24 (24).

25 Alberto Flores Galindo, *La agonía de Mariátegui: la polémica con la Komintern*, 44.

26 Melis, 'El debate sobre Mariátegui: resultados y problemas', 130. For a reading in tune with Mariátegui's anti-economism, see also Oscar Terán, 'Latinoamérica: naciones y marxismos', in *Socialismo y participación*, 11 (1980), 169–90 (172–73).

27 José Aricó, 'Mariátegui y la formación del partido socialista del Perú', in *Socialismo y participación*, 11 (1980), 139–68 (142).

28 Oscar Terán, *Discutir Mariátegui* (Mexico: Universidad Autónoma de Puebla, 1985), 88–89; Mariátegui, *Siete ensayos*, 35.

29 William Rowe, 'José Carlos Mariátegui: 1994', in *Travesía*, 3, 1–2 (1994), 290–98 (296–98).

30 Mariátegui, 'El hombre y el mito', 18–19.

31 'La imaginación y el progreso', in *El alma matinal y otras estaciones de hoy*, 36–39 (38).

32 On the vacuum of reflections on the national question within Marxist tradition and the counterweight provided by Latin American thought and particularly by Mariátegui, see especially Terán, *Discutir Mariátegui*, 83–85 and 99.

33 'La lucha final', in *El alma matinal y otras estaciones de hoy*, 23–27 (27).

34 'La realidad y la ficción', in *El artista y la época*, 22–25 (23–25).

35 'La realidad y la ficción', 23. His note published in *Amauta* entitled 'Defensa del disparate puro' was written on the occasion of the publication of Martín Adán's poem 'Gira' and summarizes the essence of both Mariátegui's aesthetic parameters and his vision of the revolutionary task and mechanisms of art: 'Martín Adán toca en estos versos el disparate puro que es, a nuestro parecer, una de las tres categorías sustantivas de la poesía contemporánea. El disparate puro certifica la defunción del absoluto burgués. Denuncia la quiebra de un espíritu, de una filosofía, más que de una técnica ... En una época revolucionaria, romántica, artistas de estirpe y contextura clásicas como Martín Adán, no aciertan a conservarse dentro de la tradición. Y es que entonces fundamentalmente la tradición no existe sino como un inerte conjunto de módulos secos y muertos. La verdadera tradición está invisible, etéreamente en el trabajo de creación de un orden nuevo. El disparate tiene una función revolucionaria porque cierra y extrema un proceso de disolución. No es un orden—ni el nuevo ni el viejo—pero sí es el desorden, proclamado como única posibilidad artística. Y ... no puede sustraerse a cierto ascendiente de los términos, símbolos y conceptos del orden nuevo ... una tendencia espontánea al orden aparece en medio de una estridente explosión de desorden' ('Defensa del disparate puro', in *Peruanicemos al Perú*, 155). A clarification: although Mariátegui does not explain those other two 'categorías sustantivas de la poesía contemporánea', perhaps a key to their understanding can be found in a paragraph in the last of his *Siete ensayos*, in which he says that 'por comodidad de clasificación y crítica cabe ... dividir la poesía de hoy [en tres categorías primarias]: lírica pura, disparate absoluto y épica revolucionaria' (306).

36 It is suggested, for instance, in his article 'Anatole France', in *La escena contemporánea*, 3rd edn (Lima: Biblioteca Amauta, 1964), 164–69 (166–67). There, Mariátegui reads the French author's position as one of transition between a decadent civilization to which he declares himself to be opposed, and a new revolutionary era to which he cannot commit himself 'spiritually', but only through an 'intellectual act'. For all his rejection of bourgeois society, says Mariátegui, France's work nevertheless draws on bourgeois aesthetic values, rather than those of popular culture.

37 The article is a follow-up to 'Nacionalismo y vanguardismo', initially published in *Mundial*, Lima, 27 November 1925. Later, Mariátegui was to combine both articles to produce 'Nacionalismo y vanguardismo: en la ideología política, en la literatura y el arte', also included in *Peruanicemos al Perú*, 72–79.

38 Mariátegui, 'Lo nacional y lo exótico', in *Peruanicemos al Perú*, 25–29 (25–26).

39 See D'Allemand, 'Art and Culture in the Discourse of José Carlos Mariátegui', *Travesía*, 3, 1–2 (1994), 299–312.

40 Mariátegui, 'Nacionalismo y vanguardismo: en la ideología política, en la literatura y el arte', 72.

41 Mariátegui, 'Indigenismo y socialismo, intermezzo polémico', in *Ideología y política*, 11th edn (Lima: Biblioteca Amauta, 1980), 214–18 (215).

42 For an analysis of Mariátegui's racist reading of the other ethnic groups in Peru, such as the population of African origin and the Chinese immigrants, see Elizabeth Garrels, *Mariátegui y la Argentina: un caso de lentes ajenas* (Gaithersburgh: Ediciones Hispamérica, 1982).

43 Cited by Cornejo Polar in 'El problema nacional en la literatura peruana', in *Sobre literatura y crítica latinoamericana* (Caracas: Universidad Central de Venezuela, 1982), 23.

44 Mariátegui, 'Pasadismo y futurismo', in *Peruanicemos al Perú*, 20–24 (23–24). For further treatment of this issue, see Cornejo Polar, 'Apuntes sobre literatura nacional en el pensamiento crítico de Mariátegui', in Xavier Abril *et al.*, *Mariátegui y la literatura*, 55–56.

45 See Cornejo Polar's books, *Literatura y sociedad en el Perú: la novela indigenista* (Lima: Lasontay, 1980) and *Escribir en el aire: ensayo sobre la heterogeneidad socio-cultural en las literaturas andinas* (Lima: Editorial Horizonte, 1994).

46 I examine this problem in connection with Angel Rama and Alejandro Losada in 'Urban Literary Production and Latin American Criticism', *Bulletin of Latin American Research*, 15, 3 (1996), 359–69.

47 Mariátegui, 'Réplica a Luis Alberto Sánchez', in *Ideología y política*, 219–23 (222).

48 Mariátegui, *Siete ensayos*, 327–28.

49 Cornejo Polar, 'Apuntes sobre literatura nacional en el pensamiento crítico de Mariátegui', 49–59 (52). The author provides an evaluation of 'El proceso de la literatura' and its place within the development of Peruvian criticism on pages 52–54.

50 D'Allemand, 'Art and Culture in the Discourse of José Carlos Mariátegui', 299–312.

51 See D'Allemand, 'Urban Literary Production and Latin American Criticism', 359–69.

CHAPTER FOUR

Doing Time in Peru: the Poetics of Multitemporality as Method for Cultural History

William Rowe
Birkbeck College, London

Any cultural condition to be described as postcolonial includes a construction of temporalities which in specific ways adjust or refuse to adjust to centralizing narratives of the modern. One of the concerns of this essay is the differential sense of time that is produced by the works of the Peruvian poet César Vallejo. Consideration of his texts places before us the way the cultural field is assembled in the study of literature in order that senses of time—and of place—can be extrapolated for discussion. There is not one way to compose that field but various, and the different choices, which are displayed in works of literature, also confront the student of literature as decisions to be taken. Not that literary works follow on after the fact, simply retracing patterns already marked out by other types of cultural action (such as sociology, philosophy or cultural studies): the most interesting works are the ones which alter available senses of time and space, inventing new ways of probing the field, which may be in advance of those produced anywhere else. Little attention is given to this fact in British universities, where the arts are virtually excluded from cultural studies. If relations are what any field is made up of and these cannot be given in advance but have to be worked out in the detailed action of exploring a specific field, then the work of a poet can be one such working out, and taken as a set of hermeneutic proposals.

To ask whether there is a Latin American hermeneutics of cultural history is not a useful way of framing the issues, however, since the question polarizes the answer into Latin American or non-Latin American, which would mean that the places from which any answer could be enunciated were already substantially given, and that the relations between terms had, to an important extent, already been decided upon. For example, to decide what is colonial or non-colonial in terms of discrete objects is not a viable proposition: objects and words became doubly inflected during the colonial period in Peru—it depended on who was using them, in what way, and where, the differences of place varying as functions of socio-ethnic location. For this reason the concept of heterogeneity became strategic in twentieth-century interpretations of Peruvian culture, because that is when it became possible to propose, more or less consistently, an alternative version of Peruvian history, no longer as an inferior and time-lagged imitation of Western history, but as a set of different possibilities, which include that of an alternative modernity.[1]

The notion that Peruvian reality is heterogeneous, because of the dual inheritance of native and Spanish cultures, as opposed to the relative homogeneity of (Western) European nations, whose culture was 'orgánicamente nacional', was first put forward by José Carlos Mariátegui (1894–1930) in the 1920s and needs to be understood in conjunction with his judgement that a key task was to 'hacer nación', given that Peru was not yet a nation in the modern sense.[2] The concept of heterogeneity was later developed by Antonio Cornejo Polar (1936–97), as a tool of literary and cultural analysis. Cornejo takes literary *indigenismo* as a key expression of heterogeneity in the sense that the world it refers to, that of native Andean populations, is different from its context of writing and reception, which is that of the non-native, urban middle classes. His most succinct definition of this sense of heterogeneity is that it consists in a 'fractura de la unidad *mundo representado y modo de representación*'.[3]

One of the purposes of the present essay is to test out what happens if one places beside the notion of heterogeneity, which is primarily a spatial concept, the question of temporality, and in particular whether different modes of temporalization have been constructed in twentieth-century Peru: in other words, to let otherness of place intersect with otherness of time. The phrase 'heterogeneidad multitemporal' appears in *Culturas híbridas* by Néstor García Canclini, who explains that what he means by it is the continued existence, alongside modernization, of 'premodern' cultural, economic and political conditions:

> Esta *heterogeneidad multitemporal* de la cultura moderna es consecuencia de una historia en la que la modernización operó pocas veces mediante la sustitución de lo tradicional y lo antiguo. Hubo rupturas provocadas por el desarrollo industrial y la urbanización que, si bien ocurrieron después que en Europa, fueron más aceleradas. Se creó un mercado artístico y literario a través de la expansión educativa ... Pero la constitución de ... campos científicos y humanísticos autónomos se enfrentaba con el analfabetismo de la mitad de la población, y con estructuras económicas y hábitos políticos premodernos.[4]

In this formulation, heterogeneity is the substantive, which suggests that it may be easier to think than multitemporality since it arises in spatial differences that are immediate because evident through social and ethnic markers. In Peru, no one could deny these differences, though of course, from the sixteenth century to the present, different ways have been proposed for incorporating them into the imagination of the national.[5] Yet the notion that there is a single temporality, that of Western modernity, has apparently received little criticism and certainly no systematic discussion in Peru. And it could be argued that García Canclini's proposal is itself partially infused by the coloniality of power when it represents the non-modern as '*pre*modern', connoting a version of linear, substitutory progress, modelled on Western modernity.

In this essay, the intention is to find out what happens if one takes certain elements of César Vallejo's poetry as initial and partial probes into these issues. The following account of Vallejo's biographical circumstances may be taken as an example of unitemporal heterogeneity:

> The geography of Vallejo's poetry is that of anachronism: time measured in arduous distance along mountain roads, towns nestling in the past, protected by the screen of provincialism from the rude awakening into the twentieth century, villages sunk in an even remoter time, sugar-estates and mines forming brutal links in the chain of Peru's dependency. The landscape unfolds in a series of shocks quite unlike the homogeneous contemporaneity of North America.[6]

The notation of spatial differences is placed within a unilinear time-frame: from the twentieth century back via mines, sugar-estates (early forms of industrial production) to remote villages outside modern communications. In other words, there is a receding perspective towards a remote past. This way of temporalizing is rejected by Vallejo himself. The poems 'A mi hermano Miguel' or *Trilce* III, which refer to the death of his brother, present coexistent parallel times which subvert the biographical notion of growing up and the historical one of progress. Childhood is placed alongside adulthood, without any sense of growing 'out' of it and 'into' something else: neither gives a hermeneutic frame for the other. Any frame of continuing meanings over time breaks down: there is no support upon which continuity could rest.

The technique used is to place voices alongside each other: voices of adulthood and childhood, of now and then, except that the juxtapositions themselves undermine such terms and the boundaries proposed by them. Thus the handling of childhood is not the simplificatory one of receding perspective: the material of childhood of lower complexity than that of the time-place of enunciation. On the contrary, memory too is delinearized into a collage of voices, which is both a form of oral memory and a compositional technique of avant-garde poetics. Moreover, the coexistent parallel times are embodied: not just the voice but the body of the child is alongside, without clear boundaries between itself and another body called adult. Therefore the voice-body is not 'back' somewhere or 'inside' because enveloped by a rational outside. We are dealing with rationalities of time, not in an absolute sense of constructs which hold a frontier against an 'irrational', but in the temporal sense of specific social ways of interpreting a biography and its geographical spaces. The place of enunciation is made strange, an alteration which affects the field where personal time and cultural temporalization intersect.

How does one get to a heterogeneous multitemporality (to make time the substantive)? Is not multitemporality *a fortiori* heterogeneous, in the sense that to criticize the singular temporality of Western modernity is to speak of the colonial spaces that it suppresses? But to say that does not help with the difficulty of defining what form multiple temporalities might take as a practice of reading, or, more widely, of cultural hermeneutics. Vallejo's phenomenology of voices that construct time gives one possible starting-point. It permits non-modern and modern cultural practices to be brought together in creative interaction, without subordination. But that ability to bring oral cultural practices and the modern urban avant-garde together was not invented by Vallejo out of nothing. It relies on an available inheritance of formal constructions of the modern in Spanish America, whose first major manifestation took place in the 1880s with the body of work (poetic, fictional, journalistic, graphic) known as *modernismo*, which in a comparative sense can be seen as the beginnings of a differential Modernism south of the border.

A useful way to get into the process of artistic modernism in Spanish America is via the state of the language. José Martí, in a magnificent essay on Walt Whitman published in 1887, works out the necessities of a language that will respond adequately to the modern city by producing the new speeds of the environment:

> ¿Rimas o acentos? ¡Oh, no!, su ritmo está en las estrofas, ligadas, en medio de aquel caos aparente de frases superpuestas y convulsas, por una sabia composición que distribuye en grandes grupos musicales las ideas, como la natural forma poética de un pueblo que no fabrica piedra a piedra, sino a enormes bloqueadas.[7]

The emphases here—to break with dominant neoclassical forms, to compose by the musical relationships of ideas—are similar to those of Rubén Darío's statements of poetics, a major dimension of which is the need to break with the literary language of nineteenth-century Spain as inadequate instrument. The intonation of Spanish spoken in Latin America, which is different from that of Spain, was able to enter literature because of the formal innovations of the *modernistas*.

But *modernismo* and the avant-garde movements that followed it were complicated in Peru by what the Peruvian poet Martín Adán called the lack of 'una forma nuestra'. Adán's study of the poet José María Eguren draws attention to the irrelevance of the scenarios of Eguren's poems to Peru. He also suggests that this makes them expressive of the situation of literature in Peru. Mariátegui, around ten years earlier, had argued that what was lacking in Peruvian literature was an engagement with popular culture.[8] The large historical factor underlying these arguments is the colonial division of cultures that began with the Conquest in 1532.[9] According to Mariátegui, literary *indigenismo* is the most dynamic cultural expression of the need to overcome that division, given that its writers, when they incorporate native themes into their work, are collaborating, whether consciously or not, in the task of creating 'el Perú nuevo'.[10]

Let us consider, once again, the place of language in these questions. The central difference, according to *indigenista* literature, is the Indian/landowning-class one, and in the *indigenista* novel it is marked phonetically and lexically in the speech attributed to native characters, which often led to the need for a glossary. The dualistic ethnic gaze and the concomitant linguistic decisions reinforce each other: we end up with a singularized axis of differentiation. This is precisely what José María Arguedas rejects, in an essay which is crucial for Peruvian cultural history, where he points out that his own writing, because of its concern with all the groups of Peruvian society, is not limited to a bipolar social vision and is therefore not *indigenista*.[11] He also explains why he had abandoned the *indigenista* attitude to language: because Indians do not speak like that, and because the necessity was to make Spanish into the most highly expressive medium that could be achieved.

Martín Adán, similarly, draws attention to the artistic incoherence of the *indigenista* handling of language. He points out that the major proponents of *indigenismo*, such as Manuel González Prada and Mariátegui, were careful not to use any vocabulary drawn from Quechua (the main Andean language) because they wished to achieve good communication.[12] Adán's own work should also be mentioned here: his major long poem, *La mano desasida*, dramatizes the need to see Andean Peru as a vast material actuality: as ontology rather than ideology, because the history of being in Peru had not included the Andean. In this sense, *La mano desasida* is comparable to Vallejo's concern with the ontology of the native Peru in poems such as 'Telúrica y magnética'. Arguedas's method, extendable into a methodology for cultural history, was to reject the lexical and morpho-syntactic interferences of Quechua (i.e. the method of *indigenismo*) which he had experimented with in his early novel *Yawar Fiesta*, and to find, instead, ways of translating the qualities of Quechua into Spanish. A crucial one of these is intonation, the modulations of the tone of the voice which constitute, as Bakhtin puts it, the relationship of language with the outside. His extraordinary novel, *El zorro de arriba y el zorro de abajo*, is the high point of the bringing into Spanish of those other intonations. That novel could not have been written without the previous translations of modern urban space into literary form carried out by *modernismo* and later by the avant-garde.[13]

The formation of *indigenismo* can be traced back to González Prada's response to the defeat of Peru by Chile in the War of the Pacific in 1879. His famous statement, 'No forman el verdadero Perú las agrupaciones de criollos i extranjeros que habitan la faja de tierra situada entre el Pacífico i los Andes; la nación está formada por las muchedumbres de indios diseminados en la banda oriental de la cordillera',[14] was part of his interpretation of the course of the war: Peru had lost because the Indians had not been incorporated into the nation. The truth was different: the Indians, as the historian Nelson Manrique shows,[15] had more commitment to Peru than the weak Lima bourgeoisie, and the war accelerated the nascent forms of regional modernity which Limeño creoles like González Prada were blind to.

Blindness to other temporalities, or the suppression of them, in favour of a central, unifying time—the time of dominant historiography—is therefore something which occurs inside Peru itself, as well as in the relationship between colonial metropolis and colony. And the War of the Pacific was a colonial war: it marks a decisive geopolitical shift from European domination of Africa and the orient to US domination of the Pacific. The importance of the coloniality of power to temporality is stressed by Peter Osborne in his crucial book, *The Politics of Time*. Proposing that the category of modernity is necessary because its 'totalizing conception of historical time' is the only way we can engage fully with the political dimensions of time, he also points out that 'this totalization of history ... homogenizes and represses, reduces or forgets, certain forms of difference'. Among the latter—i.e. the differentiation that this homogenization negates—are, most drastically, colonial spaces.[16]

The avant-garde, in its attitude to composition, is a major site of the rejection of inherited selectivities. Osborne's stress on the need to construct a conceptual ground does not give sufficient attention to the places of enunciation and surfaces of inscription that are attendant upon any critical, non-selective, investigation of time.[17] Let us consider how these issues emerge in César Vallejo's work.

Trilce, Vallejo's most formally radical book, served as a workshop for experiments which could reveal relationships between time and language. The use of numbers rather than titles for the 77 poems is part of a notion of the book as a complex spatio-temporal field. In the small selection that follows, the intention is not to exhaust the generative action of reading by imposing conceptual boundaries, but to suggest some of the ways in which the book's actions take us to questions of occurrence, its traces, and their notation that arise before any conceptual grounding of time. Poem XX delineates a scene of speaking and writing which is deeply heterogeneous: a prison in provincial Peru. One of the inmates is visited by his small daughter. The man is described as 'guillermosecundario' and 'mostachoso', Kaiser Wilhelm II, German Emperor during the First World War, serving as gross icon of history as European and as model for the creole sector of Peruvian society. While the other inmate and 'I' of the poem speaks of suffering as his only location, the other's grandiosity is vulgarly juxtaposed with the noise of his fly-buttons and urine, described as a 'desagüe jurídico', a juridical sewer, the collision of referential fields cutting through socio-linguistic hierarchies. The other body-fluids in the poem are saliva and sweat. Two people are dribbling: the speaker at the spectacle of the other's sweating happiness (and cream cake) and the little girl, whose spit is the matter of writing: while the mustachio'd man pours with sweat as he shines her shoes, the three-year-old girl

> pónese el índice
> en la lengua que empieza a deletrear
> los enredos de enredos de los enredos,
> y unta el otro zapato, a escondidas,
> con un poquito de saliba y tierra,
> pero con un poquito
> no má–
> .s.

As Julio Ortega has said, 'the tangles of tangles of the tangles' are a Vallejian image of language.[18] But the child's making letters with spit on a dusty shoe (*tierra* is actually both dust and earth) is a differential scene of writing—other, for example, than Mallarmé's 'black on white' paper[19]—and inscribes a hetero-iconology. And on that surface of inscription, time and writing occur together, as a slowness which the typography delineates.

Some but not all of the characteristics I have drawn attention to could be linked with the vulgar and the 'subaltern'. Not all, because it seems to me that in placing its own enunciative and inscriptive actions as emergences of space and time, rather than solely as locations within existing grids, the poem proposes a radical critique of existing historiography, in other words, a different way of doing history, which does not stop at reversal of values but gets into the dense stuff of writing at all and its inextricability from particular places.

The freight of Vallejo's dense writing is time, and reading it releases time. Consider poem II, where again the scenario is prison, a biographical referent in the sense that Vallejo spent four months in gaol in 1920–21. Here—in the poem as in the gaol—language can refer to and represent time, but that time is already inside the language: in its morphosyntactic articulation but also in the act of naming. And, in the social dimension, the repetitions of prison reduce time. The two dimensions intersect, to produce a place of enunciation which is highly resistant to reconciliation with dominant literary prestige. In this and other poems of *Trilce*, there is no redemption of time into continuities, the historian's dream.[20] Doing time in gaol becomes quite literally what one is doing, as the poem radiates from and simultaneously centres itself on and in gaol and its agencies, exposing it as the bottom line of modern socialized time. And time is a burden of language, in precisely that way, and not because of metaphysics—the prison is not metaphysical!

There is therefore in these poems a far-reaching critique of modernity, without reconciliation. Time and again, Vallejo blasts apart reconciliatory language. He writes, for example, in poem LV:

> Samain diría el aire es quieto y de una contenida tristeza
>
> Vallejo dice hoy la Muerte está soldando cada lindero
> a cada
> hebra de cabello perdido ...

quoting the French Symbolist's lines, 'Comme dans un préau d'hospice ou de prison, / L'air est calme et d'une tristesse contenue'.[21] Vallejo's statement does not contest the attitudes so much as the form of language which permits containment in equivalences—not for nothing is 'containment' part of the vocabulary of custodial-bureaucratic language. In Vallejo's language there are no equivalences, only micro-differences soldered together. Against the economy of containment, a discontinuous time, which penetrates between words and in the non-phonetic signs used in printing and brings down the grand narratives of history:

> Y, en fin, pasando luego al dominio de la muerte,
> que actúa en escuadrón previo corchete,
> párrafo y llave, mano grande y diéresis,
> ¿a qué el pupitre asirio? ¿A qué el cristiano púlpito ...[22]

This discontinuous time, which may be contrasted, for example, with Whitman's use of the industrial rotary printing press as image of continuity beyond individual death,[23] is related to a radical change in poetics, away from symbolism and towards an openness to pullulating micro-differences, which are, as in Brownian motion, time-events prior to the construction of time into directionalities, via—in literature—narratives.

Another poem (LVIII) constructs prison as the chemical phases of matter: solid, liquid and gas. The method serves to break the linearity imposed by society and education upon time-bound materials and to bring them into contemporaneity and comparability without dehistoricizing them: the rule of phase as a method for historiography, as Henry Adams was later to propose.[24] Multiphasic time serves as an alternative to the unilinear time of the narratives of modernity.

Vallejo's discontinuous, multiphasic time is the ground of those relative continuities of history which enter his poems: it is their ground in the sense that it is that which supplies their material and makes them comparable. Thus the later poems which respond to recession in Europe and to the Spanish Civil War, do so without redeeming discontinuities, without reconciling what in life does not become symbolic with the narrative of mass actions: both coexist.[25]

Let us consider, finally, a later poem as display of Vallejo's method. 'Telúrica y magnética' is a telluric poem in the sense that it echoes that literature of the 1930s in Latin America, sometimes called 'telurismo', which emphasized the land as marker of a difference from narratives of civilization centred on the capital cities which, in turn, stood exposed as enclaves of a narrow version of culture which excluded *mestizo* and native traditions.[26] Vallejo's poem goes further: the land does not represent these things to an interpretation situated elsewhere (as in *indigenismo*) but is the direct material of native intelligence:

> ¡Mecánica sincera y peruanísima
> la del cerro colorado!
> ¡Suelo teórico y práctico!
> ¡Surcos inteligentes; ejemplo: el monolito y su cortejo!

As Brotherston and Sá have pointed out, Vallejo takes archaeology as ontology:[27] not as an attenuated sign of a previous epoch, but as dense and actual material, no less complex than the modern. His intensely Peruvian landscape includes twentieth-century science ('¡Molécula exabrupto! ¡Átomo terso!') alongside archaeology, without subordination: '¡Rotación de tardes modernas / y finas madrugadas arqueológicas!' The archaeological and the modern, the physical and the intellectual, are placed alongside each other, without hierarchies. Barbarians, for Aristotle, for Sepúlveda against Las Casas in the debates about the nature of American Indians, and for the narrator of Conrad's *Heart of Darkness*, can only imitate, but not generate intelligence. In Vallejo's restitution, coloniality stands exposed as a sedimentation of power, as power over time, in language.

Notes

1   See Alberto Flores Galindo, *La agonía de Mariátegui*, in *Obras completas*, II (Lima: Sur, 1994).

2   Mariátegui, who had spent some time in Italy, was affected by reading Gramsci but does not simply transfer the idea of the national popular to Peru.

3   Antonio Cornejo Polar, *Literatura y sociedad en el Perú: la novela indigenista* (Lima: Lasontay, n.d.). The statement is included in Cornejo's key article, first published in 1978 and published in translation as 'Indigenismo and Heterogeneous Literatures: Their Dual Socio-Cultural Logic', in *Journal of Latin American Cultural Studies*, 7, 1 (1998), 15–27.

4   Néstor García Canclini, *Culturas híbridas: estrategias para entrar y salir de la modernidad* (Mexico: Grijalbo, 1989), 72.

5   To test the differences, one might compare three versions of Cusco: El Inca Garcilaso's, Riva-Agüero's, and Arguedas's.

6   Jean Franco, *César Vallejo: The Dialectics of Poetry and Silence* (Cambridge: Cambridge University Press, 1976), 1.

7   José Martí, *José Martí en los Estados Unidos* (Madrid: Alianza, 1968), 259.

8   See the discussion of Mariátegui by Patricia D'Allemand in Chapter Three of this volume.

9   Flores Galindo's *Buscando un Inca: identidad y utopía en los Andes* (La Habana: Casa de las Américas, 1986), which develops Arguedas's thinking, is the most coherent investigation to date of how Andean notions of utopia propose an alternative modernity.

10 José Carlos Mariátegui, *Siete ensayos de interpretación de la realidad peruana* (Lima: Amauta, 1964), 285, 289.

11 José María Arguedas, 'La novela y el problema de la expresión literaria en el Perú', *Mar del Sur*, 9, 1–2 (1950), 66–72. See also Mirko

Lauer's revaluation of *indigenismo* in *Andes imaginarios: Discursos del indigenismo–2* (Lima: Sur, 1997). Mario Vargas Llosa has entered the debate with *La utopía arcaica: José María Arguedas y las ficciones del indigenismo* (México: Fondo de Cultura Económica, 1996). My essay, 'De los indigenismos en el Perú: examen de argumentos', *Márgenes*, 11, 16 (1998), 111–20, offers a critical examination of Lauer's and Vargas Llosa's books.

12 Rafael de la Fuente Benavides, *De lo barroco en el Perú* (Lima: Universidad Nacional Mayor San Marcos, 1968), 376–77. Because the book is difficult to obtain, here is the passage referred to: 'tras de sopesar el mínimo don de lo indígena a nuestra formal literatura, podemos concluir afirmando que la literatura peruana y, extensamente, la hispanoamericana es sustantivamente la barroca española delongada e influida y que el aporte de lo indígena puro no es sino de asunto propuesto al prejuicio del criollo y de nomenclatura empleada con fines de aditivo embellecimiento o de esclarecimiento lexicológico. Recordemos que penates del indigenismo criollo, en muy diverso tiempo y designio, como Melgar y González Prada se abstuvieron de dar, ni en expresión inmediata ni en deliberado discurso, nomenclatura alguna de idioma indígena. Mariátegui, en nuestros días, la evitó con escrúpulo; y no pudo menos que obrar así el gran periodista peruano, tan interesado en la propagación de su doctrina. El indígena puro, nada criollo, no puede dar al criollo literatura indígena, porque no podría recibirla. El comercio de lo inteligible no puede ser sino de perfecta honestidad y reciprocidad.'

13 In the Peruvian avant-garde, the key names, apart from Martín Adán, are Emilio Adolfo Westphalen, César Moro, César Vallejo, and Xavier Abril. Arguedas was particularly affected by the work of Vallejo and Westphalen.

14 Manuel González Prada, 'Discurso en el Politeama', in *Pájinas libres* (Lima: Fondo de Cultura Popular, 1966), 63. See José Tamayo Herrera, *El pensamiento indigenista* (Lima: Mosca Azul, 1981), for a collection of key *Indigenista* essays.

15 Nelson Manrique, *Campesinado y nación: las guerrillas indígenas en la guerra con Chile* (Lima: Centro de Investigación y Capacitación, 1981).

16 Peter Osborne, *The Politics of Time: Modernity and Avant-Garde* (London: Verso, 1995), 29; see also 17–19.

17 See Osborne, 13.

18 Julio Ortega (ed.), *César Vallejo: Trilce* (Madrid: Cátedra, 1991), 120.

19 See Mary Ann Caws (ed.), Stéphane Mallarmé: *Selected Poetry and Prose* (New York: New Directions, 1982), 77. The statement is from *Quant au livre* (1895).

20 See Riva-Agüero's statement: 'La patria es por esencia continuidad', from the essay 'Religión, orden y estado', in *El pensamiento fascista*, ed. J. I. López Soria (Lima: Mosca Azul, 1981), 66.

21 Quoted in Ortega, *César Vallejo: Trilce*, 260.

22 'Sermón sobre la muerte', included in *Poemas humanos*.

23 'Starting from Paumanok', Section XIII.

24 Henry Adams, 'The Rule of Phase Applied to History', in *A Henry Adams Reader*, ed. Elizabeth Stevenson (New York: Doubleday, 1958), 365–92.

25 See, for example, 'Parado en una piedra', 'Salutación angélica', 'Pedro Rojas' and 'Masa'.

26 Jean Franco, *The Modern Culture of Latin America: Society and the Artist* (London: Pall Mall, 1967), Chapter Four.

27 Gordon Brotherston and Lucia Sá, 'La poética del patrimonio: "Telúrica y magnética" de César Vallejo', *Cuadernos hispanoamericanos*, 548 (February 1996), 109–19.

CHAPTER FIVE

America, Americanism and the Third World in the work of Leopoldo Zea

Robin Fiddian
Wadham College, Oxford

The work of the veteran Mexican intellectual, Leopoldo Zea, offers a wide range of connections with postcolonial theory, a fact acknowledged by Walter Mignolo in two landmark essays of the mid-1990s.[1] 'Occidentalización, imperialismo, globalización, herencias coloniales y teorías postcoloniales' (1995) and 'La razón postcolonial: herencias coloniales y teorías postcoloniales' (1997) locate Zea decisively within a two-dimensional framework of inquiry into the legacies of colonialism. On one level, Zea is related to contemporary trends in Latin American philosophy, represented— in Mignolo's account—by Enrique Dussel and Rodolfo Kusch who jointly interrogate modern Western rationality from a valorized location on the periphery ('Occidentalización', 28); on the other, he is referred (more obliquely) to the broader context of postcolonial studies represented by such figures as Homi Bhabha, Frantz Fanon, Edouard Glissant and Ella Shohat. Following on from Mignolo, the purpose of the present essay is to look more closely at Zea's connections with postcolonial discourse, through a consideration of certain historical and biographical factors which prompted Zea to identify with global processes of decolonization and to subscribe to a particular interpretation of Latin American history. Examination of a range of works written by Zea between the early 1940s and the mid-1990s will broaden considerably the temporal scope found in the essays by Mignolo and elsewhere, and allow a more sustained analysis of Zea's engagement with a number of issues that are central to the historical and discursive phenomenon of postcolonialism.

Born in Mexico City in 1912, and still an active member of the academy at the century's end, Leopoldo Zea is a unique survivor of a generation which lived through the turmoil and the aftermath of the Mexican Revolution and then bore witness, over the decades that followed, to ensuing events in Mexico, the Americas, and the world at large. A volume entitled *Filosofar a la altura del hombre* published in 1993 includes a biographical summary that is vividly evocative, in spite of the rather conventional picture that it constructs of the author's life and times:

> Se trata de un largo camino biográfico dentro del mundo que me había tocado en suerte, mi mundo. Testigo privilegiado de este mundo, con sus dos grandes guerras mundiales, sus dos grandes revoluciones planetarias: las guerras de 1914 a 1918 y la de 1939 a 1945: la revolución nacionalista y anticolonialista que se inició en México en 1910 y la revolución socialista iniciada en Rusia en 1917.[2]

Zea continues:

> La Revolución Mexicana fue captada de diversas formas en sus efectos desde mi temprana edad; la socialista, racionalizada poco a poco. Crisis de 1929, nacimiento del fascismo; los crímenes coloniales del llamado Mundo Libre. La brutalidad del nazi-fascismo. La Guerra Civil Española ... La represión neoimperialista estadounidense sobre la América Latina. Los movimientos nacionalistas y anticolonialistas del llamado Tercer Mundo y un sentimiento peculiar de dolor, como un 'Me duele España' y duelen los atropellos a los pueblos de una América que siento como parte mía. Dolor ... por Vietnam y alegría por su triunfo. Dolor por la muerte de Salvador Allende, el cerco a Cuba, a Nicaragua, la brutalidad gorila en el Cono Sur y muchas

cosas más ... Esta ha sido, más o menos atropelladamente, mi ya larga experiencia vital.

(*Filosofar a la altura del hombre*, 15–16)

Reading, in large part, like an index of the most significant political causes of the international Left in the twentieth century, this summary of interests and events foregrounds issues of colonialism to an extent that is both noteworthy (especially in regard to the characterization of twentieth-century Latin America as the continuing site of contestation of colonialism and neoimperialism a full century after the severance of formal ties with the Spanish empire), and wholly consistent with a pattern of concerns that begins to take shape in Zea's work in the 1940s, undergoes a significant transformation in the 1960s and, by the 1970s, has crystallized into a form that will remain constant in the author's production down to the century's end.

Zea's first major work was a study of the reception of European positivist ideas (especially those of Comte and Spencer) in late nineteenth-century Mexico. *El positivismo en México* (1942) addressed the question of the problematical relation between local conditions and foreign paradigms of thought, and concluded that throughout its history as a modern nation, Mexico had failed repeatedly to assimilate external paradigms to an integrated cultural project. First, Spain, then—in the nineteenth century—France and England, and subsequently the United States of America, have offered models that have proved incompatible with a national character caught up in a struggle for self-definition that continues to this day.

A couple of essays from the late 1940s provide further insights into Zea's thinking at this stage of his development. 'Norteamérica en la conciencia hispanoamericana' (1947) commemorates the centenary of the war between Mexico and the United States and surveys the attitudes to their northern neighbour of several generations of Spanish American intellectuals of the modern period.[3] Looking, first, at the nineteenth century, the essay registers the widespread call for a 'mental emancipation' to match the political freedoms gained in the initial phase of postcolonial independence. With thinkers such as Esteban Echeverría, Juan Bautista Alberdi and José Luis Mora in mind, Zea observes: 'Liberados de [España] políticamente, saben que no es suficiente, que es menester arrancársela de las entrañas. A la emancipación política debe seguir otra emancipación, lo que llaman *emancipación mental*' (*La filosofía como compromiso*, 57). Moving ahead to the twentieth century, Zea then praises José Enrique Rodó and Antonio Caso for their 'actitud de potenciar lo hispanoamericano' and identifies two strands in their attitude towards the United States. On the one hand, Rodó, Caso and others like them found much to admire in the democratic traditions of the USA; on the other, they were united in their abhorrence of 'la Norteamérica de las ambiciones territoriales, la del "destino manifiesto", la de las discriminaciones raciales, la de los imperialismos' (*La filosofía como compromiso*, 82).

The implications of Zea's historical analysis for the Spanish American intelligentsia of the day are spelt out in 'La filosofía como compromiso' of 1948. Taking for granted a connection (reminiscent of Sartre) between philosophy and ethics, this pithy and combative essay asks 'Nosotros los americanos, más concretamente los hispanoamericanos, ¿de qué hemos de responder? ¿De cuál situación hemos de ser responsables? ¿Qué compromisos tiene que asumir responsablemente nuestra filosofía?', and calls for 'una filosofía consciente de [nuestra] situación' (*La filosofía como compromiso*, 31–32), i.e. a way of thinking suited to the circumstances of Spanish American societies and the intelligentsias that serve them. For, as Zea sees it, the nature of the world around them demands an attitude of commitment; he envisages a future close to hand involving the creation of new types of community founded on solidarity between colonial peoples and their united opposition to imperialist nations—a global scenario in which the peoples of Spanish America, he claims, will occupy 'un lugar muy especial' (*La filosofía como compromiso*, 36).

Altogether, these are the first published declarations of Leopoldo

Zea that I have found on the theme of the opposition between colonial peoples ('los pueblos coloniales') and imperialist countries ('los países imperialistas'). In the context of Latin American culture at the time, they chime in with the anti-imperialist ideology of a Pablo Neruda or a Gabriel García Márquez, and could consequently be regarded as unexceptional. There are nevertheless three points worth making about them. The first point has to do with Zea's assumed role as spokesperson for Latin America and its peoples. Quite consciously and explicitly, he inscribes himself within the tradition of Simón Bolívar, José Martí, José Vasconcelos and others who had promoted the idea of a culturally and politically unified Spanish America in contradistinction to Anglo-America. A continental projection and affiliation will characterize Zea's work from this moment on. The second point of interest concerns an assumption that informs Zea's thinking, as it does that of Neruda, García Márquez and others at the end of the 1940s, which is the vulnerability of the world that they inhabit to neo-imperialist interference. Categorical distinctions between colonialism (understood as involving the conquest and control of other people's lands and goods) and imperialism (understood—after Lenin—as involving the exercise of military and economic power in the service of advanced capitalism) are essayed in many primers of postcolonial studies and shown to be inextricably entangled, against the background of the political order that emerges from the Second World War.[4] In a much-quoted essay, Anne McClintock reviews the multiple forms taken, since the 1940s, by 'the United States' imperialism-without-colonies' and documents the relentless frequency with which the nations of Latin America have proved vulnerable to north American military invasion, gunboat diplomacy, economic exploitation and gross interference in the domestic political sphere.[5] In such circumstances, the status of the majority of those nations as formally independent of an erstwhile European empire is merely a *de jure* condition, offering little or no immunity against the intrusions of a neoimperialist power strengthened both militarily and politically at the end of a global war. The image of vulnerability to neoimperialist interference that is conveyed in the work of Leopoldo Zea at the mid-point of the century has consequently to be seen as an accurate reflection of American geopolitics of the time. Finally, I stress the strong presence in Zea's writing of a sense of being at a watershed in the overall history of the world. It is commonplace in postcolonial studies (and in other historiographies) to identify the late 1940s as a crucial moment in the evolution and reconfiguration of the world order. Through his anticipation of the concerted uprising of 'los países coloniales' against 'los países imperialistas', Zea positions himself within the general parameters of revisionary thinking of the late 1940s and in a clear relation to contemporary postcolonial discourse.[6]

Moving ahead to the 1960s, we find evidence both of continuity and of significant development in Zea's thinking. The transparently titled *América latina y el mundo*, published in Buenos Aires in 1965, illustrates the author's evolved position. It also bears the imprint of two major events—one biographical, the other historical—that had influenced Zea in the intervening years. The first of these is a tour that Zea made, in 1961, of 'casi toda Africa', as he put it to me in the course of a private conversation that took place in Mexico City in March 1998. Travelling as the official envoy of the Mexican government's Dirección General de Relaciones Culturales and the Secretaría de Relaciones Exteriores, Zea visited Morocco, Tunisia and Ghana that year; amongst the people that he met were President Nasser of Egypt, President Sédar Senghor of Senegal, and King Idris—as he then was—of Libya. (To the name of Sédar Senghor I here add in parenthesis that of Aimé Césaire, whom Zea would also meet, in the early 1960s, at the headquarters of UNESCO in Paris.) Zea's African tour was followed in 1962 by a further diplomatic visit, to Japan, Hong Kong and India, adding an Asian dimension to his life-experience, which would shortly be reflected in his writings of the middle of that decade.

The historical event which made a dramatic impression on Zea, as it did on countless millions of other people at the time, was the Cuban Revolution, begun in 1959. It is difficult to overstate the impact that the Revolution had on the political attitudes and perceptions, and indeed the entire political culture, of the contemporary world. A particularly important consideration was the policy of the Revolution of reaching out to peoples and nations far removed from the Caribbean and the Americas, to areas where 'el viejo enramaje colonial' was in crisis. The author of an article published in 1966 in the official cultural magazine of the Revolution—*Casa de las Américas*—traced a continuous line beginning in 1945 (the end of the Second World War), through Revolution in China in 1949, Egypt in 1952, and Indochina in 1954, down to the present, situating recent events in Cuba in the wider context of Third World liberation.[7] As early as 1963, the Segunda Declaración de la Habana had asked, rhetorically:

> ¿Qué es la historia de Cuba sino la historia de América Latina? ¿Y qué es la historia de América Latina sino la historia de Asia, Africa y Oceanía? ¿Y qué es la historia de todos estos pueblos sino la historia de la explotación más despiadada y cruel del imperialismo en el mundo entero?[8]

Third World intellectuals and the Cuban Revolution had an immediate and long-lasting effect on Zea. In the interview mentioned above, I asked how well he knew the work of Césaire, Sédar Senghor and Fanon. He replied that he had never met Fanon, but read him in the 1960s, when all three writers 'me complementaron, ampliando mi mundo'. As a point of fact, Spanish translations of works by both Fanon and Césaire appeared in Habana in 1965 and 1966, followed by the text of an interview with Césaire in 1968 and a selection of his poetry in 1969. The material published in 1965 was a translation of *Les damnés de la terre* (1961) by Julieta Campos which was reviewed in the pages of *Casa de las Américas* by Roberto Fernández Retamar; a year later there followed an excerpt from Césaire's 'Discours sur le colonialisme', published in the same number of *Casa de las Américas* as the translation of a short piece by Fanon entitled, in Spanish, 'Antillanos y africanos'.[9] Later reprintings in Mexico of these last two items were accompanied by introductory notes penned by none other than Leopoldo Zea.

Looking closely at Zea's *América latina y el mundo*, we find that the frame of reference of the majority of the essays goes beyond Latin America to encompass the Middle East, India, Indonesia and those whom Zea calls 'los pueblos negros del continente africano' (*América latina y el mundo*, 14). What is more, Zea quotes Nehru and President Sukarno of Indonesia, on the rise of a new nationalism which is concerned with removing the inequities of former European colonial rule. Greater understanding of the humanity of other races amongst European postwar intellectuals (Camus, Sartre, Greene and Toynbee are foremost in Zea's mind) encourages the peoples of Latin America to see themselves in a new light: 'no como gentes especiales, originales o singulares, sino semejantes a la totalidad de los pueblos del mundo' (18). Writing within a time-frame that is contemporary with the war in Vietnam and later than the uprising in Algeria, Zea sees a whole range of opportunities not formerly available to colonized peoples. On his interpretation, the classic opposition between socialism and imperialism has given way to a struggle between 'el viejo imperialismo europeo y las que aún son o fueron sus colonias', on the one hand, and on the other, a new-style imperialism which 'busc[a] llenar los supuestos "vacíos" provocados por la retirada europea en el resto del mundo'. Asserting—in words reminiscent of 'La filosofía como compromiso' of 1948—that Latin America 'tiene mucho que decir, mucho que aportar en este mundo recién surgido' (32), Zea implicates Latin America in a wider narrative of decolonization, in keeping with the political ideology and territorial view of the Cuban Revolution.[10]

The relationship that I am tracing between Zea's work and mainstream currents of postcolonial thought is reinforced in a collection of essays from the early 1970s, published under the title *Dependencia y liberación en la cultura latinoamericana* (1974). At a general level, the title alludes to the role of dependence theory in Latin America and the challenge represented to it by the philosophy of liberation expounded by, among others, Enrique Dussel and Augusto Salazar Bondy. Both of these men are mentioned by Zea in the essay entitled 'La filosofía latinoamericana como filosofía de la liberación' of 1973, which reads the history of the continent as a series of failed attempts to accede to (Western) modernity and as the story of a 'permanente subordinación' still obtaining at the time of writing: 'Ahora se nos vuelve a plantear, como en el pasado siglo XIX, el problema de nuestra emancipación mental o cultural' (*Dependencia y liberación*, 37). Of especial relevance to the present enquiry is the intermingling of the names of Dussel and Salazar Bondy with those of Aimé Césaire, Leopold Sédar Senghor and Frantz Fanon, all of whom Zea quotes and invokes in the essays under review. Thus, in 'La filosofía latinoamericana como filosofía de la liberación', a critique of Salazar Bondy's vision of 'una decisiva transformación de nuestra sociedad mediante la cancelación del subdesarrollo y la dominación' (40) is bolstered by an appeal to 'Frantz Fanon, otro latinoamericano' and by a double quotation from *Les damnés de la terre*: 'La descolonización es simplemente la sustitución de una *especie* de hombres por otra *especie* de hombres', which renders the English 'Decolonization is quite simply the replacing of a certain "species" of men by another "species" of men'—from the very first paragraph of Fanon's seminal essay—and 'Por Europa, por nosotros mismos y por la humanidad, compañeros, hay que cambiar de piel, desarrollar un pensamiento nuevo, tratar de crear un hombre nuevo' (41), which translates Fanon's final sentence, 'For Europe, for ourselves and for humanity, comrades, we must turn over a new leaf, we must work out new concepts, and try to set afoot a new man'.[11]

Essentially, Zea detects in Salazar Bondy a utopian streak which requires correction. He discovers in the work of Fanon both a statement of the problem and 'acaso', he writes, 'su solución'. The problem centres on how to set colonized peoples free, without denying their particular way of being ('modo de ser'). For Zea as for Fanon, the solution involves the creation of a new humanity and its insertion into a new world order (cf. 'This huge task consists of reintroducing mankind into the world, the whole of mankind' (Fanon, *The Wretched of the Earth*, 84). Crucially, the new 'species' of human being envisaged in that scenario must be neither a copy nor a belated version of the category of 'Man' promoted for centuries by the agents of European civilization. At this crucial moment in the history of the world, what is called for is 'un orden en que todos los hombres, sin excepción, tengan el lugar que les corresponde como hombres entre hombres [ie. as human beings existing on a par with other human beings]' (*Dependencia y liberación*, 47). Zea concludes his argument by referring to the example of Fanon one final time: 'Por ello, Fanon, sin sentirse negro, latinoamericano o africano, sino hombre concreto con la concreción que es propia de todos los hombres dice [and here the words are a direct translation of Fanon's]: "si queremos que la humanidad avance con audacia, si queremos elevarla a un nivel distinto del que le ha impuesto Europa, entonces hay que inventar, hay que descubrir"' (*Dependencia y liberación*, 47; *The Wretched of the Earth*, 254).

At root, the concepts of a new man and a new humanity form part of an ideology of a new humanism which also sounds throughout the second half of *The Wretched of the Earth* and in the writings of Césaire and Sédar Senghor as well. This new humanism looks beyond national boundaries towards a set of ethical values intended to benefit people the world over. Importantly, the new humanism represents a break with the Christian and liberal humanisms of the Renaissance and the Enlightenment, which, in Fanon's view, had led Europe into moral bankruptcy and left it, after two world wars, 'swaying between atomic and spiritual disintegration' (*The Wretched of the Earth*, 251). The new doctrine must promote human values on a genuinely universal scale, leaving behind the Eurocentric prejudices of an older, colonialist dispensation.

The coincidence of Zea's and Fanon's outlook on this matter is, I think, both substantive and illuminating. In her analysis of Fanon's contribution to postcolonial thinking, Ania Loomba repeats Albert Memmi's assessment of the complex personality and motivations of the 'French-educated Martiniquan who became an Algerian nationalist' (Loomba, 180):

> Memmi astutely suggests that Fanon's revolutionary romanticism has much to do with his own rootlessness: because he was alienated from the French culture that he was brought up to revere, the Martiniquan culture that he was brought up to reject, and the Algerian culture that he espoused but was never familiar with, Fanon adopted a universalist humanism, speaking for all colonised peoples and indeed all humanity in a Messianic tone. (147)

Looked at from this perspective, Fanon exemplifies the complex and problematical relations between nationality, location and identity in colonial and postcolonial situations, as analyzed by Loomba and others.[12] Alternating between Latin American, European and African affiliations, Fanon points up the arbitrariness of standard criteria of classification, and casts some light on the profile of Leopoldo Zea who combines Mexican nationality with a continental Latin American identity and a feeling of solidarity with colonized and decolonizing peoples the world over. While clearly different from Fanon in crucial respects of race and colour, temperament and the social and professional status that he enjoys in the institutional world of the Mexican intelligentsia, Zea nevertheless echoes precisely Fanon's universalism, his refashioned humanism, and the Martiniquan's comparative perspective on decolonization in Africa and the Americas.

A full-scale engagement with the agenda of postcolonialism is the comparison which Zea traces between the ideologies of Negritude and *indigenismo* in a paper which he delivered at a colloquium on 'Négritude et l'Amérique latine', held at the University of Dakar, Senegal, in January 1974. The grounds for comparison are asserted in the introduction to the paper, which is reproduced as Chapter IV of *Dependencia y liberación en la cultura latinoamericana*:

> Negritud e indigenismo son conceptos ideológicos que tienen
> su origen en una situación que es común a los hombres de
> Africa negra y Afroamérica por un lado y de Latinoamérica o
> Indoamérica por el otro: la situación de dependencia. En uno
> y otro casos expresa la toma de conciencia de una situación de
> marginalidad y subordinación que se pretende cambiar.

Negritude and *indigenismo* are forms of consciousness which contest both the political and economic foundations of imperialism and the racialist ideologies undergirding colonialism. Focusing on the latter, Zea stresses the common opposition of Negritude and *indigenismo* to a white mythology that had relegated non-whites to the category of 'lo subhumano', and whose founding assumptions they turn upside down: 'La negritud y el indigenismo, al ser enarbolados como banderas de reivindicación del hombre en Africa y América Latina invierten la connotación que el dominador ha querido darles'. In line with the revised humanism that he advocates elsewhere, Zea categorizes Negritude and *indigenismo* as 'simplemente expresiones concretas del hombre', which counter an exclusive ideology of 'blanquitud' with a discourse of racial and cultural difference committed to a non-exclusive definition of the category of the human (*Dependencia y liberación*, 57). This reading concurs generally with the characterization of Negritude provided by Césaire and Sédar Senghor, who explained the inspiration behind the movement of which they were spokesmen and champions, partly in terms of 'una voluntad de desafío, una afirmación violenta' of black (French-Caribbean) values over and against 'la civilización racionalizante del Occidente', and partly in terms of a transcendent will to 'ir hacia lo universal profundizando en lo particular. Desembocar siempre en lo universal.'[13]

As early as the third paragraph of his essay, Zea has to concede a major difference between the two ideologies, admitting that:

> Si bien negritud e indigenismo son expresiones de una toma de
> conciencia común a los que enarbolan uno y otro concepto, es
> decir, la de dependencia, su origen no es el mismo. Negritud

> es un concepto que nace del mismo hombre que ha sufrido dominación y discriminaciones en nombre de la supuesta superioridad del hombre que no es negro ... El indigenismo, por otro lado, no tiene su origen en el propio indígena, en el indio de América ... Es parte de un programa para incorporar al indígena, esto es, al indio ... a una comunidad creada por el criollo y el mestizo. Es éste, el que llamaremos latinoamericano, el que ha enarbolado la bandera del indigenismo como un complemento ineludible de su afirmación de hombre concreto de esta América. (*Dependencia y liberación*, 59)

The problematical implications of the question, 'Who speaks for the subaltern?', are sidestepped in Zea's account of the promotion of the cause of the Indian populations of Latin America, which he seems content to present uncontroversially as subordinate to a wider project concerned with the fulfilment ('realización') of 'el hombre americano'. The strands of subalternity, *mestizaje*, Americanism and humanism introduced in the first part of the essay are thereafter woven into a dense web of argument and brought to a conclusion which resolves only some of the issues involved.

Parts two and three of 'Negritud e indigenismo' survey the history of the ideology of *indigenismo* in Latin America, with particular reference to Mexico and Peru. A 'preocupación por valorar al indio y su cultura' is traced back to the end of the eighteenth century in the work of a number of historians and natural scientists such as 'Francisco Javier Clavijero en México, Juan Ignacio Molina en Chile, el catalán Benito María de Moxó, [e] Hipólito Unanue en Perú'. Crucially, these (predominantly *criollo*) intellectuals rejected the colonial discourse of Europeans 'tales como Jean Louis Leclerc Buffon y Cornelio de Pauw respecto a la inmadurez o decadencia de la naturaleza americana y como parte de ella la inferioridad, degeneración y bestialidad del indio americano' (*Dependencia y liberación*, 60). That discourse of racist disparagement would be rearticulated in the mid-nineteenth century by the likes of Domingo Faustino Sarmiento, who would claim that the Indians 'no piensan porque no están preparados para ello' (61).[14] Subsequently, it is contested in the twentieth century by thinkers allied to the nationalist movements of the 1920s, the most prominent being Manuel González Prada and José Carlos Mariátegui in Peru and José Vasconcelos in Mexico. Closer to the time of writing, Zea identifies the Peruvian philosopher, Francisco Miró Quesada, and the Director of the Instituto Nacional Indigenista of Mexico, Gonzalo Aguirre Beltrán, as heirs to the tradition of *indigenismo* whose history he has outlined in parts two and three of his essay.

What is also plotted there is the cooption of *indigenismo* by a Marxist nationalist ideology in mid-twentieth-century Peru and by the official rhetoric of the Mexican Revolution still operating in the late 1960s and 1970s. And it is here that Zea's account of *indigenismo* acquires a crucial inflection, as a result of aligning itself with the 'anti-oligarchic' and 'anti-imperialist' philosophy of the one (*Dependencia y liberación*, 66), and the doctrine favouring the assimilation of the Indian to a national cultural project, advocated by the other. Such a manoeuvre enables Zea to effect a double domestication of *indigenismo*. He can view it, first, as an aspect of a larger, and ideologically irreproachable project, which is that of 'latinoamericanismo': in the case of Peru, Zea observes how in the hands of the leaders of 'la revolución nacionalista ... de nuestros días', 'El indigenismo se transforma así en latinoamericanismo' (66). And secondly, he can view it as an ideological tool compatible with his own particular brand of humanism: in the Mexican context, the discourse of cultural assimilation provides a ready-made narrative which envisages the transformation of the Indian 'simplemente en un mexicano. En un hombre con su concreta y especial personalidad, la que le dan sus orígenes y la forma como asimila la cultura nacional, pero también como un miembro activo de ella'. The example of Benito Juárez as a one-time subaltern who 'actuó ... como miembro de la comunidad cuya cultura había asimilado' and reached the highest pinnacle of political achievement 'no sólo a nivel nacional, mexicano, sino a nivel americano' (69), is invoked to justify a policy of cultural assimilation. Yet, events in our time in Chiapas and other parts of Mexico seriously discredit the proposition that cultural assimilation can be generally beneficial to the nation's Indian populations.

Zea's understanding of the nature and history of Latin American *indigenismo* inevitably colours his perception of its relation to Negritude, which he returns to in the fourth and final part of 'Negritud e indigenismo'. Here, questions of race and skin colour are first brought to the fore and then elided as Zea again characterizes the two ideologies as pursuing the same goal, which is the affirmation of the humanity of all species of men (sic). As he puts it, 'el hombre negro, al afirmar su negritud afirma su humanidad'; 'el indio', represented as a socially marginalized, economically disadvantaged and politically disenfranchised member of 'his' national community, 'debe dejar de ser indio y transformarse en un latinoamericano concreto, en un americano u hombre sin más' (*Dependencia y liberación*, 70).

It is important to note that the Indian referred to in the above quotation is both a social category, whose lot can potentially be improved, and an ethnic category, whose exclusion from the project of the nation ('la cultura nacional') can be remedied through a process of 'mestizaje racial y cultural'. Indeed, according to Zea, 'es éste su mestizaje el que afirma frente a filosofías políticas de dominación' (70). Not the least of the problems generated by this formulation is the attribution, to the Indian, of a measure of political agency earlier denied him in Zea's account of the history of *indigenismo*. More controversial still is the vision of the Indian's absorption into a grand narrative of racial and cultural mixing ('mestizaje'), which is none the less questionable for the pedigree that lies behind it. Some twenty years before Jorge Klor de Alva penned his polemical essay,[15] Zea invokes the history of the concept, which has all the force of a myth, of 'Latinoamérica como crisol de razas' and celebrates its 'exemplary' expression in 'el libro de José Vasconcelos, *La raza cósmica*' of 1925 (*Dependencia y liberación*, 70). As Klor de Alva observes, 'mestizaje' is a term which has been used at critical moments in Spanish American history to define and affirm nation-state identities; from a perspective informed by postcolonial theory, it belongs to a larger set of 'categories/practices of contestation' which oppose racialist discourses of the sort referred to above in connection with Buffon and De Pauw (Klor de Alva, 244). Yet, for all its serviceability as a form of oppositional consciousness, the more serious issue here is how the concept of 'mestizaje' is used by Zea to bolster a comparison between *indigenismo* and Negritude.

Zea achieves his aim through a stratagem of reinterpreting Negritude as an ideology inspired by that same 'preocupación por el mestizaje': 'El negro, al afirmar su negritud afirmará, al mismo tiempo, su derecho a hacer suyas las expresiones de la cultura de otros hombres, concretamente la del blanco. Se afirma el ser negro, pero no para quedarse en esta afirmación, sino para hacer de ella el instrumento de asimilación de otras culturas' (71). But there is a fundamental asymmetry between the project of Negritude, as described here, and that of *indigenismo*, which resides in the fact that the 'mestizaje' that Zea attributes to Negritude is operative only in cultural terms: nowhere does he state that Negritude pursues a goal of 'mestizaje cultural *y racial*' (my emphasis), presumably because such a claim is untenable. When he eventually reaches the end of his argument in support of the comparison that he has been making all along, the conclusion that he offers follows only in part from what has gone before: 'Negritud e indigenismo tienen *así* [my emphasis] una preocupación común, el mestizaje cultural a partir de la situación concreta del hombre que sostiene la una y el otro, la dependencia' (73). The different conceptions of 'mestizaje' that inform the two ideologies represent a fissure in a term which ultimately fails to mediate dialectically between those of Negritude and *indigenismo*. None of which weakens the claim of this essay to be regarded as one of the most serious and complex engagements with a top-priority item on the agenda of postcolonialism in Latin America, Africa, and elsewhere.

A less controversial, but no less substantial, contribution to that broad subject is Zea's *Discurso desde la marginación y la barbarie*, of 1988.[16] In a nutshell, the book surveys five hundred years of European imperialism and its assignment of other peoples to the categories of barbarians and savages. Descartes, Rousseau, Hegel, Marx and Engels are points of reference in a narrative of global expansion driven by a Eurocentric view of history. In a chapter entitled 'Eurocentrismo', Zea considers the dialectical relationships between colonizer and colonized, and valorizes the efforts made by the periphery to resist and displace the centre. From the Habsburgs to Queen Victoria, the European powers assumed moral and political supremacy in the world, taking for granted their identification with the values of civilization. However, their treatment of the Other did not often accord with the identification of the West with civilization and that of the Other with barbarism or savagery; as the mid-nineteenth-century Mexican patriot Gabino Barreda remarked apropos the invasion of Mexico in 1864 by forces supporting the Emperor Maximilian, the real savages in the Franco-Mexican conflict were the French and Belgian army, whose aggression, he remarked, was 'la negación misma de la civilización que ahora encarna América' (*Discurso desde la marginación*, 56). In recalling Barreda, Zea makes the same point as Césaire in 'Discours sur le colonialisme', where European colonization, far from carrying out a civilizing mission, actually results in the 'salvajización' of the metropolis and its agents.[17] Also evoked here is the narrative of Caliban's revenge, in which the colonized Caliban turns the instruments of colonization against the colonizer, in a strategic reversal adumbrated in Shakespeare's *The Tempest* and reformulated by a clutch of American writers including Césaire, Roberto Fernández Retamar[18] and Leopoldo Zea in the concluding chapters of *Discurso desde la marginación y la barbarie*.

The presence of the Caliban motif in Zea's work fits perfectly well into the framework of beliefs and assertions being examined here. What I want to stress in the final paragraphs of this study is not so much the coincidence, though that in itself is noteworthy, as Zea's elaboration on the theme of Caliban, through his discussion of an essay by the North American academic, Richard Morse. Morse published 'El espejo de Próspero: un estudio de la dialéctica del nuevo mundo' in 1982, in a Spanish translation only.[19] In his essay he invited North America to look at its Hispanic American counterpart, no longer as 'víctima', 'paciente' or 'problema'—i.e., as alien and monstrous—but rather as a reflection of 'sus propias dolencias y "problemas"'. Morse reminds his reader that the image reflected in a mirror is an inverted image, and he explains that it is his intention to 'dar la vuelta a la superficie reflejante', thus facilitating a reversal of Anglo-American perceptions of Ibero-America (*El espejo de Próspero*, 7). Zea, of course, leaps at the chance to exploit this new reading of the Caliban–Prospero motif. Without lessening its force as a paradigm of anti-colonial resentment and resistance, he takes Morse's image of Prospero's mirror as the basis for a new model of political and moral relationships between Anglo- and Ibero-America and, more widely, between the West and the non-West, the centre and the periphery, generally. 'Al otro lado del espejo del sistema, frente al que ya viene reaccionando Europa y Occidente', Zea declares, 'están los pueblos que lo han sufrido y sufren, pueblos que han tomado conciencia de la manipulación de que han sido objeto durante casi cinco siglos, que se saben obligados a barbarizar el discurso de su señor y colonizador' (*Discurso desde la marginación*, 277). Citing two contemporary Africans—Amadou Mahtar M'Bow and M'Bounoua—as well as the older examples of José Martí and Justo Sierra, Zea insists that the time has come to 'ir más allá de la supuesta marginación y barbarie' (282).

The fact that Zea remains tied to the selfsame binary that he otherwise purports to dismantle, inevitably limits the extent of his critique. Arguably, by simply inverting the values of *civilización* and *barbarie*, as Barreda had done, Zea does little to subvert the paradigm itself. This failure to assimilate the lessons of post-structuralism is a disabling feature of *Discurso desde la marginación y la barbarie*. On the other hand, Zea keeps faith with the principles of a high-minded humanism that he had espoused in the late 1940s, calling now for improved inter-American understanding and respect for 'expresiones del hombre que no por ser distintas son menos humanas' (*Discurso desde la marginación*, 24). His continuing support for the peoples of Latin America and the Third World demonstrates a consistency in his moral and political outlook which may perhaps be judged to outweigh the failure to renovate his mind-set. Ideological objections aside, the voice and the writings of Leopoldo Zea resonate powerfully beyond the political boundaries of Latin America and illuminate the field of postcolonial relations in the world at large, at the end of the twentieth century.

Notes

1 Walter Mignolo, 'Occidentalización, imperialismo, globalización, herencias coloniales y teorías postcoloniales', *Revista iberoamericana*, LXI, 170–71 (1995), 27–40, and 'La razón postcolonial: herencias coloniales y teorías postcoloniales', in *Postmodernidad y post-colonialidad: breves reflexiones sobre Latinoamérica*, ed. Alfonso de Toro (Frankfurt: Vervuert; Madrid: Iberoamericana, 1997), 51–70.

2 Leopoldo Zea, *Filosofar a la altura del hombre: discrepar a la altura del hombre* (Mexico City: UNAM, 1993), 15.

3 Zea, *La filosofía como compromiso* (Mexico: Tezontle, 1952), 55–84.

4 See, for example, Ania Loomba, *Colonialism/Postcolonialism* (London: Routledge, 1998), 1–7, and Patrick Williams and Laura Chrisman, *Colonial Discourse and Post-colonial Theory: A Reader* (New York and London: Harvester Wheatsheaf, 1993), 2–3.

5 Anne McClintock, 'The Angels of Progress: Pitfalls of the Term "Post-colonialism"', in Williams and Chrisman, *Colonial Discourse*, 291–304 (295).

6 Williams and Chrisman, 3. See also Robert Young, *White Mythologies: Writing History and the West* (London: Routledge, 1990), 119–21.

7 Ricardo Alarcón, 'América latina y la Conferencia Intercontinental', *Casa de las Américas*, 35 (March–April 1966), 4–10 (4).

8 Alarcón, 7.

9 The Campos translation appeared under the title *Los condenados de la tierra* (Habana: Ediciones Venceremos, 1965). Roberto Fernández

Retamar hailed its Martinican author in 'Fanon y América latina', *Casa de las Américas*, 31 (July–August 1965), 89–94. As for Césaire, a sign of the high profile accorded to him is the two-part interview conducted by Sonia Aratán and René Depestre, 'Entrevistas con Aimé Césaire', *Casa de las Américas*, 49 (July–August 1968), 130–42.

10 The Revolution's self-identification with the Third World is attested to in Alarcón, 'América latina y la Conferencia Intercontinental', and by Roberto Fernández Retamar, 'Hacia una intelectualidad revolucionaria en Cuba', *Casa de las Américas*, 40 (January–February 1967), 4–18. Particularly enlightening are the following statements by Fernández Retamar apropos the pioneering role of José Martí, which clearly identify Martí as a precursor of the Third World intellectual: 'En efecto, el primer intelectual en comprender a plenitud nuestra pertenencia a eso que iba a ser llamado "tercer mundo" fue José Martí' (14); 'Martí [fue] el primer pensador del tercer mundo'; and, most evocatively, 'Volver a Martí después de haber conocido a Fidel, al Che, a Fanon, a Amílcar Cabral, es por lo menos un sacudimiento' (15).

11 Frantz Fanon, *The Wretched of the Earth*, trans. Constance Farrington, with a Preface by Jean-Paul Sartre (Harmondsworth: Penguin, 1967; reprinted 1990), 255.

12 Loomba, *Colonialism/Postcolonialism*, 173–78.

13 These two quotations are from the interview with Césaire conducted by René Depestre, 'Entrevistas …', 141 and 135.

14 On the ideology of Sarmiento, compare the reading offered by Else Vieira in Chapter Two of this volume with the more indulgent assessment volunteered by Peter Hulme in 'Including America', *Ariel: A Review of International English Literature*, XXVI, 1 (January 1995), 122.

15 J. Jorge Klor de Alva, 'The Postcolonization of the (Latin) American Experience: a Reconsideration of "Colonialism", "Postcolonialism", and "Mestizaje"', in *After Colonialism: Imperial Histories and Postcolonial Displacements*, ed. Gyan Prakash (Princeton, NJ: Princeton University Press, 1995), 241–75.

16 *Discurso desde la marginación y la barbarie* (Barcelona: Anthropos, 1988).

17 See Aimé Césaire, *Discurso sobre el colonialismo*, which in reality is an excerpt from that essay, reprinted as a booklet with an introduction by Zea (Mexico: UNAM, 1979). The reference to 'salvajización' is to be found on page 7.

18 Ania Loomba pays significant attention to Fernández Retamar's exploitation of the Caliban theme, in *Colonialism/Postcolonialism*, 174–75 and 189.

19 Richard Morse, *El espejo de Próspero: un estudio de la dialéctica del nuevo mundo* (Mexico City: Siglo XXI, 1982).

CHAPTER SIX

Fernando Ortiz's Transculturation: the Postcolonial Intellectual and the Politics of Cultural Representation

Catherine Davies
University of Manchester

One of the major contentions in the postcolonial debate is the appropriateness of the term 'post(-)colonial' in a multitude of historical contexts. This essay argues that Cuban polymath Fernando Ortiz (1881–1969), although still relatively unknown outside the Spanish-speaking world, ranks among the most important theorists of the postcolonial condition. Consideration of his extensive work within its specific historical context will enable us to further refine the terms commonly employed in Anglo- and Franco-centric discourses. To more fully appreciate the significance of Ortiz's work for postcolonial theorization, the political status of post-independence Cuba must be taken into account. That Cuba passed from a colonial to a postcolonial status vis-à-vis metropolitan Spain in 1898 is indisputable. The fact that the end of European colonialism was concomitant with the onset of US neocolonialism on the island is well documented. As military governor General Wood wrote at the time, 'I believe that [Cuba] is a very desirable acquisition to the United States. The island will be gradually "Americanized" and in due course we will have one of the most rich and desirable possessions existing in the world.'[1] The US occupation of Cuba, which led Lenin to formulate his theories on the highest (or latest) forms of capitalism (monopoly capitalism),[2] was the very first example of US global imperialism. Cuba became a political protectorate of the United States until 1934 and an economic dependency until 1959. From the 1920s on, Ortiz and other Cuban intellectuals struggled to gain control of the means of cultural production in an effort to resist the hegemony of the United States.[3]

It is important to remember that Ortiz was born and educated within a colonial regime. He was seventeen when Cuba secured formal independence, but his education continued in Spain. Like many postcolonial writers of the white intellectual elite, Ortiz adopted a metropolitan perspective in his early work, particularly with respect to Cuban blacks. Later, in the mid-1920s, when the full implications of US intervention became clear, his viewpoint shifted markedly. If his first book can be said to mimic colonial discourses, with the proviso that for him the colonized other was alive and well at home, his later studies demonstrate a keen awareness of the need to encourage the recognition and expression of an autonomous, hybrid national culture. His project, to create a Cuban national consciousness, necessitated a radically different attitude to African-Cuban culture on both a personal and collective level. Despite his acceptance of the evolutionary paradigms typical of nineteenth-century social thought, Ortiz realized that it was black popular culture that made Cuba distinctive. He thus took up the ambiguous role of the postcolonial intellectual; on the one hand appropriating and rationalizing these cultures as objects of knowledge and, on the other, associating himself with the popular resistance to neocolonialism and imperialism they were seen to represent. His project involved not only the reinscription of African-Cuban cultures into white areas of knowledge, but also their legitimation and, indeed, celebration. Though groundbreaking, however, Ortiz's work was not revolutionary. He was politically active and contributed to the overthrow of the dictator Gerardo Machado in 1934, but he could never quite shake off the ideological premises of his Eurocentric formation. His work corresponds most closely to Frantz Fanon's second or 'remembrance' phase in the native intellectual's evolution from colonial complicity to postcolonial opposition, produced at the point when the intellectual 'decides to remember what he is'. Fanon's description of remembrance writing as 'literature of just-before-the battle ... dominated by humour and allegory; but often ... symptomatic of a period of distress and difficulty' is particularly relevant to Ortiz's work.[4]

Nevertheless, Ortiz should be credited with a fundamental insight that provided the basis for the regeneration of Cuban national identity at a time of crisis: that foreign domination needed to be contested by popular cultural resistance, and that this was to be found among the African-Cuban population. By the 1930s, in the wake of large-scale US purchases of Cuban territory, the Cuban nation, 'such as it was', became progressively identified with the descendants of slaves, with 'the people, the workers, the millworkers, the Negroes, "los humildes"'.[5] For Ortiz, for whom culture was the living expression of social and political relationships, the colonialist strategy of separating the Cuban elites from the masses that embodied the national culture was to be challenged. In choosing to dedicate his life's work to the study of African-Cuban culture, and in recognizing its key place in an anti-imperialist strategy, Ortiz came close to fufilling the role of the Gramscian 'organic' intellectual.

In this essay I will focus on one aspect of Ortiz's work: his invention of the term 'transculturation' in 1940. In many ways this marks the high-point of Ortiz's career, the moment when he most successfully entered into constructive dialogue with representatives of imperial hegemony. That this should happen at a time when Cuba had become a client state of the USA, when the American way of life threatened to swamp Cuban cultural values, is no coincidence. The level of success of the term 'transculturation' was indicative of the extent to which the subaltern could have some impact on neocolonial discourse. What, then, did this word mean for Ortiz, and what significance is there in the fact that it was coined in Cuba in 1940?

Intellectual genealogy

Ortiz's first book *Los negros brujos (apuntes para un estudio de etnología criminal)* (Madrid, 1906) was prefaced by Italian criminologist Cesare Lombroso and his *Contrapunteo cubano del tabaco y del azúcar* (Havana, 1940) by anthropologist Bronislaw Malinowski. This has led critics to associate Ortiz's ideas with these two systems of social thought: criminology and functionalism. Without wishing to deny this association, I would like to counter the assumption that Ortiz merely borrowed exogenous methods and terminologies and suggest that he developed his own ideas concurrently, ideas which were firmly grounded within a Hispanic intellectual tradition. Just as important in Ortiz's early formation was his teacher Manuel Salas y Ferré, Chair of Sociology at the Universidad Central (Madrid) from 1899, founder of the Instituto de Sociología in Madrid. Salas y Ferré, whose *Tratado de sociología* (4 vols) appeared between 1899 and 1904, was a pupil of Krausistas Julián Sanz del Río and Fernando de Castro. Salas y Ferré was interested in positivism and evolutionism and translated the works of Herbert Spencer into Spanish.[6] This end-of-century interest in post-Krausist German thought was potentially conducive to an appreciation of the rich constellation of ideas regarding history, society, the nation and cultural diffusion emanating from central Europe. This included the work of Herder, Hegel, Frobenius (whose *Der Schwarze Dekameron* was published in 1910) and, latterly, the counter-evolutionists Franz Boas (founder of cultural anthropology in the United States) and the 'Young Pole' Malinowski, both contemporaries of Ortiz.[7]

During a discussion at the Instituto de Sociología of Bernaldo de Quirós and José María Llanas Aguilaniedo's recently published *La mala vida en Madrid* (1901), a naturalistic study of psychic and spiritual degeneracy, Ortiz was asked to compare criminal life in Madrid with that of Havana. He knew nothing of the subject, but he hit on a suitably exotic line of enquiry after seeing 'ñáñigo' costumes and instruments in the Museo de Ultramar in Madrid.[8]

That he should look with 'imperial eyes' on his own culture is explained by his intellectual formation. Ortiz was born in Cuba but was raised and educated in Menorca until he was fourteen.[9] In 1895, he returned to Cuba where he studied for three years, throughout the Wars of Independence (1895–98). In the critical year 1898 he left for Spain, to study Law at the Universities of Barcelona and Madrid (1899–1900), culminating in a doctorate in Civil Law (Universidad Central, 1901). He returned to Cuba in 1902, the year the US troops withdrew from the island and the first Cuban Constitution, incorporating the infamous Platt amendment, was approved. Ortiz's formation takes place then at a crucial moment of transition (1898–1902), when Cuba switches from colonial to neocolonial dependency, and his ideas later developed in the context of the Cuban 'pseudo'-Republic (1902–59) in which the founding of an autonomous, national identity was to become a collective imperative.

When the young Ortiz first saw the 'ñáñigo' exhibits in metropolitan Madrid, looking from the centre to the periphery, he adopted the colonial gaze. His appreciation of Cuban difference was still mediated by the museum, the colonial institution (although Cuba had been politically independent from Spain for three years). This moment of identification and (collective) self-recognition must have shocked him. He realized that what differentiated Cuba from Spain was the presence of a vibrant, undocumented black culture, and that what differentiated Cuba from the USA was its large mulatto population. James Shepherd Pike had referred to Cuba as an island filled with 'black, mixed, degraded and ignorant, or inferior races' and therefore unsuitable for annexation to the USA.[10] The more hybrid the Cuban population could be proven to be, the safer it was from US designs. The purpose of Ortiz's research was to develop, substantiate and legitimate his newly acquired insider's view, the view of the Cuban ethnologist working at home. This development was gradual, lasting some forty years, from the publication of *Los negros brujos* to *La africanía de la música folklórica de Cuba* (1950). At the same time, Ortiz's intentions became increasingly political.

Although the term 'transculturation' was not made public until 1940, Ortiz had been mulling over the concept, in need of a label, since the turn of the century. By 1939, the year he met Malinowski in person, he had already coined the word and tried to persuade Malinowski to use it. Following his Spanish university education and his first encounter with 'ñáñigo' ritual on foreign soil, Ortiz spent three years in Italy studying positivist criminology with Lombroso. His first important essay, 'Las supervivencias africanas en Cuba', appeared in Cuba in two parts (in 1905 and 1908) and his book *Los negros brujos* in 1906 (definitive edition: *Hampa afrocubana: los negros brujos [apuntes para un estudio de etnología criminal]*, Madrid, 1917). The initial framework for this research was undoubtedly Lombroso's biological determinist views that criminal tendencies are innate in certain degenerate individuals in whom the survival of traits of a more primitive stage of human evolution may be detected by phrenology. However, this kind of atavistic, anthropometric explanation was much discredited during the first two decades of the century and replaced by ideas on social (rather than individual) pathology and the cultural transmission of delinquency: groups of people were socialized into a tradition of crime. This was the view of the Chicago School. Ortiz developed his ideas (on 'demopsicología')[11] concurrently with this line of thinking. In fact, in the 'Carta Prólogo' to *Los negros brujos*, Lombroso praised Ortiz's work on suicide among the black population but lamented the omission of data on craneal and physiognomical anomalies.[12] Ortiz studied criminal activities among the black Cuban population, the first to do so in a systematic way, and in so doing he stressed the diversity of groups and the transmission of cultural traditions. Like his mentor, Salas y Ferré, Ortiz considered himself a positivist: true knowledge was obtained from the description and explanation of observable social and physical phenomena, and the scientific study of society using methods associated with the physical sciences would lead to social improvement. Thus he aimed to engage in observing the black population as objectively as possible.[13] This was no mean task in racist Cuba where the white elites were so loath to acknowledge African influence that they attributed all cultural features not overtly Hispanic to the extinct Amerindian cultures ('siboneyismo'). As Ortiz later explained, 'hasta hablar en público del negro era cosa peligrosa'.[14] But Ortiz also challenged positivist assumptions based on induction (that is, generalizations derived from empirical observation) by inferring crucial questions such as what constituted deviancy, which norms were infringed, and according to whom? Ortiz came to view transgression as a relative term explained by cultural rather than biological factors. As he stated many years later (1939), it was taken for granted, by the 'blancos dominantes', that Cuban blacks were included *ipso facto* in 'la mala vida', 'Es decir, de la vida no aceptada como la buena, que era, naturalmente! la del grupo social predominante, política y jurídicamente coactivo'.[15]

Similarly, it is clear from his work that he considered himself a functionalist: social institutions, including religions, could be explained in terms of the functions they perform; society was a system of interacting, interdependent parts working together to meet different social needs. At times he favoured the biological, organic or geological analogies associated primarily with Herbert Spencer, but the matrix of his research after *Hampa afrocubana* is the kind of functionalism practised by the founders of twentieth-century social anthropology: Malinowski and Radcliffe-Brown.[16] Malinowski's founding works were published in the 1920s (*Crime and Customs in Savage Society*, 1927; *Sex and Repression in Savage Society*, 1927). His methodology (detailed, participant observation leading to a monograph on a particular 'people': an ethnography) was made public in *Argonauts of the Western Pacific* (1922). Ortiz, participating in the same tradition as Malinowski, though not as Professor of Anthropology at the London School of Economics (1927–38), but alone at home in Vedado (Havana), had been 'doing' ethnography since 1906. From 1921, the year in which he published his study of black institutions ('Los cabildos afrocubanos'), through to 1940 when his status was formally recognized by Malinowski, and on into the 1960s, Ortiz practised a similar methodology. He studied all facets of Afrocuban (a term he coined) culture (organization, religion, language, food, music, instruments, dances, theatre, oral history) to produce a massive corpus of ethnographical and ethnological studies. Ortiz's method was functionalist, but unlike most functionalists of the 1920s and 1930s, he did not neglect the importance of individual human agency (see Malinowski's Preface to *Contrapunteo*) and his ethnographies of African-Cuban culture were complemented by an ethnological and historical interest in the mapping of cultural diffusion (see Coronil, 1995).

Crucially, however, Ortiz lacked the institutional support or authority of an academic establishment that might have contributed to the development of a Hispanic sociological/anthropological tradition. One of the corollaries of this situation, typical of the Latin American intellectual, was his recourse to creative writing as a form of empowerment. As Jean Franco explains, 'because it was blocked from making contributions to the development of scientific thought, the [Latin American] intelligensia was forced into the one area that did not require professional training and the institutionalization of knowledge—that is, into literature'.[17] Ortiz's apparently undisciplined writing, lacking the stylistic rigour expected in sociological monographs, is as literary and historical as it is anthropological. His art was that of rhetorical persuasion in the public arena, a skill that was to prove useful in a society where the facts did not speak for themselves.

Transculturation: a political project

Ortiz's most famous work, *Contrapunteo cubano del tabaco y el azúcar*, published when he was 60, is neither a positivist-functionalist ethnography nor a monograph. It is here that the term 'transculturation' first appears. Interestingly, it appears as the solution to a translation problem as well as a distinctive concept.

The term in use at the time, primarily in US cultural anthropology, to describe what in Britain was referred to as 'cultural contact' was 'acculturation'. This term had been legitimated by Melville Herskovits in his book *Acculturation: The Study of Cultural Contact* (New York, 1938). It describes a process in which continuous contact between different cultural groups leads to the acquisition of certain cultural traits by one or all groups as they mutually adapt to part or all of each other's culture. Herskovits's fieldwork had been in Haiti where he studied (like Ortiz, through historical documentation and direct contact) the interactions of French and African cultures. In certain circumstances, it was noted, a syncretic culture had developed, resulting in cultural loss (displacement, deculturation) and the formation of new customs (neoculturation). Herskovits stressed that there were diverse French cultures (for example, aristocratic and regional) and numerous African tribal cultures: neoculturation would take place only when similar aspects of these diverse cultures came into contact. Herskovits claimed he had initiated this type of study in 1930, whereas Ortiz had been pursuing similar objectives in Cuba since 1906.[18] However, the term 'acculturation' did not take into account issues such as power, control, inequality, whether the transference was unidirectional, or if one culture was thought of as 'inferior' to another. Ortiz was not satisfied with the concept: it was too mechanistic. For him culture was a dynamic, creative social fact and he was more interested in the dialectical process itself rather than the resulting syncretisms. He explained this in his conversation with Malinowski (in 1939).[19]

Typically (Ortiz was a keen etymologist), he challenged the concept 'acculturation' by deconstructing the word. In Spanish, the Latin prefix 'ac' means 'a' or 'hacia' whereas in Anglo-Saxon 'a' may mean 'on' or 'and', implying supplementation. Thus 'acculturation' means 'a tendency towards culturation' with, as Malinowski points out, a 'terminus ad quem', a finishing point. This suggests that the 'uncultured' person receives the benefits of 'our' culture, so becoming 'one of us'. Malinowski, for whom the word 'acculturation' sounded like a cross between a hiccup and a belch, wrote: 'It is an ethnocentric word with a moral connotation. The immigrant has to "acculturate" himself; so do the natives, pagan, heathen, barbarian or savage, who enjoy the benefits of being under the sway of our great Western culture.' These values, he adds, 'radically vitiate the real understanding of the phenomena'.[20] 'Transculturation', that avoided accumulative models, was a more accurate term for the complex process of cultural contact in which both cultures experience change:

> [It] is a process in which something is always given in return for what one receives, a system of give and take ... a process from which a new reality emerges, transformed and complex, a reality that is not a mechanical agglomeration of traits, or even a mosaic, but a new phenomenon, original and independent ... an exchange between two cultures, both of them active, both contributing their share ... (Malinowski, x–xi)

Ortiz himself introduces the neologism, usually written in italics, with a diffidence which belies his audacity. He switches the agenda, however, from the universal to the local:

> Hemos escogido el vocablo *transculturación* para expresar los variadísimos fenómenos que se originan en Cuba por las complejísimas transmutaciones de culturas que aquí se verifican, sin conocer las cuales es imposible entender la evolución del pueblo cubano, así en lo económico, artístico, lingüístico, psicológico, sexual ... La verdadera historia de Cuba es la historia de sus intricadísimas transculturaciones. ... Entendemos que el vocablo *transculturación* expresa mejor las diferentes fases del proceso transitivo de una cultura a otra, porque éste no consiste solamente en adquirir una distinta cultura, que es lo que en rigor indica la voz anglo-americana *aculturation* [sic], sino que el proceso implica también necesariamente la pérdida o desarraigo de una cultura precedente, lo que pudiera decirse una parcial *desculturación*, y, además, significa la consiguiente creación de nuevos fenómenos culturales que pudieran denominarse *neoculturación*. (99, 103)

'Transculturation', then, should replace the defective (US) term 'acculturation' because this does not account for the Cuban situation and therefore is theoretically flawed. 'Transculturation' is a more encompassing label, conceived from within a local, peripheral but uniquely complex culture. Ortiz is suggesting here that the Cuban term has the authority to explain other cultures, including those of the United States, whereas the US term does not. He also implies that the racialist premises of Anglo-Saxon Manifest Destiny should be rejected in favour of Cuban (Hispanic) hybridization. In this way Ortiz launches the Cuban term for world export, as Cuban tobacco was launched centuries before. In fact, in his work tobacco stands as a metaphor for transculturation. Through the cultural diffusion of these empowering home-grown products, the subaltern asserts its authority.[21]

Ortiz's explanation of a term that clearly defies easy definition is six pages long. In attempting to synthesize these pages, I suggest that what he meant by 'transculturation' was on-going cultural contact in a bounded space (the island, Cuba) in a (more or less) bounded period of time (450 years, though he refers also to cultural contact in medieval Spain and between pre-Columbian indigenous populations). Cuba exemplifies transculturation. His interpretation is far from mechanistic; he consistently deconstructs binary or Manichean conceptualizations of colonial cultures. His writing—lyrical, suspenseful, witty, chaotic, exciting—captures all the dizzy turbulence, violence, panic, terror, pain, hopes, struggle and disillusions of this complex, overlapping series of traumatic cultural 'encounters'. Reading the compressed evocation of the dramatic process of Cuban cultural life gives the impression of whizzing through a tunnel in a time machine:

> Después, la *transculturación* de una corriente incesante de inmigrantes blancos. Españoles, pero de distintas culturas y ya ellos mismos *desgarrados*, como entonces se decía, de las sociedades ibéricas peninsulares y transplantados a un Nuevo Mundo que, para ellos fue todo nuevo de naturaleza y humanidad, donde tenían a su vez que reajustarse a un nuevo

sincretismo de culturas. Al mismo tiempo la *transculturación* de una continua chorrera humana de negros africanos, de razas y culturas diversas, procedentes de todas las comarcas costeñas de Africa, desde Senegal, por Guinea, Congo y Angola, en el Atlántico, hasta las de Mozambique ... Todos ellos arrancados de sus núcleos sociales originarios y con sus culturas destrozadas, oprimidas bajo el peso de las culturas aquí imperantes ... Y todavía más culturas inmigratorias, en oleadas esporádicas o en manaderos continuos, siempre fluyentes, influyentes y de las más varias oriundeces: indios continentales, judíos, lusitanos, anglosajones, franceses, norteamericanos y hasta amarillos mongoloides de Macao, Cantón y otras regiones del que fue el Imperio Celeste. Y cada inmigrante como un desarraigado de su tierra nativa en doble trance de desajuste y de reajuste, de *desculturación* o *exculturación* y de *aculturación* o *inculturación*, y al fin de síntesis, de *transculturación*.

... Los *ciboneyes* pasan a siervos *naborias* o huyen a las serranías y selvas, a los *cibaos* y *caonaos*. Luego un huracán de cultura; es Europa. Llegaron en tropel el hierro, la pólvora, el caballo, el toro, la rueda, la vela, la brújula, la moneda, el salario, la letra, la imprenta, el libro, el señor, el rey, la iglesia, el banquero ... Y un vértigo revolucionario sacudió a los pueblos indios de Cuba, arrancando de cuajo sus instituciones y destrozando sus vidas. ... Si estas Indias de América fueron Nuevo Mundo para los pueblos europeos, Europa fue Mundo Novísimo para los pueblos americanos. Fueron dos mundos que recíprocamente se descubrieron y entrechocaron. El contacto de las dos culturas fue terrible. Una de ellas pereció, casi totalmente, como fulminada. *Transculturación* fracasada para los indígenas y radical y cruel para los advenedizos. ... Curioso fenómeno social éste de Cuba, el de haber sido desde el siglo XVI igualmente invasoras, con la fuerza o a la fuerza, todas sus gentes y culturas, todas exógenas y todas desgarradas, con el trauma del desarraigo original y de su ruda transplantación, a una cultura nueva en creación.

('Del fenómeno social de la "transculturación"
y de su importancia en Cuba', *Contrapunteo*, 99)

The point is that the term 'transculturation', rubber-stamped by Malinowski, was developed in Cuba by Ortiz at the same time as the term 'acculturation' was gaining credence in the United States. But by the 1930s and 1940s, social/cultural anthropology was a recognized discipline in the English-speaking world. Numerous institutions, university departments, professorial Chairs and so on were founded to fund, legitimate, authorize and diffuse its (Anglo-American-centric) discourses. This was not the case in the Spanish-speaking world, including Cuba—despite its close connections with the United States. Ortiz was fully aware of writing in an institutional void, which he attempted to remedy. He resurrected the *Revista Bimestre Cubana* (1910–30) as a publishing outlet for his work; he set up the 'Sociedad de Estudios Afrocubanos' in whose journal he published in the 1940s; he gave public lectures in the Sociedad de Amigos del País (of which he was President 1923–30) and in the Institución Hispano-Cubana de Cultura (which he re-established); he encouraged the founding of the *Archivos de Folklore Cubano*, and organized public performances of African-Cuban music and drama in the 1930s. But from an ethnological point of view, his was a lone voice. His only 'disciple' was his wealthy sister-in-law, Lydia Cabrera,[22] who had no anthropological or sociological training.[23]

Nevertheless, Ortiz's work proved to be indispensable for the Cuban aesthetic avant-garde (the *Grupo minorista*) of the mid-1920s, participating in what Nestor García Canclini refers to as the 'desajuste entre modernismo y modernización' and seeking to 'edificar campos artísticos autónomos'.[24] Other like-minded intellectuals of the centre left were Emilio Roig de Leuchsenring and Ortiz's secretary, Rubén Martínez Villena.[25] As Alejo Carpentier explains in *La música en Cuba* (1946):

> La presencia de ritmos, danzas, ritos … que habían sido postergados durante demasiado tiempo … abría un campo de acción inmediato, que ofrecía posibilidades de luchar por cosas mucho más interesantes que una partitura atonal o un cuadro cubista.

Those who had heard *The Rites of Spring*, he continues:

> comenzaban a advertir, con razón, que había en Regla [suburb of Havana], del otro lado de la bahía, ritmos tan complejos e interesantes como los que Stravinsky había creado ... Los ojos y los oídos se abrieron sobre lo viviente y lo próximo ... La posibilidad de expresar lo criollo con una nueva noción de sus valores se impuso en las mentes. Fernando Ortiz, a pesar de la diferencia de edades, se mezclaba fraternalmente con la muchachada. Se leyeron sus libros. ... Súbitamente, el negro se hizo eje de todas las miradas.[26]

The African-Cuban cultural movement, which lasted some ten years (1930–40), was made possible by Ortiz's research which, from the 1930s on (coinciding with the Harlem Renaissance), focused on black performance arts: music, dance, instruments and theatre. It is in these cultural studies that he explains some of his most interesting and surprisingly modern views relating to ethnogenesis.

In retrospect, *Contrapunteo*—for some critics an avant-garde work in its own right[27]—marks a turning point for Ortiz and for Caribbean postcolonial discourse. It had been praised by the founder of modern anthropology (whose research had taken a similar direction in *Methods of Study of Culture Contact in Africa*, 1938), as an 'obra maestra' that should be translated into English and read by students, politicians and the general US public (*Contrapunteo*, xv). At the VIII American Scientific Congress, held in Washington in 1940, Ortiz's proposal for the establishing of Social and Economic Research Institutes in the Americas, including one in Cuba, had been unanimously agreed. Yet nothing came of this, despite the fact that in 1954 he was awarded the title Doctor Honoris Causa by Columbia University and that in 1956 Sidney Mintz referred to him as the father of Afroamerican studies,[28] nor was the term 'transculturation' used in anthropological circles. The reason is, of course, political.

Ortiz belonged to the first generation of intellectuals of the newly constituted Cuban Republic. He lived through a period of collective crisis (from 1902 to the 1933 Revolution against Gerardo Machado) experienced not only by the intellectual elite but at all levels of society. As the poet José María Poveda wrote at the time, 'somos la sombra de un pueblo, el sueño de una democracia, el ansia de una libertad. No existimos.'[29] Ortiz was one of the more active members of the Cuban Generation of 1898, the existence of which is incontrovertible. The collected articles and reviews, written from 1906 to 1911, published in the book *Entre cubanos: psicología tropical* (1913) makes this quite clear. The book, with an introduction entitled 'Al dormido lector'[30] in which Ortiz addresses the 'soñoliento hijo de los trópicos ... a ti que dormido, sueñas y que soñando desprecias a los que trabajando vencen; a ti que sólo piensas en el modo de no pensar nunca y que sólo quieres no querer nada' (1), reprints two emotive letters to Unamuno pointing out that Cuba was in a worse state than Spain, 'es que Cuba, en no pocos aspectos, es más española que España'.[31] The articles, including several hard-hitting attacks on the Cuban governing elite and proposals for improvement (the setting up of a Popular University and a Museum of Social History), describe a pathologically dependent society in desperate need of rapid modernization. Despite his positivism and his polemical attack on the concept of a 'raza hispánica' or, in his words, 'racismo panhispanista',[32] Ortiz's preoccupations were similar to those of the Spanish 'Generation'. However, he was much more politically engaged[33] and fully aware of the specific problems posed by the United States in Latin America. In the article 'Labor de Titanes' in the collection, he uses a comment by Salas y Ferré (that the Aqueduct of Segovia could only have been built by slave labour) to attack the methods used in the recent construction of the Panama Canal. 'Nicaragua Intervenida' is an angry blast against US imperialist aggression and international indifference, 'engendros anémicos de un imperialismo que moría, hemos [Cuba and Nicaragua] seguido embrutecidos en la modorra tropical ... Sólo una civilización intensa y difundida podría salvarnos; siendo cultos, seríamos fuertes' (*Entre cubanos*, 47–48, 76–78).

There was one overriding purpose to Ortiz's studies of black culture in Cuba, and that was political: to found the scientific basis for (to prove the existence of) a politically and culturally independent, multi-racial Cuban nation. Such a collective identity was seen as the result-in-process of on-going transculturation of distinct cultures. There was no national essence but an interactive confluence of cultures. Ortiz's works functioned not only as description and explanation, therefore; they were also a political statement and were themselves a part of the transculturation process in dialogue not only with African and European cultures but, more importantly, with the United States. As Malinowski perceived in the preface to *Contrapunteo*, transculturation stressed the cultural contact beween Cuba and the United States as a two-way, dialectical process; the impact of Cuban ideas on the United States was as significant as those of the imperial power on the neocolonial dependency.

Ortiz's project, though frustrated in the short term, was crucially important from the point of view of objectification and the control of knowledge. At a time when US anthropological interest concentrated on the remnants of (virtually eradicated) native cultures at home, and British interest on the suitably distanced living cultures of the Empire, Ortiz's field work represented an independent postcolonial perspective that focused, from the periphery, on its own ethnographically rich, vibrant cultures. A great opportunity was lost for postcolonial theory when this mode of enquiry did not take hold, for here was an instance of the subaltern playing a constitutive role in colonial discourse.

Transculturation: 'scriptive survival'

Ortiz's work has proved to be seminal in recent studies of African-American culture, not only for the rare data he collected but also in view of his emphasis on process rather than form. This emphasis preempted Sydney Mintz's thesis (1976) that African-American cultures were new, synthetic formations produced by rapid creolization in response to Old and New World exigencies and possibilities. Stephan Palmié has looked to Ortiz's work for corroboration of the view that while the rapid creolization theory might stand, it is also the case, certainly in the Cuban 'cabildos de nación' and the Brazilian 'irmandades' (originating in fifteenth-century Seville and Lisbon respectively), that African cultures did not simply persist in the New World but were recreated anew in a process of ethnogenesis. This depended not on descent or ethnicity but on the institutional frameworks already in place into which individuals were initiated as 'fictive religious kinship' (for example, the Abakuá/Ekpe cult).[34] African societies are not therefore 'the doubtful exporters of the personnel of New World "nations"' but providers of 'models for corporate aggregation' (Palmié, 343). This idea is supported by Ortiz's work, in particular by his study of the sacred batá drums (used in santería), secular instruments first consecrated by blacks in Cuba and institutionalized so that one set of drums ritually 'gives birth' to another in the 'cabildos'.[35] Thus the cultural reproduction of nascent (Cuban) institutions and the 'transgenerational maintenance of a common culture' (Palmié, 338) was made possible by existing social organization. Ethnogenesis is certainly the most prevalent motif informing Ortiz's work, not the word itself, but recurrent images relating to an aesthetic of desire: copulation, intercourse, child birth, family relations, promiscuity and even orgasm.[36] So, for example, Cuban music is the 'engendro de negros y blancos; producto mulato', born from the 'abrazo cruzador' of different cultures; 'música eurocubana [y] afrocubana' 'se maridaron':

> amores de la vihuela española con el tambor africano. Cosquillas a la blanca guitarra rasgueando sus tripas sobre la entraña abierta entre sus caderas; caricias al negro tambor y manoseo de su piel caliente. Engendro mestizo ... la mulatez o mestizaje no es hibridismo insustancial ni eclecticismo, ni descoloración, sino simplemente un *tertium quid*, realidad vital y fecunda, fruto generado por cópula de pigmentaciones y culturas, una nueva sustancia, un nuevo color.[37]

It could also be argued that Ortiz was carrying out an ethnography of the city which bridged traditional anthropological and sociological approaches, in the tradition of the Chicago school, long before the issue was taken on board in Latin America in the 1970s.[38] His work on the traumatic alienation of blacks in white colonial society, on the devastating effects of colonial domination on the psyche and culture of the Cuban slaves and their descendants, anticipates in some ways Fanon's *Black Skins, White Masks* (1952).[39] Finally, although he has been criticized for lamenting the existence of 'negative' African-Cuban cultural values that should, in his opinion, be eradicated, his views were not so distant from those of Amílcar Cabral, who also thought it was necessary to 'combat with flexibility but with rigour the negative and reactionary elements' of African cultures.[40]

Ultimately, 'transculturation' was not a term favoured by the social sciences. The fact that it has reappeared on the Anglo-American academic agenda in the field of literary and cultural studies is significant.[41] In the 1970s, Angel Rama studied transculturation and 'culture shock' through the prism of Marxist dialectics (Adorno and Benjamin) in his work on the Latin American novel.[42] More recently, Mary Louise Pratt's *Imperial Eyes* features the term 'Transculturation' on its glossy cover. This would have pleased Ortiz, but less so the fact that he does not make it to the index and merits only five lines of small print in a note. Pratt defines the term as serving 'to describe how subordinated or marginal groups select and invent from materials transmitted to them by a dominant or metropolitan culture'—which falls short of Ortiz's more dynamic conception, though her further elucidation of the term broadly coincides with Ortiz's.[43] Pratt also introduces further useful terms such as 'autoethnography' and 'contact zone' which develop the concept, although Ortiz would have queried if there is such a thing as a non-contact zone, a non-dialogical cultural formation. He might have been happier with García Canclini's term, 'un escenario', a place 'donde un relato se pone en escena' (García Canclini, 339).

In 1989, two books appeared which did Ortiz some justice,

though they focus on stylistics rather than political import. Both were published by Cuban literary theorists in post in the United States. In *La isla que se repite* (translated as *The Repeating Island*) Antonio Benítez Rojo considers *Contrapunteo* as a disorganized, multi-disciplinary, 'dialogic, uncentred', postmodern text inscribing 'a plurality of voices and rhythms'. He is interested in *Contrapunteo*, 'because it offers a method by which one can conduct a reading of the Caribbean that has an outcome different from any that might have been done from the perspective either of modernity or of postmodernity, which are, finally, strictly Western perspectives and Western readings'.[44] The three chapters dedicated to Ortiz in Gustavo Pérez Firmat's *The Cuban Condition* (1989) present *Contrapunteo* as an exemplary model of deconstruction. Pérez Firmat's point that Ortiz's narratorial stance is one of constant exaggeration through understatement (paralepsis), consistently undermining all authoritative versions and voices by endless deferral, in *Contrapunteo* and his entire oeuvre,[45] and actively creating new hybrid terms to indicate this process, such as 'ajiaco'[46] and 'contrapunteo' (signifying the play between identity and difference) is well taken. However, Pérez Firmat downplays the theoretical legitimacy of the term 'transculturation' and, despite his discussion of another neologism, 'cubanía', Ortiz's political intentions. Benítez Rojo and Pérez Firmat are interested in *Contrapunteo* as a work of literature. *Contrapunteo* is certainly a funny, ironic, outlandish book. The reader is never sure when to take the author seriously; and the light-hearted verbal mockery, Cuban 'choteo', is itself an idiosyncratic feature of Cuban culture. But both these readings defuse the political impact of Ortiz's work.

A more incisive reading of *Contrapunteo* is that of Venezuelan historian/anthropologist Fernando Coronil. Locating Ortiz firmly in the political scenario of the late 1930s (when he featured as the proponent of a plan of national unity, 1933)[47] and picking up on the personification of the commodities sugar and tobacco, the products of human activity, and their constantly shifting identities, Coronil reads the book as a thinly veiled attack on US capitalist encroachment on Cuba and the mechanization of social relations.[48] As Coronil notes, by means of extensive analogy, Ortiz proposes an alternative utopian outcome: Don Tabaco and Doña Azúcar, representing respectively black and white cultures (with a marked preference on Ortiz's part for 'tobacco') marry and give birth to alcohol, the essence of an autochthonous, independent Cuban vitality. 'El alcohol, hijo de tales padres, es fuego, fuerza, espíritu, embriaguez, pensamiento y acción', whose glory the 'vates del pueblo de Cuba' might one day sing (*Contrapunteo*, 94).[49]

In sum, how relevant is the term 'transculturation', as Ortiz understood it, today? A recent article by curator Ben Genocchio suggests an answer. Genocchio discusses the contemporary politics of representation and exhibition of Latin American art in Europe and the USA and the subsequent objectification of Latin American culture 'largely in the name of difference'.[50] Latin American culture is still represented as exotic and Other by means of three interpretative strategies: 1) essentialist and homogenizing claims for a more natural, passionate, authentic Latin American essence; 2) claims for cultural diversity resulting from a polarization of Latin American difference that nevertheless incorporates European (universal) modernism into its own aesthetics; and 3) a concept of Latin America as a distinctive locus of hybridity which, while presenting 'a useful dialectical model of transcultural interaction characterized by constant and unstable processes of hybridization' (9), is still predicated on a 'murky' in-betweenness which retains binary oppositions, constitutes a new form of exoticism, ignores the fact that all cultures are hybrid, and, above all, does not challenge Eurocentric academic establishments. Genocchio asks, then, 'what cultural apparatus exists for speaking about artistic practice and expression from Latin American countries which avoids totalising and/or appropriating it?' (11). Ortiz's work is a corrective to such objectification. First, for Ortiz, Cuba is a locus *sui generis* not to be conflated with 'Latin America'. Second, his concept of a national identity is radically non-essentialist (in Perez Firmat's words 'the essence of Cuba lies in not having one').[51] Third, he recognizes the hybridity of all cultures, though Cuba is distinctive due to the intensity (in time and space) of hybridization. Fourth, he views identity as produced by its contrapuntal relation to difference and is not interested in 'vague pluralism' or eclecticism. And, fifth, his concept of hybridity is part of a national political project which aims to set up a resistance to imperialist discourses and cultural establishments: 'Si no tan grave como el imperialismo económico, que succiona la sangre del pueblo cubano, es también disolvente el imperialismo ideológico que le sigue. Aquél le rompe su independencia económica; éste le destroza su vida moral. El uno le quita el sostén, el otro el alma.'[52] It could be said that Ortiz faced the dilemma of the postcolonial intellectual in deciding who to address—the (white) academic elites or the (African) Cuban people—on whose behalf, and from which perspective (as a personally involved insider or an objective outsider). In fact, Ortiz's stand is the more decisive in that he assumes what Bhabha refers to as 'the right to signify from the periphery of authorised power'.[53] His project is one of political empowerment. His radical rejection of notions of permanence constantly undercuts colonial discourse, which depends on a 'concept of "fixity" as the ideological construction of otherness' (66). Ortiz is thus an exemplary model of postcolonial agency and accomplishment.

Notes

1   Quoted in Peter Marshall, *Cuba Libre: Breaking the Chains?* (London: Victor Gollantz, 1987), 33.

2   For Lenin, monopoly capitalism gave rise to imperialism, a new form of capitalist exploitation. The two events which mark the transition are the Spanish–American War (1898) and the Boer War (1899–1902).

3   See Ann Wright, 'Intellectuals of an Unheroic Period in Cuban History, 1913–1923: The "Cuba Contemporánea Group"', *Bulletin of Latin American Research*, VII, 1 (1988), 109–22. Wright locates the

turning point from acquiesence, and even enthusiastic acceptance, of US hegemony to outright resistance around 1923, following the economic crisis of 1920 and the intervention of General Enoch Crowder in 1921.

4   See Frantz Fanon, 'On National Culture', in *The Wretched of the Earth* (1961) (Harmondsworth: Penguin, 1967), 179.

5   Hugh Thomas, *Cuba, or the Pursuit of Freedom* (London: Eyre and Spottiswoode, 1971), 601.

6   Salas y Ferré (1843–1910) wrote his *Filosofía de la muerte* (1877) using manuscripts left by Sanz del Río and was entrusted by Fernando de Castro to complete his unfinished works after his death (for example, *Historia de España*, 1899).

7   Cesare Lombroso, 1836–1909; Franz Boas, 1858–1942; Bronislaw Malinowski, 1884–1942. Ortiz visited Germany in 1909.

8   Fernando Ortiz, 'Brujos y santeros', *Estudios afrocubanos*, III, 1–4 (1939), 85–90 (86): 'pero salí airoso hablando de algo allí tan exótico como los ñáñigos ... pero en realidad yo nada sabía de cierto de los ñáñigos'. Ñáñigos are priests or 'babalao' of the Abakuá sect (originating in Cameroon and Guinea).

9   His mother was Cuban and his father Spanish. He and his mother moved to live with his uncle, Mayor of La Ciudadela, Menorca.

10 See Reginald Horsman, *Race and Manifest Destiny: The Origins of American Racial Anglo-Saxonism* (Cambridge, MA and London: Harvard University Press, 1985), 282. Horsman explains how US expansion was limited by racial ideas from 1850 on.

11 'Las supervivencias africanas en Cuba' (1905), in *Entre cubanos, psicología tropical* (Paris, 1913) (Havana: Editorial Ciencias Sociales, 1993), 86.

12 *Los negros brujos* (Miami: Ediciones Universal, 1973), 1.

13 Many of Ortiz's comments are considered racist today. To this effect, see Robin Moore, 'Representations of Afrocuban Expressive Culture in the Writings of Fernando Ortiz', *Latin American Music Review*, XV, 1 (1994), 33–54, Martin Lienhard, 'El fantasma de la oralidad y algunos de sus avatares literarios y etnológicos', *Les Langues Néo-Latines*, 297 (1996), 19–33, and Aline Helg, *Our Rightful Share: The Afro-Cuban Struggle for Equality 1886–1912* (Chapel Hill

and London: The University of North Carolina Press, 1995), 112–13, 280. However, I believe Ortiz should be understood relative to his time. Later in life he challenged rather than replicated predominant assumptions on race. His shift towards anti-racist views reflects the shift towards anti-imperialism. I would like to thank Miguel Arnedo, currently writing a doctoral thesis on Afrocubanist expression at Queen Mary and Westfield College, University of London, for drawing my attention to the above articles. Lombroso's use of literary quotations, proverbs and contrived etymologies as part of his 'evidence' must also have influenced the young Ortiz.

14 Quoted in *Los negros brujos*, xvii.

15 'Brujos y santeros', *Estudios afrocubanos*, 89.

16 For a more detailed discussion and alternative views see Fernando Coronil's excellent introduction to his edition of *Cuban Counterpoint: Tobacco and Sugar* (Durham, NC and London: Duke University Press, 1995), xx–xxxvii.

17 Jean Franco, 'Beyond Ethnocentrism: Gender, Power and the Third-World Intelligentsia', in *Marxism and the Interpretation of Culture*, ed. Cary Nelson and Lawrence Grossberg (Basingstoke: Macmillan, 1988), 504 (also in *Colonial Discourse and Post-Colonial Theory: A Reader*, ed. Patrick Williams and Laura Chrisman [Hemel Hempstead: Harvester Wheatsheaf, 1993], 359–69 [360]).

18 Herskovits's ideas on originary African traits taking root in America (acculturation) became unfashionable in the 1960s, primarily because it is no longer feasible to talk of fixed tribal identities: 'whole people may, upon historical investigation, turn out to be something quite different from what we (or they) think they are' (Stephan Palmié, 'Ethnogenetic Processes and Cultural Transfer in Afro-American Slave Populations', in *Slavery in the Americas*, ed. Wolfgang Binder [Wurzburg: Konigshausen and Neumann, 1993], 337–63 [343]).

19 In the Spanish text, the date is given as 1929, and in the English translation, 1939. The conversation is described by Malinowski in the preface to *Contrapunteo*. However, in a speech read at Havana University in 1981, Roberto Fernández Retamar refers to the first encounter between Ortiz and Malinowski having taken place in 1937 in Yale. This information was provided by José J. Arrom who was also

present at the meal. I would like to thank Rogelio Escudero for his generous advice on this matter.

20   *Cuban Counterpoint: Tobacco and Sugar*, trans. Harriet de Onís (New York: Alfred Knopf, 1947), x. All English quotations are from this edition. The original text is not translated in its entirety and the following chapters (including some of the most interesting) are omitted: 5, 6, 10, 11, 14, 15, 17, 19, 21, 22, 24 and 25. All Spanish quotations are from Fernando Ortiz, *Contrapunteo cubano del tabaco y el azúcar (Advertencia de sus contrastes agrarios, económicos, históricos y sociales, su etnografía y su transculturación)* (rev. edn Las Villas: Dirección de Publicaciones Universidad Central de las Villas, 1963). Malinowski understood Spanish (he was partially brought up in the Canary Islands) but no doubt wrote the prologue in English. It is signed 'Yale University 1940'.

21   See in particular the chapter 'De la transculturación del tabaco' in *Contrapunteo*, 237–336. Ortiz describes the process of diffusion and, more importantly, the transference of cultural values of the natural substance, tobacco. The smoking of the leaf had religious significance for the indigenous peoples and acquired medicinal value among the black slave population; later, they too incorporated it into their religious rituals. At the same time, for the white population tobacco was taboo associated with devilry, only later acknowledged for its medicinal, hedonistic and commercial possibilities. The seafaring men, black and white, took tobacco to Africa and Spain, from where it reached Europe and the East. From a substance connoting diabolical filth among the whites, by the eighteenth century tobacco had become an object associated with status and wealth, and by the nineteenth century a commodity, cultivated (now by white landowners) for profit and a lucrative source of revenue for the state.

22   Ortiz was married to Esther Cabrera, Lydia's sister, the daughter of leading Cuban intellectual Raimundo Cabrera who founded the newspaper *Cuba y América* in New York.

23   Lienhard prefers Cabrera's less rigid 'horizontal' methodology to Ortiz's 'vertical' approach. See 'El fantasma de la oralidad y algunos de sus avatares literarios y etnológicos'.

24 Nestor García Canclini, *Culturas híbridas: estrategias para entrar y salir de la modernidad* (Mexico City: Grijalbo, 1989), 67, 76. See Ana Cairo, *El Grupo Minorista y su tiempo* (La Habana: Ciencias Sociales, 1978). I would like to thank Carmen Barrionuevo for this reference and for her particularly informative seminar paper on Juan Marinello and Jorge Mañach read at the University of Manchester, 23 February 1999.

25 See Ann Wright, 'Intellectuals of an Unheroic Period in Cuban History', 118–19.

26 Alejo Carpentier, *La música en Cuba* (Mexico City: Fondo de Cultura Económica [1968]), 235–36. Ortiz's position can be favourably compared to the white elitism of the 'Orígenes' group, in particular of José Lezama Lima, who rejected the 'síntesis apresurada' of a Cuban cultural 'mestizaje'. See Jesús J. Barquet, 'El grupo Orígenes ante el negrismo', *Afro-Hispanic Review*, XV, 2 (1996), 3–10 (3). *Iniciación a la poesía afro-americana*, ed. Oscar Fernández de la Vega and Alberto Pamies (Miami: Ediciones Universal, 1973) includes two essays by Ortiz on 'la poesía mulata'.

27 Roberto González de Echevarría, 'El *Contrapunteo* y la literatura', *La Gaceta de Cuba* (marzo–abril 1996), 23–26 (25).

28 Jorge Ibarra, 'La herencia científica de Fernando Ortiz', *Revista Iberoamericana*, 152–53 (julio–diciembre 1990), 1339–51 (1349, 1341).

29 Jorge Ibarra, *Un análisis psicosocial del cubano 1898–1925* (Havana: Ciencias Sociales, 1985), 32; see also 267–337. In 1899, a third of the population of 1.5 million was 'coloured' and 64 per cent of the total population illiterate (Fernando Ortiz, *El pueblo cubano* [Havana: Ciencias Sociales, 1997], 20, 37). In 1907, 53 per cent were illiterate. However, these figures were much better than those in Brazil which, according to García Canclini, are as follows: in 1890, 84 per cent of the population was illiterate, and in 1920, 75 per cent (García Canclini, *Culturas híbridas*, 66).

30 Strongly reminiscent of several poems, for example, 'A una España joven' and 'El mañana efímero' in Antonio Machado's *Campos de Castilla* (1912).

31 *Entre cubanos: psicología tropical* (Havana: Ciencias sociales, 1993), 13. This book demonstrates that a Cuban Generation of 1898

existed alongside its Spanish counterpart. For an overview, see Ricardo Viñalet, '*Entre cubanos* y el regeneracionismo', *La Gaceta de Cuba* (marzo–abril 1996), 27–29. See also Carlos Serrano, 'Miguel de Unamuno y Fernando Ortiz. Un caso de regeneracionismo trasatlántico', *NRFH*, XXXV, 1 (1987), 299–310.

32 'Ni racismos ni xenofobias', *Revista Bimestre Cubana* (enero–febrero 1929), pp. 6–19. This talk, delivered in the 'Sociedad Económica de Amigos del País', Havana, refers to a previous lecture given by Ortiz at a reception (in the Lhardy Restaurant) organized by the Económica in Madrid in November 1928. It was at this splendid event, attended by numerous ambassadors from South America as well as the Spanish commercial, governmental and intellectual elite, that Ortiz chose to speak of the 'Racismo panhispanista'. He rejected the concept of a 'raza hispana' and proposed instead the recognition of a 'cultura hispánica'. This caused shock waves in the Spanish press. Benjamín Jarnés was one of Ortiz's most fervent supporters.

33 Ortiz was elected MP in 1916 for the Liberal Party and was a member of Parliament until 1927. He became increasingly disillusioned with politics on account of the fraud and corruption. He was sent into exile (to the USA) between 1930 and 1934 by the Machado dictatorship. He was President of the Cuban Society against Racism (1936–40) and headed the Cuban Alliance for a Free World (1941–45).

34 Stephan Palmié, 'Ethnogenetic Processes and Cultural Transfer', 337–63.

35 Ortiz refers to this music as '"música de color" que, para encubrir su canela, va embijada y con indio plumerío. No quiere ir en cueros, en cueros de tambores' (in *La africanía de la música folklórica de Cuba* [Havana: Editorial Universitaria, 1965], 98). See also Nicolás Guillén's 1931 poem 'La canción del bongó'.

36 For a lengthy discussion of the conflation of sexual and (post)colonial discourses, see Robert J. C. Young, *Colonial Desire: Hybridity in Theory, Culture and Race* (London and New York: Routledge, 1995).

37 Fernando Ortiz, *La africanía de la música folklórica de Cuba*, 1, 3, 4. Other clusters of recurrent images in the early works relate to stratification (geological strata, levels in buildings), geometrical shapes (triangles, parabolas) and chemical processes (metallurgy,

crucibles, alchemy). A constant feature is the personification of substances and objects, as with tobacco and sugar.

38 See García Canclini, *Culturas híbridas*, 228–35. García Canclini laments that 'menos frecuentes aún, son las investigaciones que encaminan los procedimientos por los cuales las culturas tradicionales de los indígenas y campesinos convergen sincréticamente con diversas modalidades de cultura urbana y masiva, estableciendo formas híbridas de existencia de "lo popular"' (*Culturas híbridas*, 230). This is precisely what Ortiz was doing in his studies of black culture (religion, theatre, dance and music) in Havana.

39 See 'La poesía mulata', *Revista Bimestre Cubana*, XXXIV, 2–3 (1934), 205–13.

40 Amílcar Cabral, 'National Liberation and Culture' (1973), in Williams and Chrisman, *Colonial Discourse and Post-Colonial Theory*, 62–80.

41 M. Taussig, *Mimesis and Alterity* (London and New York: Routledge, 1993) uses the term in an ethnographical sense. See *Key Concepts in Postcolonial Studies*, ed. B. Ashcroft, G. Griffiths and H. Tiffin (London and New York: Routledge, 1998), 233–34. The entry outlines Pratt's description of the term, and Ortiz's (briefly), as interpreted by Pratt.

42 Angel Rama, *Transculturación narrativa en América Latina* (Mexico: Siglo XXI, 1982).

43 Mary Louise Pratt, *Imperial Eyes: Travel Writing and Transculturation* (London and New York: Routledge, 1992), 228, 6.

44 Antonio Benítez Rojo, *La isla que se repite* (Hanover, NH: Ediciones del Norte, 1989); *The Repeating Island*, trans. James Maraniss (Durham, NC and London: Duke University Press, 1992), 156–58.

45 For Pérez Firmat, Ortiz adopts a 'duplicitous authorial stance ... according to which a writer simultaneously avoids and assumes the responsibilities of authorship' (*The Cuban Condition: Translation and Identity in Modern Cuban Culture* [Cambridge: Cambridge University Press, 1989], 54).

46 See 'La cubanidad y los negros', *Estudios afrocubanos*, III, 1–4 (1939), 3–15 (5).

47 *Contrapunteo* was published the year Batista was elected to government.

48 Fernando Coronil, 'Challenging Colonial Histories: *Cuban Counterpoint*/Ortiz's Counterfetishism', in *Critical Theory, Cultural Politics and Latin American Narrative*, ed. S. M. Bell, A. H. Le May and L. Orr (Notre Dame and London: University of Notre Dame Press, 1993), 61–80. Note also Silvia Spitta's shrewd comments in *Between Two Waters: Narratives of Transculturation in Latin America* (Houston: Rice University Press, 1995), 1–6.

49 'La caña del azúcar y el tabaco son todo contraste. Diríase que una rivalidad los anima y separa desde sus cunas. … Blanca es la una, moreno es el otro. Dulce y sin olor es el azúcar; amargo y con aroma es el tabaco. Contraste siempre! Alimento y veneno, despertar y adormecer, energía y ensueño, placer de la carne y deleite del espíritu, sensualidad e ideación, apetito que se satisface e ilusión que se esfuma, calorías de vida y humaredas de fantasía … El azúcar es *ella*; el tabaco es *él* … En la industria: el tabaco es de la ciudad y el azúcar es del campo. En el comercio: para nuestro tabaco todo el mundo por mercado, y para nuestra azúcar solo un mercado en el mundo. Centripetismo y centrifugación. Cubanidad y extranjería. Soberanía y coloniaje. Altiva corona y humilde saco' (*Contrapunteo*, 4–5). Of course, all kinds of objections may be raised against Ortiz's concept of utopia as interracial marriage and alcoholic drink.

50 Ben Genocchio, 'The Discourse of Difference: Writing "Latin American Art"', *Third Text*, 43 (Summer 1998), 3–12 (4).

51 Gustavo Pérez Firmat, *The Cuban Condition*, 26.

52 'De la música afrocubana: un estímulo para su estudio', *Universidad de La Habana*, I, 3 (1934), 113. Quoted in Diana Iznaga, *Transculturación en Fernando Ortiz* (Havana: Ciencias Sociales, 1989), 26.

53 Homi Bhabha, *The Location of Culture* (London and New York: Routledge, 1994), 2.

CHAPTER SEVEN

Caribbean Masks: Frantz Fanon and Alejo Carpentier

Stephen Henighan
University of Guelph

Early in Alejo Carpentier's novel *El siglo de las luces* (1962), Esteban, a young late eighteenth-century Cuban intellectual intoxicated with the rhetoric of the French Revolution by his French mentor, Victor Hugues, has the opportunity to visit Paris. As Roberto González Echevarría has demonstrated, this section of the novel swarms with deliberate, half-masked anachronisms. Carpentier coyly dresses up the Paris of the early 1790s in homage to the Paris of the 1920s and 1930s, where the Cuban novelist had undertaken his own intellectual apprenticeship. As Esteban walks the eighteenth-century streets, descriptions of Daliesque paintings mingle with references to automatic writing.[1] Yet, arguably, González Echevarría overlooks one anachronistic allusion crucial to the deliberately inverted perspective through which Carpentier's novel assesses the French Revolution in terms of its political and intellectual impact on the Caribbean. Visiting a masonic lodge which serves as a meeting place for foreign supporters of the revolution, Esteban is pleased to discover that this establishment appears to have been liberated from racial prejudice:

> No podía decirse, por lo demás, que no reinara una sana mentalidad democrática donde un Carlos Constantino de

Hesse-Rotenburg trataba familiarmente al patriota de color quebrado, venido de la Martinica.[2]

The evidence suggesting that this Martinican friend of the Revolution might represent a respectful nod towards Frantz Fanon, though circumstantial, is by no means trivial. Like Esteban, Carpentier had experienced the tutelage of his own French intellectual mentor-cum-father-figure, André Breton, whose influence, like that of Victor Hugues in the novel, had proved at first illuminating but ultimately distorting, patronizing and oppressive. In 1947, Breton—whom Carpentier had by then rejected as his mentor[3]—published a preface to the first postwar edition of *Cahier d'un retour au pays natal* (1939), a groundbreaking suite of polemical poems and lyrical reflections by Fanon's mentor, the Martinican poet Aimé Césaire.[4] Césaire rooted his perceptions within the context of a distinctly Afro-Caribbean history of slavery: 'J'accepte. / J'accepte. / et le nègre fustigé qui dit: "Pardon mon maître" / et les vingt-neuf coups de fouet légal …' (52).

Césaire's work laid the intellectual foundations for both Fanon's *Peau noire, masques blancs* (1952) and Carpentier's *El siglo de las luces*. In addition to the serendipitous connection of Carpentier's mentor having helped to pave the way for the European success of Fanon's primary role model, the two men's lives followed not dissimilar trajectories. Fanon left Martinique at 22, never to return; Carpentier fled Cuba at 24, spending less than a decade of his remaining 52 years of life in the country where he had grown up. By the time Carpentier was putting the finishing touches on *El siglo de las luces*, around 1960, he and Fanon enjoyed analogous positions of revolutionary ascendancy within what was coming to be known as the Third World: Fanon as ambassador to Ghana of the provisional government-in-exile of revolutionary Algeria, and Carpentier as director of the state publishing house in Fidel Castro's Cuba. In retrospect, both writers are viewed as foundational figures. Carpentier and his thematic concerns provided a model for younger novelists such as Carlos Fuentes and Gabriel García Márquez, who during the 1960s would lead the Latin American novel into a period of innovation, mass popularity and, initially, solidarity with Third World revolutionary struggles. Fanon, meanwhile, is often identified by contemporary postcolonial theorists as one of the crucial pioneering figures—perhaps *the* crucial pioneering figure—of their discipline.[5]

The gesture of tipping his hat to Fanon was, for a number of reasons, a natural one for Carpentier to make during this period. The juxtaposition of Fanon's Caribbean treatise *Peau noire, masques blancs* and Carpentier's Caribbean novel *El siglo de las luces* opens up the thorny question of the usefulness and consequences of meshing postcolonial discourse with Latin American cultural production. What, if anything, do these two fields have to gain from each other? The popular culture of contemporary Latin America, replete with pungent subversions of ruling paradigms, requires little instruction from North Atlantic postcolonial theorists;[6] Latin American cultural criticism,[7] from Sarmiento to Martí to Rodó to Mariátegui to García Canclini,[8] has cut its own arc from the nineteenth century to the present. The suitor in the proposed marriage of the Latin American cultural product and postcolonial practice is, unavoidably, the foreign academic. A jaundiced observer might view this foraging abroad for material as itself a kind of academic colonization of new territory. The most prominent figures in postcolonial criticism—Edward Said, Gayatri Spivak and Homi Bhabha—all seem to have published their respective climactic statements. Bart Moore-Gilbert has written of the 'weariness' which during the 1990s has been 'symptomatic of the sub-field [i.e. postcolonial theory] as a whole'.[9] The postcolonial theorist, one could argue, his local resources exhausted, is now striking out to plunder the riches of Latin America. This suspicion was voiced recently by the Uruguayan critic Hugo Achugar. Refuting attempts to assimilate Latin American culture into the skeins of North Atlantic postcolonial theory, Achugar commented: 'La globalización leída desde el *Commonwealth* parece no haber abandonado ciertos hábitos y ciertas memorias de la historia imperial en lengua inglesa'.[10]

Yet, despite Achugar's valid preoccupations, postcolonial theory does share certain coordinates with dominant trends in Latin American literature, music and film. Both often strive to dismantle imperial and colonial assumptions; both, at certain points, have placed a positive emphasis on hybridization as a strategy for vitiating the oppressive force of hegemonic cultures. The most salient objection to the introduction of postcolonial theory into the realm of Latin American studies—one which has been put to me verbally by colleagues—is that it is ahistorical. Postcolonial theory, this argument goes, developed through the scrutiny of direct colonial relationships: Fanon's study of the psychological impact of French colonialism in the Caribbean, Bhabha's and Spivak's respective probings of the residue of British colonialism in India. To then 'apply' these theories to a relationship which is not one of direct colonial tutelage, such as, for example, Latin America's relationship with the hegemonic discourses of the contemporary United States, is, one is sometimes told, a violation of postcolonial theory's own tenets. But is this really an inconsistency? Postcolonial theory, from the outset, has been a diverse, multiform movement; a cluster of wide-ranging approaches rather than a defined doctrine. The text which has done more than any other to legitimize postcolonial theory as a field of study within the academy, Edward W. Said's *Orientalism* (1978), does not study a direct colonial relationship, but rather the construction of Western 'knowledge' and how this has been used, primarily in the French- and English-speaking traditions, to represent, imagine, define and dominate the 'East'. Said's focus expands steadily over the course of *Orientalism*, so that by the book's closing chapter he is applying the concept of Orientalism to societies as remote from the Arab world, where his inquiry originated, as that of Japan.[11]

This sometimes indiscriminate foraging across the boundaries of cultural traditions and academic disciplines has been the trait of postcolonial theory which has aroused the greatest hostility among traditionalist scholars. Said's authority to include Japan within his analytical frame, like his qualifications to wade into debates concerning anthropology or classical music, has been severely challenged.[12] The same objection contributes to some of the institutional reluctance to embrace postcolonial approaches to Latin American culture.

The potential relevance to Latin America of the postcolonial approach resides, among other features, in its ability to pinpoint key moments of cultural contradiction. Here it is Homi Bhabha who brings us back to the issues raised by the juxtaposition of Carpentier and Fanon, when, in *The Location of Culture* (1994), he follows up an acerbic critique of the cultural specificity of the notion of 'modernity', as generally employed in Western discourse, by suggesting that:

> The ethnocentric limitations of Foucault's spatial sign of modernity become immediately apparent if we take our stand, in the immediate postrevolutionary period, in San Domingo [sic] with the Black Jacobins, rather than Paris. What if the 'distance' that constitutes the meaning of the Revolution as sign, the *signifying lag* between event and enunciation, stretches not across the Place de la Bastille or the rue des Blancs-Monteaux, but spans the temporal difference of the colonial space? ... What do we make of the figure of Toussaint—James evokes Phèdre, Ahab, Hamlet—at the moment when he grasps the tragic lesson that the moral, *modern* disposition of mankind, enshrined in the sign of the Revolution, only fuels the archaic racial factor in the society of slavery?[13]

This passage illustrates the claim to efficacy of a postcolonial approach to Latin American culture, as well as some of its drawbacks. Venturing into territory he does not know well, Bhabha gets the name of the location of the 1793 slave uprising wrong. (It is, of course, Santo Domingo in Spanish, Saint-Domingue in French.) Bhabha's halting prose, characterized by clumsy repetitions and ungainly word choices, is alien to the Latin American tradition, where the most trenchant cultural critics have been, in many cases, masters of Spanish or Portuguese rhetoric.[14] Tellingly, perhaps, the aspect of C. L. R. James's account of the uprising which

Bhabha has chosen to emphasize—the comparison of the slave leader Toussaint L'Ouverture to the protagonists of classical Western tragedies—reinforces the centrality of the assumptions of North Atlantic culture. Arguing for cultural difference, Bhabha nonetheless perpetuates some of the 'limitations' he decries by interpreting the experience of the slaves in terms of an analogy to Western literary archetypes implicitly deemed to be central and universal. His habit of referring to the slaves as 'Black Jacobins' confirms this foundation of European centrality. Yet Bhabha's awareness of the patterns of colonial power enables him, without possessing any particular expertise in Spanish American or Caribbean culture, to pick out one of the most vital moments of contradiction in Latin American colonial history. Bhabha evinces no awareness of Alejo Carpentier's fiction (he is, obviously, aware of the work of Fanon), yet he has stumbled upon the disjuncture—the slaves' insistence on taking seriously the French Revolution's slogan of *'liberté, égalité, fraternité'*—which fuels two of the most significant novels of one of Latin America's most important writers, *El reino de este mundo* (1949), set during and after the 1793 revolt in Saint-Domingue, and *El siglo de las luces*.

At this point I would like to return from the general and theoretical plane to that of the local and the specific. This is necessary to anchor my discussion of Carpentier and Fanon; but the oscillation between these two extremities, it seems to me, also constitutes the central tension to be taken into account when observing the interplay of postcolonial theory and Latin American culture (or, indeed, any culture from the periphery). The strongest resistance to postcolonial theory often originates not from traditionalist Western scholars suspicious of Foucault and Derrida, but from the writers who find themselves cast as that theory's imputed object.[15]

The tension between the need to theorize in order to explain, understand and confront hegemonic cultural forces, and the antipathy to theory as a process through which the cultures of the periphery are generalized, objectified, reified and exoticized resounds through Fanon's early writing. If *Peau noire, masques blancs* is the ancestor of *Orientalism*, and of Bhabha's insistence on the historicity of purported Western universals (*Location*, 237), then it is also the ancestor of the attacks on postcolonial theory launched by politically committed Third World intellectuals who see those who have joined the Western academy as traitors.[16] The fear of theory itself as a mask—a distorting misrepresentation of the culture of the periphery—runs through Fanon's life and thought. His decision to leave his post as psychiatrist at the French hospital in Blida in favour of a life of direct revolutionary action casts a reproachful shadow over the comfortably tenured existences of later generations of postcolonial theorists.[17] While Fanon's focus is on the impact of the colonial experience on the colonized, he remains scathingly aware of the construction of the colonizer's discourses. In his rebuttal of Octave Mannoni's *Psychologie de la colonisation* (1950), Fanon insists on the objective reality of the world of the *bossale*: the African slave displaced to the colonies of Guadeloupe and Martinique.[18] Responding to Mannoni's distinctions between different forms of exploitation, Fanon proclaims:

> L'auteur parle de phénoménologie, de psychanalyse, d'unité humaine, mais nous voudrions que ces termes revêtent chez lui un caractère plus concret. Toutes les formes d'exploitation se ressemblent. Elles vont toutes chercher leur nécessité dans quelque décret d'ordre biblique. Toutes les formes d'exploitation sont identiques, car elles s'appliquent toutes à un même 'objet': l'homme.[19]

In asserting the unity of all forms of exploitation, Fanon is at once rejecting the fine distinctions of Mannoni's theorizing, and smearing together a range of disparate colonial experiences into a single, generalized state. Fanon imposes his own theory of the unity of the experience of the colonized. At the same time, paradoxically, he couches his attack on the authority of the universalizing metropolis in terms of a humanist universal: 'l'homme'.

This tension between the local and the universal, the specific and the theorized, recurs throughout *Peau noire, masques blancs*. Refuting the Marxist theorist Pierre Naville, Fanon insists on the concrete historical reality: 'Le fusil du tirailleur sénégalais n'est pas un pénis, mais véritablement un fusil Lebel 1916' (86). By providing the make and year of the rifle, Fanon deflects the sexual stereotypes projected on to men of African descent through the assertion of local particularities. Elsewhere in *Peau noire, masques blancs*, Fanon berates Carl Gustav Jung for the universalizing presumption of the collective unconscious (154). He is drawn into a lengthy, footnoted theoretical digression, however, concerning the implications of Jacques Lacan's mirror stage for interracial perceptions of identity (131–32); yet the discussion soon descends from the abstruse to concrete examples of precisely delineated childhood memories of Martinique. Having concluded that for the Afro-Caribbean '[c]'est en termes de Blanc que l'on perçoit son semblable' (132), Fanon describes how, during his youth, students in Martinique classified their examiners according to their 'blackness':

> Pendant la guerre, des professeurs guadeloupéens venaient à Fort-de-France corriger les épreuves du baccalauréat et, poussés par notre curiosité, nous allions voir, jusque dans l'hotel où il est descendu, M. B., professeur de philosophie, qui avait la réputation d'être excessivement noir; comme on dit en Martinique, non sans quelque ironie, il était 'bleu'. Telle famille est très bien vue: 'Ils sont très noirs, mais ils sont tous bien'.
>
> (132)

In addition to reiterating the importance of the local and the particular, this passage draws a sharp line between Fanon's point of origin and that of Carpentier. If Fanon is divided from later generations of postcolonial theorists by his not having worked within the legitimizing structures of the Western academy, he is divided from Carpentier by race. Both writers may be motivated by Caribbean concerns, and at different stages associated with revolutionary regimes, but only Fanon—though belonging to the relatively privileged stratum of the *gens de couleur libres*—is black. Carpentier's approach to the question of racism (and by extension, to the issue of Caribbean identity) reflects his origins as the Cuban-reared child of a French architect father and a Russian linguist mother. His engagement with the problem is more intellectual than visceral, and hence more prone to theorization. In *El siglo de las luces* race is the lever which sets rolling the novel's obsession with questions of centre and periphery. Where the young Fanon and his friends were intrigued by examiners darker than themselves, Carpentier's novel—opening in the bosom of a white bourgeois Havana family where the father has died and been swiftly replaced as an authority figure by the enlightened French adventurer, Hugues—must first establish the credibility of black people of any shade to exercise a profession. The resistance of Sofía, the daughter, to allowing Ogé, the black doctor, to enter the house to treat her cousin Esteban's asthma is depicted as emblematic of the ideology of a slaveholding society:

> Quien fuera negro, quien tuviese de negro, era, para ella, sinónimo de sirviente, estibador, cochero o músico ambulante—aunque Víctor, advertido el gesto displicente, explicara que Ogé, vástago de una acomodada familia de Saint-Domingue, había estudiado en París y tenía títulos que acreditaban su sapiencia … 'Pero … ¡es un negro!' cuchicheó Sofía, con percutiente aliento, al oído de Víctor. 'Todos los hombres nacieron iguales' respondió el otro, apartándola con un leve empellón. El concepto acreció su resistencia … Nadie encomendaría a un negro la edificación de un palacio, la defensa de un reo, la dirección de una controversia teológica o el gobierno de un país. (119–20)

For Victor Hugues, Caribbean emissary of the ideals of the Enlightenment, Ogé's 'color quebrado' (120) masks his essential humanity—the fact that, in Fanon's terms, he belongs to 'l'homme'. In Ogé, Carpentier has endowed Vincent Ogé, the historical leader of a 1791 slave uprising, brutally executed by the French, with a fictional brother;[20] Dr Ogé incarnates the revolutionary tradition in Afro-Caribbean culture. Yet Victor, later appointed governor of Guadeloupe and French Guyana, becomes instrumental in snuffing out the slave emancipation he has earlier championed: the freedom manifested most dramatically in the 1793 slave revolt which led, for the first time—in opposition to the ironic final line of the preceding citation—to a black man governing a modern republic.

Returning to the Caribbean in his new guise as French government official, Victor brings with him not only copies of the 1794 decree outlawing slavery in the French colonies, but a guillotine. Carpentier is careful to underline the irony: 'Con la Libertad, llegaba la primera guillotina al Nuevo Mundo' (*El siglo*, 205). The contradiction dramatizes Carpentier's insight that freedom can never be granted to the periphery by the metropolis; the metropolis—represented here by the controlling French father-figure, Victor—always stifles in the periphery the social advances it promotes at the centre. 'Si el gobierno de la Metrópoli transigía con sus ministros liberales, estaba muy resuelto, en cambio, a extirpar las ideas avanzadas de sus colonias', the narrator observes (149). Just as the ideals of the French Revolution spurred the slaves of Saint-Domingue to revolt, so Sofía and Esteban, once they have been infused with Enlightenment ideals, surpass Victor's radicalization. Esteban serves a long prison sentence for translating into Spanish and disseminating throughout the Caribbean revolutionary French pamphlets. Sofía, who is both politically and sexually liberated by Victor, proves capable, once he betrays his ideals, of demonstrating her emancipation by breaking with him on both fronts, finding for herself new revolutionary struggles and new lovers. The novel's anti-colonialist logic dictates the inevitability of both the French reinstitution of slavery in the Caribbean in 1802, and Victor's unblinking compliance with this reversal in policy: the metropolis, ultimately, can only uphold oppressive institutions.

Like Fanon, Carpentier finds himself caught between the particular—in this case, the imperative to narrate the details of the lives of a group of individuals enmeshed in making Caribbean history—and the need to theorize: to erect a counter-ideology as a barrier against French cultural dominance. The kernel of this impulse may be discerned in Carpentier's idealization of the historical figure of Victor Hugues, upon whom the character in the novel is loosely based. In the novel, Victor's decline from impassioned apostle of equality to slaveholding local tyrant parallels the corruption of the French Revolution and the growing support for independence from Spain among the Spanish American colonies. Historians, on the other hand, portray Hugues's support for the rights of slaves as always having been purely an expedient military strategy to defeat the British in the Caribbean: 'Hugues ... was prepared to use the most formidable weapon of all by encouraging slave risings' (Augier *et al.*, *The Making of the West Indies*, 114).

By modifying Hugues's historical role, Carpentier provides himself with a scale by which to measure the inapplicability to the Caribbean of European ideologies. Disillusionment with Europe leaves the Caribbean without the option of either full acceptance of European culture, or total rejection. The residue of European influences cannot be denied, yet neither can it be uncritically absorbed; a strategy of hybridization is required. For Carpentier, this takes the form of the Caribbean baroque. At the time he was writing *El siglo de las luces*, Carpentier had rejected his own earlier formulation of Latin American identity, 'lo real maravilloso', as excessively dependent on a European concept—the marvellous— which required the objectification of Latin American reality, since scrutinizing this reality too closely would dissolve the observer's sense of wonder. 'Lo real maravilloso' condemned the Latin American writer to view his own society with an imperial gaze.[21] The baroque, also, was a European concept, but one which, Carpentier believed, would enable Latin American, and particularly Caribbean, writers to celebrate the peculiar conjunctions of their heritage by conglomerating the vestiges of oppression into the foundations of a new identity.

Part of Carpentier's ideological inheritance from European culture is betrayed by his inability to let 'lo barroco' arise in the novel purely from the collision of disparate cultures. Just as the nineteenth-century European nation-states presented themselves as the expressions of discrete ancestral tribal essences, so Carpentier roots his ideology of the Caribbean baroque in natural essences. Primary among these are an elaborate spiral shell and a coral reef, discovered by Esteban on a beach: '[L]os primeros barroquismos de la Creación' (*El siglo*, 248). The European flotsam which accretes on these natural essences brings with it a history and culture whose significance is worn down and recast by the tides of the New World:

> De sorpresa en sorpresa descubría Esteban la pluralidad de las playas donde el Mar, tres siglos después del Descubrimiento, comenzaba a depositar sus primeros vidrios pulidos; vidrios inventados en Europa, desconocidos en América; vidrios de botellas, de frascos, de bombonas, cuyas formas habían sido ignorados en el Nuevo Continente; vidrios verdes, con opacidad y burbujas; vidrios finos destinados a catedrales nacientes, cuyas hagiografías hubiera borrado el agua ... (249)

The New World annihilates traditional metropolitan connotations, introducing new meanings and human possibilities through its multiplication of forms and peoples. Carpentier's appeal in this lauding of diversity is to the traditional tenets of Western humanism. Like Fanon conflating all forms of exploitation on the grounds that they share as their object a universalized human subject, Carpentier builds his anti-European ideological edifice on European assumptions. The Caribbean becomes a new Mediterranean, flaunting a human diversity which the ever more centralized nation-states of Europe, by this point embroiled in the Napoleonic Wars, are extirpating from their own increasingly rigid national profiles.

> En Francia había aprendido Esteban a gustar del gran zumo solariego que por los pezones de sus vides había alimentado la turbulenta y soberbia civilización mediterránea—ahora prolongada en este Mediterráneo Caribe, donde proseguíase la Confusión de Rasgos iniciada, hacía muchos milenios, en el ámbito de los Pueblos del Mar. Aquí venían a encontrarse,

> al cabo de larga dispersión, mezclando acentos y cabelleras, entregados a renovadores mestizajes, los vástagos de las Tribus Extraviadas, mezclados, entremezclados, despintados y vueltos a pintar, aclarados un día para anochecerse en un salto atrás, con una interminable proliferación de perfiles nuevos, de inflexiones y proporciones, alcanzados a su vez por el vino que, de las naves fenicias … había pasado a las carabelas del Descubrimiento, con la vihuela y la tejoleta, para arribar a estas orillas propiciadoras del trascendental encuentro de la Oliva con el Maíz. (256)

As this passage illustrates, Esteban has acquired his taste for racial and cultural mingling in the bustle of Paris. New World hybridization, in *El siglo de las luces*, is as changeable as many of the human intersections it praises: now a strategy of resistance to European hegemony, now a paradisal prolongation of essences which, in their original, Old World incarnations, have become sullied or corrupted. Carpentier's celebration of diversity alternates almost schizophrenically between these poles. Victor's authority, at times conveyed in terms of sexual dominance, celebrates the implantation in the Caribbean of the seeds of Enlightenment idealism. Sofía, travelling to meet Victor in Cayenne in order to renew their sexual relationship, thinks: 'Víctor … estaba penetrando … en esta Tierra Firme de América llevando a ella, como antes, las luces que en el Viejo Mundo se apagaban' (371). Yet the novel closes with Sofía and Esteban hurling themselves into an insurrection in Madrid in 1808 to the cry of '¡Mueran los franceses!' (412), sacrificing their lives in order to overturn French dominance, even though it is French culture which has inspired them to develop into revolutionaries.

The contradictions in Carpentier's novel cluster around the cultural power struggle between the colonized territories of the Caribbean and Paris, perceived as the epicentre of cultural modernity. Racial issues serve as a kind of gauge of the various characters' respective positions within this cultural nexus. Hence Dr Ogé, an important figure in the narrative's early stages, vanishes once he has served the purpose of establishing each of the white characters' locations on the spectrum of racial tolerance and political engagement. Ogé's final appearance occurs when he announces to Victor that his brother has been executed by 'Ustedes' (164), that is, by the French. The incompatibility of the undiluted essences of black and white prepares the ground for Carpentier's argument in favour of a hybridized culture.

After Ogé's disappearance, characters of African descent act as backdrop and local detail; the only black character of even passing significance is Mademoiselle Athalie Bajazet, the Guadeloupean woman with whom Esteban has the sort of casually exploitive sexual liaison typical of relations between white men and black women in a colonial context. Defined in terms of her sexual availability and her untrustworthiness, Mademoiselle Athalie betrays Esteban's confidences, prompting him to retaliate with a colonialist vengeance: 'le había amoratado las nalgas a bofetones' (245).

Esteban's abuse of Mademoiselle Athalie as a woman in this scene does not detract from the fact that she is far more freely abused because she is black. His beating of his Guadeloupean mistress recalls Césaire's 'nègre fustigé[e]', adumbrating a crucial difference in emphasis between Carpentier's assumption of a multi-racial mask and Fanon's deconstruction of the white masks layered over black faces. For Carpentier, the crime of racism inculpates mechanistic, univocal European discourses, signalling the necessity of the elaboration of a baroque, Utopian, crossroads culture in the Caribbean. The articulation of this culture is Carpentier's central project; for Fanon, anti-colonial (and postcolonial) theorizing arises, involuntarily and often irrelevantly, from the primary struggle against racial oppression. Formed by a brutally racist society which even in 1998 was bitterly divided by the celebration of the sesquicentenary of the definitive abolition of slavery in the French Caribbean,[22] Fanon is interested in the colonial condition purely in so far as it perpetuates the racial oppression of people of African descent. At the close of *Peau noire, masques blancs*, writing of the struggle confronting the colonized African or Afro-Caribbean, Fanon argues:

> Et cette lutte, il l'entreprendra et la mènera non pas après une analyse marxiste ou idéaliste, mais parce que, tout simplement, il ne pourra concevoir son existence que sous les espèces d'un combat mené contre l'exploitation, la misère et la faim …
> La découverte de l'existence d'une civilisation nègre au XVe siècle ne me décerne pas un brevet d'humanité. Qu'on le veuille ou non, le passé ne peut en aucune façon me guider dans l'actualité. (181–82)

This is a very different Fanon from that habitually vaunted by contemporary postcolonial theorists. At a conference held in London on Fanon's work in 1996—sponsored, it is worth noting, by Toshiba—Homi Bhabha described Fanon's contemporary relevance as follows:

> Fanonian 'continuance' is the temporality of the practice of action: its performativity or agency is constituted by its emphasis on the singularity of the 'local': an iterative structuring of the historical event and political pedagogy and an ethical sense constructed from truths that are partial, limited, unstable. Fanon's dialectic of the everyday is, most significantly, the emergency of a new historical and theoretical temporality generated by the process of revolutionary transience and transformation.[23]

What Bhabha seems to be saying here, as he drops condescending quotation marks around 'local', is that, from the perspective of the metropolitan postcolonial theorist, Fanon's unwavering focus on the problems surrounding him and his refusal to be drafted into elaborating an Afrocentric counter-history represent, nonetheless, a way of interpreting history. There is, Bhabha argues, no escape from historicity. Or, to put it a little differently, all intellectuals from the periphery, whether they like it or not, can be drafted into the postcolonial theorist's all-encompassing reimagining of history.

It is at this point that the prospect of the convergence of

metropolitan postcolonial theory and Spanish American culture appears least productive and most troubling, as postcolonial theory seems to cast itself in the role of simply one more metropolitan master-discourse devoted to assimilating and eliding the local details which obsess a Frantz Fanon or an Alejo Carpentier. But Fanon himself, as noted earlier, is trapped in the same oscillation between the particular and the general. *Peau noire, masques blancs* may end in a lyrical assertion of the value of the encounter of two individuals outside the net of theories of black and white, but Fanon went on to write *Les damnés de la terre* (1961), which opens with a lengthy theorization of the process of decolonizing violence.[24]

I would like to close on a more optimistic note by descending from the general to the particular, and casting a final glance at how the two books I have been discussing illuminate the historical predicament of each other's respective authors. Carpentier's history of the French Caribbean alerts us to the contradictions of the context which created Frantz Fanon. Part of the extra-territorial legacy of the French Revolution was to create a paradoxical situation where francophone Afro-Caribbeans identified with the metropolis as a source of liberating ideas, while reactionary and colonialist elements rejected the centre. (This dynamic is incarnated in *El siglo de las luces* by Dr Ogé on the one hand and on the other by the figure of the old Acadian who worships prerevolutionary France [285–88].) Richard D. E. Burton, arguing that this conundrum prevented Martinique's development from leading, like that of Jamaica or Barbados, to independence, writes:

> The pattern in Martinique between 1789 and 1794 of alignments with and dissociations from the Revolution in France provides the paradigm for almost all subsequent political developments in the island and defines the basic problematic in which almost all subsequent intellectual reflection and discussion will be conducted. To put a bewilderingly complex situation very simply ... while the *gens de couleur libres* identified with the Revolution and sought to assimilate and make their own its values, meanings and benefits, the slave-owning whites

sought to distinguish themselves and the colony they still dominated from the political and intellectual logic that lay at the Revolution's core.[25]

Carpentier's novel helps us to understand Fanon's origins in a class which had thwarted its own aspirations by embracing the metropolis as the source of values capable of leading to liberation from colonialism.[26] Having read *El siglo de las luces*, with its final image of the two French-inspired Caribbean revolutionaries rushing into the street to the cry of '¡Mueran los franceses!', we understand why Fanon's engagement with France is so much more claustrophobic than the engagement with Spain or Great Britain of a Cuban or Jamaican intellectual of the same generation. We are conscious that Fanon, acclaimed as the ancestor of contemporary postcolonial theory, was, in a chronological sense, not a postcolonial writer: still today, Martinique remains a colony of France.

Having read *Peau noire, masques blancs*, however, we are driven to ask why a Cuban writer should devote his most ambitious novel to tracing French, rather than Spanish, colonial intrusions into the Caribbean. Fanon's work establishes French colonialism as the logical concern of people ruled by France. Carpentier's complex relationship with his own French father does not explain quite enough, particularly since Carpentier is far from alone in his fixation with France. Generations of Spanish American writers adopted France as the source of their intellectual and artistic models.[27] One of the insights which Fanon in particular and postcolonial theory in general may be able to offer Latin American culture lies in this awareness of a central, but highly unusual, disjuncture in Latin American history: the comparatively feeble relationship with and consciousness of the former colonizing power. In the aftermath of independence in the early nineteenth century, most of Spanish America (the case of Portugal and Brazil, obviously, is radically different) severed its ties with Spain; only Cuba and Puerto Rico remained colonies. Parisian Enlightenment writers and London merchant bankers ensured that the region was strongly influenced by French culture and British economic power, which was displaced after the Spanish-American War by United States economic and political dominance. It was only after the mass exodus of Spanish intellectuals to Mexico in the wake of the Spanish Civil War that Spain regained a tentative presence in Spanish America as a significant cultural source. Postcolonial theory, with its usefulness for drawing attention to cultural contradiction, facilitates the appreciation of the incongruity of this skewed, remote relationship with the former colonizer; it helps us to perceive the oddity of a phenomenon that is sometimes overlooked in Latin American studies simply because Spain's relative absence is so much taken for granted. Metropolitan postcolonialism may also help to alleviate Latin American solitude by offering a context capable of illuminating the internal colonizations committed by Spanish American elites. By seeing Rigoberta Menchú's need to learn Spanish in order to express herself in the public sphere against the backdrop of Chinua Achebe's or Ngugi wa Thiongo's early decisions to write in English (sustained in the former case, though afterwards reversed in the latter), one becomes even more intensely aware of the colonized nature of a society such as that of Guatemala. Conversely, making the acquaintance of Spanish America's 200-year-old tradition of cultural criticism should induce North Atlantic postcolonialists to look beyond the consecrated trinity of Said, Bhabha and Spivak to other writers, in South Asia, the Arab world and elsewhere, who criticized unequal cultural relations from within the frameworks and languages of their own societies.

Notes

1. Roberto González Echevarría, *Alejo Carpentier: The Pilgrim at Home* (Ithaca and London: Cornell University Press, 1977), 233–34.

2. Alejo Carpentier, *El siglo de las luces* (1962; rpt. Madrid: Cátedra, 1989), 177. After the initial reference to each text cited, subsequent unambiguous references will be incorporated into the main body of the essay, with the page number given in parentheses.

3. Carpentier broke with Breton during the 1929 schism in the Surrealist movement. See Maurice Nadeau, *Histoire du Surréalisme* (Paris: Éditions du Seuil, 1945), 170–95.

4. Aimé Césaire, *Cahier d'un retour au pays natal* (1939; rpt. Paris-Dakar: Editions Présence Africaine, 1983), 77–87.

5. González Echevarría, for example, writes of 'the paternity rights that [Carpentier] was exercising over younger novelists such as Carlos Fuentes, who had spent time in Cuba in the early sixties and had written his best-known novel, *The Death of Artemio Cruz*, under the influence of Carpentier'. González Echevarría, *Alejo Carpentier: The Pilgrim at Home*, 222. In his novel *Cien años de soledad*, García Márquez executes a bow in Carpentier's direction by inserting an allusion to Victor Hugues. See García Márquez, *Cien años de soledad* (1967; rpt. Madrid: Cátedra, 1994), 188. Fanon's groundbreaking importance to North Atlantic postcolonial theorists is evident in Robert Young's assessment: 'What has been new in the years since the Second World War during which, for the most part, the decolonization of the European empires has taken place, has been the accompanying attempt to decolonize European thought and the forms of its history as well ... This project could be said to have been initiated in 1961 by Fanon's *The Wretched of the Earth*.' Young, *White Mythologies: Writing History and the West* (London and New York: Routledge, 1990), 119.

6. See William Rowe and Vivian Schelling, *Memory and Modernity: Popular Culture in Latin America* (London and New York: Verso, 1991), 49–150.

7. I draw my use of this term from Patricia D'Allemand, *Latin American Cultural Criticism: Reinterpreting a Continent* (Lewiston, Queenston and Lampeter: Edwin Mellen Press, 2000).

8   This necessarily skimpy and partial list refers to works such as Domingo Faustino Sarmiento, *Facundo: civilización y barbarie* (1845; rpt. Buenos Aires: Editorial Losada, 1963); José Martí, *Cuba, Nuestra América, los Estados Unidos* (México: Siglo Veintiuno Editores, 1973); José Enrique Rodó, *Ariel: liberalismo y jacobinismo* (1900; rpt. México: Editorial Porrua, 1968); José Carlos Mariátegui, *Siete ensayos de interpretación de la realidad peruana* (1928; rpt. Lima: Biblioteca Amauta, 1968); Nestor García Canclini, *Culturas híbridas: estrategias para entrar y salir de la modernidad* (Buenos Aires: Editorial Sudamericana, 1992).

9   Bart Moore-Gilbert, *Postcolonial Theory: Contexts, Practices, Politics* (London and New York: Verso, 1997), 187.

10 Hugo Achugar, 'Leones, cazadores e historiadores, a propósito de las políticas de la memoria y del conocimiento', *Revista Iberoamericana*, LXIII, 180 (Julio–Setiembre 1997), 382.

11 Edward Said, *Orientalism* (New York: Vintage, 1979), 322.

12 See, for example, Ernest Gellner, 'Culture and Imperialism', *Times Literary Supplement*, 9 April 1993, 15.

13 Homi Bhabha, *The Location of Culture* (London and New York: Routledge, 1994), 244.

14 The obvious exception to this statement arises in *testimonio* narratives such as *Me llamo Rigoberta Menchú y así me nació la conciencia*, ed. Elisabeth Burgos (Barcelona: Argos Vergara, 1983). Here, however, the linguistic eccentricities stem from the dynamic of a 'native informant' for whom Spanish is an acquired language. The 'private language' of English-language academics—even those who trace their origins to former colonies—reflects an Anglo-American tradition in which scholars and intellectuals usually remain remote from public debate, while the generally more accessible language of many (though by no means all) Latin American cultural critics springs from a tradition in which the 'organic intellectual' has been presumed to be an able communicator within the public sphere.

15 Here I speak less as a university-based critic of Spanish American literature, than as a Canadian novelist who sometimes feels boxed in by postcolonial interpretations of Canadian literary production.

16 See Aijaz Ahmad, *In Theory: Classes, Nations, Literatures* (London: Verso, 1992).

17 This reproach does not apply, obviously, to Edward Said, who for many years put his beliefs into practice on the Palestinian National Council.

18 For an analysis of the culture of the *bossale*, see Maryse Condé, *La Civilisation du bossale: Refléxions sur la littérature orale de la Guadeloupe et de la Martinique* (Paris: Editions L'Harmattan, 1978).

19 Frantz Fanon, *Peau noire, masques blancs* (1952; rpt. Paris: Éditions du Seuil, 1995), 71.

20 F. R. Augier, S. C. Gordon, D. G. Hall and M. Reckord, *The Making of the West Indies* (Harlow: Longman, 1960), 113.

21 For a brief account of Carpentier's disillusionment with '*lo real maravilloso*', see Stephen Henighan, 'Alejo Carpentier and the Surrealist Legacy in Spanish American Fiction', *International Quarterly*, III, 1 (1998), 29–31.

22 See Béatrice Bantman, 'Abolition de l'esclavage: l'anniversaire ambigu', and 'Martinique, terre des castes', *Libération*, 25 et 26 avril 1998, 2 and 3–4.

23 Homi Bhabha, 'Day by Day ... with Frantz Fanon', in *The Fact of Blackness: Frantz Fanon and Visual Representation*, ed. Alan Read (London: Institute of Contemporary Arts, 1996), 190.

24 Frantz Fanon, *Les Damnés de la terre* (1961; rpt. Paris: Gallimard, 1991), 65–141.

25 Richard D. E. Burton, 'Between the Particular and the Universal: Dilemmas of the Martinican Intellectual', in *Intellectuals in the Twentieth-Century Caribbean. Volume II. Unity in Variety: The Hispanic and Francophone Caribbean*, ed. Alistair Hennessy (London and Basingstoke: Macmillan, 1992), 189.

26 Carpentier's theory of baroque cultural mixing also suggests that Fanon's identity as *noir* was not inevitable, but dictated by Martinique's stark racial divides and the historical legacy of slavery—and, to some extent, by Fanon's own choice of identity. As Gendzier points out, Fanon, by far the darkest of his parents' eight children, was born into a family of mixed Indian, Alsatian and African ancestry. In a different time, or a less narrowly oppressive environment, he might have

celebrated the multiple threads of his background—including his Alsatian name—as a 'baroque' or 'hybridized' Caribbean heritage. See Irene L. Gendzier, *Frantz Fanon: A Critical Study* (London: Wildwood House, 1973), 10.

27 Describing the years leading up to the opening of *El siglo de las luces*, Edwin Williamson writes: 'Within the Indies themselves the ideological separation from Spain was more gradual, but from the 1770s, too, elements of the creole intelligentsia began to lose their inherited respect for the motherland as the standard bearer of a universal Christian order. France increasingly became the beacon of civilization, since the Enlightenment in the Iberian world was but an extension of French ideas. In the arts, the latter decades of the century saw Hispanic baroque styles give way to a neo-classicism of French inspiration associated with modernity and progress.' Edwin Williamson, *The Penguin History of Latin America* (London: Penguin, 1992), 163. For a concise survey of this attraction on Carpentier and other later Spanish American writers, and a sample bibliography on the subject, see Verity Smith, 'Paris', in *Encyclopedia of Latin American Literature*, ed. Verity Smith (London and Chicago: Fitzroy Dearborn, 1997), 626–27.

CHAPTER EIGHT

Colonial Crosswords: (In)voicing the Gap in Mia Couto

Maria Manuel Lisboa
University of Cambridge

Mia Couto, author of chronicles, novels, short stories and some poetry, has emerged as perhaps the best known writer of post-independence Mozambique. His works, published in large editions in both Mozambique and Portugal, have also been translated into several languages, including English. As was also the case with almost all pre-independence Mozambican literature, important aspects of his work have to be contextualized through an awareness of the political background, in his case the events that beset Mozambique in the decades following its political separation from Portugal, attained after ten years of a conflict which, immediately after independence was gained, was followed by a civil war that lasted almost twenty years, finally ending in 1994.

The civil war between the post-independence Marxist-Leninist FRELIMO[1] government and the resistance movement, RENAMO,[2] supported initially by Rhodesia (as it then was) and subsequently by South Africa, created in the ideological but also psychic life of the country, and of its intellectuals, a conflict not previously posed by the much simpler, straightforward, inimical categories of black and white, Portuguese and Mozambican of the pre-independence war years. In the context of a conflict which, albeit not on the whole tribal, led to the killing of blacks by blacks, the pre-independence utopia of homogeneous black pan-Africanism and brotherhood gave way instead to the awareness of what for want of a better term might be seen as a potential for balkanization in the region, a Rwanda-type scenario, emerging in antithesis to the dream of black unity nationwide. The awareness of this forcible discarding of the hope of straightforward national categories and of a unified identity in a post-independence Mozambique purged of heterogeneous (namely European) variations becomes, I think, relevant to the discussion that follows of certain themes in Mia Couto's narratives. It is so, certainly, in the short story I shall be concentrating on, dealing as it does with the dream of linear and monodimensional racial and/or national identity, in the face of disturbing heterogeneity. In this connection, too, it is worth mentioning that in Mia Couto, as made explicit by him in a variety of newspaper interviews given during and in the aftermath of the civil war, the poignancy of the reality of this war and its associated ills is not, however, treated as an absolute negative.[3] Somewhat perversely, Couto seems to see this period in Mozambican history (and the concomitant international isolation in which the country found itself during the decades of the civil war), as the enablers of conditions which permitted the newly-born nation to evolve a cultural and social specificity which might otherwise have become diluted, had the birth of the country as an independent entity taken place under less dramatic circumstances, and under the inevitable intervention, or interference, of a variety of foreign interests.

The analysis that follows of one of Mia Couto's short stories from his volume *Vozes Anoitecidas* (*Voices Made Night*)[4] will lead me through a contemplation of certain themes pertaining to the question of race identity to an investigation of the deployment of myth in the charting out of the boundaries of that identity, or identities. I should like to begin, therefore, with some remarks on the nature of myth-making, and myth-reading, to use a Barthesian terminology, in the work of this writer. I would wish to argue that Mia Couto employs a two-pronged approach to myth in narrative: on the one hand he adapts old, European as well as African myths to a Mozambican reality, and on the other he adapts a present, Mozambican reality to fit in with a variety of old, Euro-perceived folkloric and mythical archetypes. He does so, specifically, in what emerges as the attempt through narrative to come to terms with, or come to an understanding of, two issues more than commonly pressing in this region of southern Africa: death, in a country where the peacetime life expectancy is at present approximately 45; and identity, in a country which surfaced from five centuries of imperial and colonial occupation into a civil war that led to the creation of over one million refugees exiled from the boundaries of their homeland, and only slightly less violently, from their linguistic, emotional and existential selves.

Mozambique is a country born out of one war (the struggle against Portuguese colonialism) and beset until recently by another (the civil war that followed independence) for most of its life as an independent nation. It is also a country which has been classified on and off by a number of international agencies including the United Nations, the World Bank and the International Monetary Fund as the poorest country in the world. In these circumstances, death—the absolute loss of identity—becomes much more than an abstract phenomenon, be it death through famine, sickness or violence. The consciousness of death as an immediate possibility, and of the transience of life, is of the essence in the experience of Mia Couto's protagonists. But their reaction to these facts tends to be, by less perilous European standards, peculiar, literally Antiquated, a species of smiling resignation which is, paradoxically, very close to Stoicism as it was originally, philosophically understood by the Greeks. Thus, where reason and understanding are by definition not possible in a world of more than usually random brutality, they must be invented. The persuasion of a universal underpinning rationality, which is the Stoical view of the world, is rephrased in Mia Couto through the finding of mythical and folkloric explanations for a very present reality, for example that of haphazardly exploding landmines in stories such as 'O dia em que explodiu Mabata-bata'.[5] In this tale, a child, Azarias, watches an ox,

Mabata-bata, being blown to pieces by a landmine in the field where it is grazing. Azarias explains the explosion to himself in terms of a folkloric tale of his childhood, as the advent of a fire-bird, the Ndlati, which in dying consumed by fire falls to earth and in the aftermath of the impact creates a teluric thirst which gives origin to rivers and springs. The fact that immediately after arriving at this life-enhancing explanation, prosaic reality impinges and Azarias is himself blown up by yet another mine does not, somehow, detract from what emerges as the attempt at an African fabular explanation, alternative to the one of a Europe-originated war-weapon, through the recapturing of the Africanity of an old tale. Contemporary reality is thus here reformulated through the vocabulary of ancestral folklore, which reflects back upon the specificity of an appallingly commonplace aspect of the local day-to-day, namely death by landmines. But if the prosaic truth kills Azarias, the facts which constitute that truth become nonetheless reprocessed into a modified reality within which living with and dying as a consequence of the mines becomes analogous to, and therefore as comprehensible (or rational) as, living and dying through climatic or geophysical disasters. The mines (like the *bandidos*, the RENAMO fighters of the civil war) become *both* re-articulated through an African myth *and* assimilated as natural phenomena, partaking of a revised status quo and modus vivendi, in a suitably adapted human cosmogony.

It is this dynamic interaction between the universalizing nature of myth and its specificity as regards local explanatory imperatives that is skilfully deployed in Mia Couto's writing, so that, to the European reader's literarily well-trained eye, certain familiar aspects of the African myths deployed clash creatively with regional specificity, to create an effect of defamiliarization and give rise to meaningful cultural crossover: a crossover all the more to be expected, given this writer's hybrid position as a white Mozambican writer, and one, therefore, at a crossroads of races and cultures. The creative potential of this crossover, however, emerges as clearly qualified through the fate of protagonists such as Azarias, who experiences the encounter of cultures (African cattleherding and European landmines), not positively but destructively, or Ascolino do Perpétuo Socorro, who, as I shall go on to argue, is left stranded in a no-man's-land of self-dispossession. Thus, we might find similarities between certain aspects of the corpus of mythical figures (whales, flying witches, serpents, firebirds) which accumulate in these stories and the parallel corpus of folk, fairytales and fables that underpin the Western European fabular imagination. The differences, difficulties and impasses of interpretation and synthesis, however, are made sufficiently palpable by the author to force upon us, as European readers, an uneasy awareness of a cultural gap that runs deep, and which discloses an entire other set of concerns not fully accessible to those (European) others who stand removed from them.

Although, of course, an alternative angle on the problems posed by the type of recourse to myth we see in the writing of this author (who is, after all, white and therefore schooled, under the old colonial system, in a European education system, raised with European stories, tales and fables), is that he lures European readers with cultural references they and he share. By this means, he draws his readership into a complicitous reading of familiar myths (rendered more palatable still by a dash of pleasantly exotic local flavouring), thus introducing references which are eminently readable by that European public, while remaining overall inaccessible to the Mozambican audience he purports to address but whose language he might not after all truly speak. I will return to this problem at the end of the present discussion.

I want to move now, however, to another aspect of this writer's work, partly connected with what I shall term his neo-Romantic preoccupation with myth-revival, which is the drive towards the creation of new, African, nobly savage, prelapsarian heroes with an African difference, but still clearly allusive to a series of epic and Homeric, or medieval and Arthurian, or biblical and Christ-like European forerunners. The quest of the heroic wise fool—directly inherited from the sister European tradition—who, like Ernesto Timba in the story 'Os pássaros de Deus',[6] echoes but also re-writes and to some extent questions the theme of Christ's Passion in that tradition, is repeated by Mia Couto, in a puzzlingly failed manner, through the moving and contemptible figure of the nationally-uprooted, identity-hungry Ascolino do Perpétuo Socorro, in the story I principally wish to discuss here, 'De como se vazou a vida de Ascolino do Perpétuo Socorro'.[7]

Any delving into questions of identity within a postcolonial framework cannot bypass the by now canonical theoretical insights of Homi Bhabha. Following Bhabha,[8] positions of power and powerlessness within a colonial context, and the identity-demarcating possibilities that these positions signpost, are not mutually impregnable or absolutely distinct, but, as Firdous Azim explains, echo each other.[9] The Other which the European gaze thinks it glimpses in the colonial mirror is the black Double whose attributed primitiveness and savagery the white man seeks out as the necessary underpinning in a process of shoring up his own identity. According to Bhabha, however, the image in the mirror, disturbingly, is not that of the unequivocal Other but rather an ambivalent and faithless replica, which is a mimic, a double, but not a perfect one, rather a flawed simulacrum, reflecting back at the colonial gazer an unfamiliar, distorted image of himself: an image which is, moreover, non-authoritative, non-viable, weakened, and therefore colludes, to draw upon another set of theoretical terms, in that murderous act which Baudrillard identified as being performed by icons, representations, or simulacra, upon a reality they proclaim to represent but which in fact they destroy, substituting themselves for its now redundant, vacated essence.

If, following Bhabha and Azim, 'it is in the confrontation or encounter with its colonized subject that the colonizing power defines the terrain against which it would like to be identified',[10] I shall argue that what the character of Ascolino extends to us, or imposes upon us, may be, indeed, at one level, the moving sand upon which that authoritative colonial discourse loses its standing. This is so, undeniably, since what Ascolino offers to the readerly gaze is the representation of a maladaptive hybridity (Goan Indian and white Portuguese) which is the fundamentally unsound palimpsest

Colonial Crosswords: (In)voicing the Gap in Mia Couto 197

of a Portuguese imperial adventure that resulted in some degree of miscegenation. His is, after all, also the plight that confronts a number of nations which are the whole in relation to which Ascolino's individual dilemma stands as the metonymical part: first, of course, the ruinous long-term legacy of imperialism for the former colonies; but also, and more unexpectedly, some consequences for Portugal itself, as the European metropolis. If Portuguese historians and writers since Gil Vicente in the fifteenth century have been warning against the disastrous long-term outcome for Portugal of placing all its eggs in the same imperial basket, Ascolino, who is intentionally subservient to, but unintentionally subversive of, that sea-going colonizing imperative, will stand, at the end of the story, as the poignant, quixotic and grotesque representation of its abysmal failure. He will stand as such, in admirably Bhabha-like fashion, through that paradoxical propinquity to, yet difference from, the Portuguese, expansionist, territorial ideal which he believes in but could never simulate, even were it a reality, and whose ultimate failure his own fragile subject status exemplifies. But, at another level, if Ascolino's identity dilemma unwittingly problematizes the colonial discourse he consciously seeks to emulate, it also, as I shall be arguing later, raises a series of difficult questions regarding the demarcation of a viable Otherness in a postcolonial national, political and theoretical context.

The protagonist of this story, Ascolino do Perpétuo Socorro, is a mixed-race man of Indo-Portuguese extraction living in Mozambique, where Indians and Indo-Portuguese originating from Goa, Damão and Diu, the former Portuguese holdings in India, formed a sizeable fraction of the otherwise black or white population. Ascolino declares all-round pride in his mixed-race status and dog-like devotion to Portuguese, and, beyond them, European traditions. His speech is an aberrant, idiosyncratic pidgin rendering of exaggeratedly elaborate Portuguese, and his dress apes colonial attire in the bush:

> Vestia sempre de rigor, fato de linho branco, sapatos de igual branco, chapéu de idem cor. Ceremonioso, emendado, Ascolino

costurava no discurso os rendilhados lusitanos da sua admiração. Enfeitava os ditos com advérbios sem propósito nem cabimento. Uma imensa lista dava entrada nas frases, mal faladas de sotaque:
—*Não obstante, porém, todavia, contudo ...* (67–68)

Relaxing on his veranda, Ascolino, a peculiar hybrid of Indian and Portuguese, colonizer and colonized, doubly dispossessed as the expatriate Indian who left one occupied land (his own) for another equally occupied one (Mozambique under the Portuguese), sits on his veranda and recalls:

> Goa, sua terra natal. Caneco se negava:
> —*Indo-português sou, católico de fé e costume.* (67)

Ascolino has been married for thirty years to Dona Epifânia, to whom he refers repeatedly as 'Epifane, sagrada esposa. Contudo, porém, trinte anos di casamento' (68). He also has a servant, Vasco João Joãoquinho, in whom are reproduced all the colonial hierarchies which, in this instance, locate, at the apex of the pyramid, Ascolino (a deficient mimicry of colonial mastery), over his makeshift chauffeur and man for all service:

> Hora respeitada, mais sagrada que a esposa, era das cinco da tarde. Houvesse ou não visitas repetia-se o ritual. Vasco João Joãoquinho, fiel e dedicado empregado, surgia da sombra das mangueiras. Fardava caqui, balalaica e calção engomado. Aproximava-se trazendo uma bicicleta. Ascolino Fernandes, protocolar, inclinava-se perante ausentes e presentes. ... Acomodava-se, com cuidado de não manchar as calças na corrente. ... Vasco João Joãoquinho montava no selim e ... os dois, Ascolino e o seu biciclitista, seguiam de adeuses em diante, rumo à cantina do Meneses. ... Seguiam, obedecidos à vontade viciosa de Ascolino, pedalando contra a sede e a distância.
> (68–69)

Meneses's bar is named Viriato, after the Lusitanian hero who, during the period of Roman occupation of the Iberian Peninsula, led a prolonged and successful resistance to the occupiers. His name thus offers a neat historical reversal of the colonizer/colonized position, with Portugal, or the territory that would later become Portugal, itself at that point an occupied province of a far-reaching Roman empire. But it offers also a painful allusion to heroic colonial resistance (Viriato's), here rendered farcical through the pusilanimous posturing of Ascolino, his undignified twentieth-century alter ego. Complexly, then, not just the colonial gaze (Portugal's), but that of the doubly colonized Ascolino (an Indian in Mozambique), capture in the colonial mirror a glimpsed simulacrum of their two respective positions (colonizer and twentieth-century colonized), each ingloriously mimicked.

In Bar Viriato, while Vasco regales his fellow servants with tales of Ascolino's drunkenness and conjugal quarrels of the night before, Ascolino, on the other side of the bar, indulges in false memories of a colonial past which from his curiously ambiguous, hybrid position he nonetheless succeeds in viewing with the uncomplicated and fond eye of someone rejoicing in irreproachably unmixed European credentials. But he does so while simultaneously becoming progressively drunker, thereby betraying in the self which he has imaginatively whitened, that stereotyped taint of native racial degeneracy and unreliability which the colonizer's position would be prompt in attributing to him: 'Na mesa reservada, Ascolino demora seus modos, relembra Goa, Damão e Diu, repuxa advérbios. Não obstante, porém. —*Sai mais dose dele, rebise o visqui*' (74).

Ascolino is a self-denominated Indo-Portuguese, but with declared aspirations to full, white, Portuguese status, while being dismissed by others as a 'darkie',[11] or 'caneco' (67), or 'monhé' (74). His euphemistic Indo-Portugueseness does not deter him from identifying with the figureheads of the Portuguese occupation of India (its sixteenth-century viceroys), and with a racial ranking that sees him in a position of power over blacks and Indians alike, a slippery status that rapidly becomes exposed as a fiction sustainable only through alcohol: 'Ascolino bebe com a certeza de um vice-rei das Índias. Ascolino superior a Ascolino, o indo-português vencendo, pelo alcóol, o caneco' (74). As his inebriation increases, Ascolino becomes entangled in a fight with some Portuguese soldiers at the next table, presumably part of the vast military presence of over 70,000 men sent to Mozambique by Salazar in the 1960s to attempt to quell the then escalating war of independence. To their taunts, couched in the vocabulary of the outraged colonizer against mutinous native rebels ('—*Goa, lá se foi. Sacanas de monhés, raça maldita!*' [74]), Ascolino retorts with persistent attempts at appeasement and identification as a loyal, emotionally if not genetically full-blooded Portuguese patriot, and therefore one of them:

> —*Monhés, sacana sim senhor. Aliás, porém, indo-português qui sou, combatente dos inimigos di Pátria lusitane.*
> Os soldados entreolham-se, desconfiados. Mas o Ascolino leva mais alto a afirmação da lusitanidade. ... Uma cruzada, sim, uma cruzada para recuperar o nome de Goa para uso português. À frente, comandando os pelotões, ele, Ascolino Fernandes do Perpétuo Socorro. Atrás, soldados e missionários, navios carregados de armas, bíblias e umas garrafitas de visqui.
> (75)

The attempted identification with the aggressor, a Freudian European father and fatherland appeased at the price of the treacherous and, as it turns out, self-destructive dismissal of the original Indian motherland ('—*monhés, sacana sim senhor*'), in any case fails. Ascolino, thrown out of the bar on his ear, declares the crusade postponed, re-assembles about his person the shreds of his tattered dignity, consults his vanished watch and laments the lateness of the hour. He summons his 'chauffeur' and sets off in a cloud of vaporous alcoholic confusion, imprecations and variously compromised identities: his own, now no longer unequivocally Indo-Portuguese, Goan or 'darkie' but a combination of all three; and the chauffeur's to whom he proffers sticky kisses, mistaking him for Epifânia:

Colonial Crosswords: (In)voicing the Gap in Mia Couto 201

> —*Sou caneco de cu lavado. Primeir catégoria, si fassfavor.*—E gritando com toda a alma: *Viva Nehru!* ...
> O goês ... insiste, açucaroso. Tenta beijar o empregado que se esquiva com vigor. Insistência aumenta, respeito diminui. O Vasco já que empurra o patrão:
> —*Deixa-me, não sou tua mulher.* (77)

The ride ends in slapstick disaster with the bicycle overturned in a ditch and Ascolino, unable to move, spending the night out in the open, watched over by Vasco. When the latter finally reaches home the following morning, leaving Ascolino still asleep, he encounters Epifânia, a sacred spouse who, having finally had her fill of her husband, is preparing to leave him and the marital home, taking its contents away with her in a lorry. This she does, under the astounded eyes of the finally awakened Ascolino:

> Ali, frente aos olhos desinstruídos de Ascolino, se vazava sua vida, sem notícia nem reparo. Passada a poeira, Vasco está de um lado da estrada, funeroso. Do outro lado, Ascolino vai subindo a valeta. Durante o tempo da visão, segue o camião que se afasta. (81)

Astounded and disbelieving, Ascolino contemplates the clouds of dust in the wake of the disappearing lorry before making a decision no less manly for being qualified by temporal hedonistic needs:

> —*Traz bacecola, Vassco. Vamos perseguir esse camião. Depresse.*
> —*Mas, patrão, se o camião já vai na distância.*
> —*Cala, vucê não sabe nada. Carrega velocípede, rápido.* ...
> —*Pedal, pedal depresse. Não obstante, temos que chegar cedo. Hora de cinco hora temos que voltar na cantina de Meneses.*
> (81–82)

I will return presently to the significance of this last episode, but I want first to consider the meaning of Ascolino's 'caneco', hybrid status in this narrative. 'Caneco' is the derogatory Portuguese term for a mixed-race, half-Indian half-Portuguese individual, the 'caneco' individual therefore occupying in the Portuguese African colonies an analogous position in the socio-racial spectrum to that of the 'mestiço' or mulatto, but with the added diasporic component of exile from the colonized land of origin of his Indian parent (usually the mother), to a territory equally colonized (in this case Mozambique) in which he experiences a double dislocation. The 'mestiço' has attracted disparate interpretations in the Lusophone imagination. At one end of the spectrum, the Brazilian critic Afrânio Coutinho—in a digression from the traditional Brazilian rescue of the mulatto as the purveyor of pathos who, in much nineteenth-century abolitionist literature, became the focus of the anti-slavery debate as a figure considered to be more likely to enlist the sympathies of white audiences than a black hero or heroine[12]—has the following to say about his mixed-race fellow citizens:

> It is however true that our mulatto ... is still full of defects of temper, psychology and character, with clear repercussions on his mental life. If the Brazilian mulatto is intellectually capable and sometimes superior, he is not yet good, he has no inner stability or equilibrium, or strength of character. And from the moral and psychological point of view he still evinces great inferiority ... An inferiority complex can go hand in hand, in the same individual, with a superiority complex, an air of seeming to think he is above the common run of humanity, that he sees as necessary to level off differences and preconceptions which he thinks prevail against him. And then there is the pride, which leads them to insubordination, criticism, posing, arrogance, so typical of certain mulattos who are intelligent but pedantic, over-familiar and *arriviste* ... These are the traits which demonstrate the *arrivisme* of the mulatto ... or else its opposite expression, cordiality, an excessive desire to please and be helpful, to create intimacy, ... the subservient tone, a sticky flattery which can be disagreeable.[13]

The above can of course be inserted into a familiar current of racist colonial perceptions which identified certain character flaws as accruing to insidious touches of the tar brush, and as rendering those afflicted by them subservient, over-familiar, ingratiating, unreliable and unstable. In somewhat less loaded language, Manuel Ferreira, one of Portugal's first *africanista* critics, remarks:

> The concept of racial bivalence [introduced by the figure of the mestiço] ... extends and is split into more complex dimensions along social, cultural and linguistic lines. Because the 'mestiço', the mulatto, is so not merely through a miscegenation of bloods, but rather, and principally, through a syncretism of cultures. Hence his transformation into what some theorists denominate the man from two worlds: the modern, more or less acculturated (or, as some would have it, deculturated) African. Hence his bipolarity, his dual cultural condition, and the references to his nature as a 'problematic' individual. ... Problematic, therefore unbalanced? Unstable or stable?[14]

Ferreira's open-ended considerations lead me back to Ascolino's plight, in Mia Couto's story, and to his triangular Indian, Portuguese and Mozambican hall of mirrors, reflective of a multiplicity of labyrinthine, evasive identities, via Robert Young's reflections on the condition of hybridity in recent and not so recent race theories. If, as Young maintains, there prevails, in the English novel of the last two-and-a-half centuries, a clearly identifiable impetus which, driven by the desire for the cultural Other, effects a forsaking of its own culture,[15] the resulting Kiplingesque 'monstrous hybrid between East and West'[16] finds in the figure of Ascolino an additionally complex tripartite configuration: namely the pull of the unclassifiable, impossible to demarcate, triangular psychic *ménage à trois*, within one single individual, of colonizer/doubly-colonized desire: Portuguese, Mozambican and Indian. A desire which is, moreover, commensurate with rejection, in himself, of that very otherness he desires, by the self-same he who desires it. This is the plight of the Indo-Portuguese 'darkie' who, in Mia Couto, wishes himself, as we shall see, fundamentally and absolutely Portuguese (while ostensibly vaunting his *Indo*-Portugueseness), and who, in desiring himself Portuguese, European, white, feels himself to be touched by a series of geographical and blood markers (Mozambican, Indian) which are themselves echoes of Portuguese imperial sojourns abroad. These are sojourns, moreover, towards whose final bankruptcy Ascolino's maladaptive narrative presence and pitifully posturing linguistic deficiencies gesture, reflecting back at the European self an unsatisfactory view of its colonial achievement, while Ascolino himself is left in the undesirable, non-desiring limbo of unresolved and for him unsatisfactory pluralism of multiple identities.

In an interview with Sneja Gunew, Gayatri Spivak stated that 'for me, the question "Who should speak?" is less crucial than "Who will listen?"'[17] Robert Young discusses linguistic paradigms as the most productive models of the complexities of cultural exchange in colonial contexts, and the pidgin or creolized languages as preserving the historical palimpsest of cross-cultural contact. Invoking Bakhtin, he rephrases a concern with racial hybridity in linguistic terms which nonetheless stress the potential for ironization and destabilization of a discourse (the colonial) revealed to be double-voiced rather than monologic. This model is only at first glance applicable to Ascolino's curious linguistic idiolect, comprising (as we have seen) over-embroidered, ultimately ridiculous mannerisms, and depicted by Mia Couto as immediately risible. Ascolino's speech, a hybrid of Portuguese basic structure, Indian grammatical alterity, Mozambican vocabulary, and accent and intonation which are a mixture of all three, never however becomes, in Couto's presentation, truly dialogic or capable of carnivalizing the colonial blueprint it deforms even while revering it. Instead, disquietingly, it resuscitates nineteenth-century race theory notions of hybridic infertility (or non-viability, here articulated as unsuccessful verbal communication). W. F. Edward and Robert Knox's theory of the reversion of races held that the hybrid products of interracial unions are either infertile or, 'if fertile, will, after a few generations, revert back to one or other of the origins from which they sprang'.[18] The unhappy hankering of the hybrid for reversion to an either/or (literally black or white) departure point is in no way akin, but rather directly antithetical, to Homi Bhabha's radical undermining of Self/Other categories, and to Bakhtin's revolutionizing dialogism. Yet it is, clearly, the invidious position imposed by his creator upon Ascolino do Perpétuo Socorro, in the shape of the latter's comic but also pathetic attempted escape from his own hybridity, back to the (w)hol(l)y European Grail which his speech, embroidered with the brocades of an old Portugal he so much admires, seeks to reinstate.

In Ascolino's case, therefore, I should wish to argue, hybridity, both racial and linguistic, expresses neither a Bakhtinian polemical dialogism of two different world views, nor a newly-synthesized one, nor even the radical mimicry of a discourse thereby disauthorized *à la* Bhabha. It conveys merely the nostalgia for a homogeneous, monologic, monodimensional, univocal, old Portugueseness anchored, as I shall go on to suggest, in a mythical Greek cradle or origin, through the plumbing of the epic, Homeric Antiquity which represents the cultural point of origin with which he would wish himself to be exclusively identified.

The conjugal tragedy of Ascolino and Dona Epifânia is flippantly allusive to a series of European wifely elopements, from Helen of Troy to the Arthurian Guinevere. This present-day Indian/African Helen, however, does not escape to the arms of any visible lover, compensating for this lack by taking the kitchen sink with her on the back of a lorry, and leaving her Menelaus dispossessed of wife, goods and chattels. The previous allusions to Viriato and to associated pre-historic Lusitanian episodes of resistance against Roman colonizers (those colonizers, incidentally, who more than any other shaped the language which Ascolino now worships), and to medieval or renaissance crusades in the name of the European fatherland, culminate here in the *opera bufa* of this comic Iliad, and in the spectacle of a skinny-legged Menelaus headed for the walls of Troy. He travels unheroically on a rickety bicycle pushed by an impatient servant, urged on by the afflicted husband variously preoccupied with the necessity of recovering his wife in time to imbibe his five o'clock whisky in Meneses's Bar Viriato:

> E o empregado prepara os assentos. No quadro, sem almofada,
> se senta o patrão. No selim, o criado. E começam a bicicletar,

estrada fora. O sulco da roda vai-se desfiando na manhã. Já nem sequer o ruído do camião se sente nos arrozais em volta. Ascolino, vice-rei, comanda a impossível cruzada para resgatar a esposa perdida.

—Pedal, pedal depresse. Não obstante, temos que chegar cedo. Hora de cinco hora temos que voltar na cantina de Meneses.

(81–82)

Vasco, himself the downgraded version of that Vasco da Gama who led the Portuguese to India, leads Ascolino in a reversal of that epic route: a route here mimicked, and deheroicized, by this reduced-scale Vasco who now leads India—in the person of Ascolino—on a failed quest for those European (Portuguese, Greek) roots (the Homeric lost wife), before which the latter willingly bows. Thus Viriato, the crusades, the Trojan war, the mapping of the Portuguese sea-borne empire, all the old feats, mythical and historical, are hereby reduced to un-noble proportions by Ascolino, no longer, even in his own imagination, a viceroy, but only vicedead,[19] a man whose identity has been truly lost, set adrift, appropriately *at sea*, in the wreckage of a dubious colonial adventure of which he himself is the sorry detritus.

If Ascolino is the unstable hybrid in search of an original homogeneity only attainable at the price of discarding the Indian half of himself, his flight to an epic mythical Greece, or to a conquering Portuguese empire, or to a medieval Christian crusade, is the flight back to any number of misconceived cultural departure points for the European in himself: a hypothetical self for which he opts in preference to the Indian or the Mozambican, in a dysphoric reach towards a lost, illusory, pre-hybridic origin, before a hypothetical Portuguese paternal sperm, embarking upon oceanic and territorial conquests, fertilized (or cross-fertilized) a racially different maternal egg. That original, pre-fecundation, pre-embryonic white self is targeted by Ascolino as the point from which he can begin to rewrite himself as exclusively European. However, the desire to do so entails the denial of the mixed-race consequences of the Portuguese imperial saga in which paradoxically he glories (as a loyal Portuguese patriot), while simultaneously seeking to elide precisely the miscegenation resulting from that saga, and which gave rise to his own hybrid Indo-Portuguese, or Goan, or 'darkie' being.

For Ascolino, therefore, the hybridity of his Indo-Portuguese position does not present itself as an acceptable option. But the alternative, the reinvention of the self as non-hybrid (white), simultaneously betrays the quest for radical Otherness, and results in the lampooning of the heroic myth hereby re-rendered as dystopian farce: the wrath of Achilles at the walls of Troy is rewritten as the drunkenness of Ascolino, and the ten-year-long siege is revised as a mission of marital recovery which must, 'notwithstanding, however, nevertheless, perforce',[20] be concluded by five o'clock, in time for the opening of the bar.

Homi Bhabha talks about the 'range of culturally and racially marginalized groups [which] readily assume the mask of the Black not to deny their diversity but to audaciously announce the important artifice of cultural identity and its difference'.[21] When Ascolino dons and then discards the mantle of Indo-Portugueseness, or of the 'caneco' or mulatto or darkie or white crusader or epic hero, he does so not audaciously, or achievingly, but rather fearfully and tentatively. His uncertain yearning is non-radical fissure, unprofitable dislocation, most emphatically *not* an illustration of Bhabha's slippery interstitial third space, which, according to the latter, is the stage upon which might be enacted the ongoing spectacle of a discontinuity of categories of racial and cultural identity.[22] Ascolino's precarious sense of self does not render the fluidity of his identity destabilizing, but merely shows it to be itself unstable. It *may*, possibly, be interpreted as reflecting back at and commenting upon a twentieth-century Portugal still nostalgic for its sea-faring past, and upon the reality of the present postcolonial economic dead-end which was the historical and political outcome of that colonial past. This, possibly, is the moral effect of the snapshot of Ascolino, the shipwreck of one imperial possession (India), stranded in the ruins of another (Mozambique), the latter a country still attempting to settle the invoice of misery the colonial experiment left behind. But that reflection, involuntary on the part of Ascolino himself, coexists, undeniably and demoralizingly, with a regressive yearning back to an imagined primordial state of purified, essentializing categories, and particularly the category of a whiteness which is also unrepentantly colonially driven to 'reconquer the name of Goa for Portuguese usage'.[23] Ascolino's frame of mind, therefore, still and enduringly gestures towards the two separate, disparate, anti-dialectical points of origin (black/white, Indian/white) of the—as it turns out, unsynthesized—hybrid, and reinstates, too, their coterminous territories of political and colonial power and powerlessness.

Ascolino's longing, then, is the ultimate reactionary, aggressor-identified trajectory of the man whose imitation of the European model to which he remains subservient is the best form of flattery. And, postcolonially, it is at best cold comfort that the impetus he personifies, and which so persistently eulogizes the aped, idolized European, Greek, Homeric, conquering model, is after all a flawed simulacrum which, as Baudrillard suggests, in the end assassinates the original model, through the revelation of its own inadequacies, in the brutal carnival of this comic and tragic diaspora.

I would like to conclude with a series of points regarding some linguistic aspects of Mia Couto's work, departing from the assumption that, in the case of this writer, the linguistic becomes willy-nilly political. His position as undoubtedly the foremost writer in post-independence Mozambique, and one moreover of considerable international projection, raises of course questions regarding whom he might speak *for* and *to*. Mozambique, as stated previously, is a country in which twenty years of civil war had, among other effects, that of creating over one million refugees in neighbouring Anglophone countries. With the advent of peace came the return of a generation of these homebound war exiles, for whom Portuguese possibly never was, but in any case certainly is not now, the official language, much less the mother tongue. As regards the rest of the population, their relationship to language, any language, continues to be one of largely pragmatic, unliterary usage and of orality (illiteracy rates in Mozambique running at an estimated 95%). Against this background Mia Couto's virtuoso deployment of Portuguese, with all its foregrounding of linguistic play, neologism, syntactical and grammatical challenges and punning word games, begs questions as to where these exhibitions of highly skilled manipulation and subversion of the language leave the reality of generalized linguistic accessibility in his ostensible (Mozambican) reality.

Linguistic enrichment, and the stretching of the limits of a language which is after all that of the colonizer, but, so innovated by the input of the colonized voice as to amount to a transgression (or Bakhtinian dialogization) of that European voice, is already an established trait of Mozambican writing under and after colonialism. The dense introduction of Ronga and Kimbundu terms by José Craveirinha and Luandino Vieira in Mozambique and Angola respectively, might be said to have offered, textually, an obstacle to European penetration (comprehension), which became a political but also a very concrete correlative of military, physical resistance to territorial occupation. *Não passarás*. Therefore, whatever the sources, allegiances and motivations behind Mia Couto's undeniable linguistic originality, upon which so many critics have commented[24]—be they rooted in a neo-Romantic drive towards innovation, or in indigenous input, or in a throwback reference to the Portugese medieval *estilo engenhoso*, or simply in personal idiosyncrasy—language as an exercise in power, both by the author himself, and within the textual worlds he brings into existence, becomes a pressing consideration.

When, in 'O último aviso do corvo falador',[25] Mia Couto tells us that the chatty eponymous raven of this story speaks with a bad accent but with conviction, he is alluding partly to the power *of* language and partly to power *over* language, as crucial in the process of carving out personal and national realities. In Ascolino's re-scripted African picaresque, language first, and then loss of control over it, determine his precarious hold over identity, and subsequent fall and disintegration. It is through language that he is successively demoted from Indo-Portuguese to Goan and then to 'darkie', and from viceroy to vicedead. Language is that which makes him ('se no viver era calado, no falar se levantava' [74]), and then breaks him. And some political significance, therefore, must be supposed to be invested, albeit not in a straightforward manner, in a literary style such as that of Mia Couto, which clearly emerges as inaccessible, in all its punning agility and neologistic revisionism, to any except the highly educated, literary sophisticated, *native speakers* of Portuguese. It is beautiful. But is it Mozambican? Who is Mia Couto (himself a curious hybrid, a white, culturally European writer, but the holder, emotionally and bureaucratically, of a Mozambican passport)? Who is he addressing? Who is his intended audience? Who does he claim to speak for? Speak with? Who should speak? Who will listen?

Notes

1   The acronym for Frente de Libertação de Moçambique.

2   Resistência Nacional de Moçambique.

3   Mia Couto in interview with Nelson Saúte. 'Mia Couto: Disparar contra o tempo', *Jornal de Letras, Artes e Ideias*, XII, 549 (12–18 January 1992), 9.

4   Mia Couto, *Vozes Anoitecidas* (Lisbon: Editorial Caminho, 1987).

5   Mia Couto, 'O dia em que explodiu Mabata-bata', *Vozes Anoitecidas*, 45–54.

6   Mia Couto, 'Os pássaros de Deus', *Vozes Anoitecidas*, 55–64.

7   Mia Couto, 'De como se vazou a vida de Ascolino do Perpétuo Socorro', *Vozes Anoitecidas*, 65–82.

8   Homi Bhabha, 'Remembering Fanon', in *Colonial Discourse and Postcolonial Theory: A Reader*, ed. Patrick Williams and Laura Chrisman (New York and London: Harvester Wheatsheaf, 1993), 112–23.

9   Firdous Azim, *The Colonial Rise of the Novel* (London and New York: Routledge, 1993), 11.

10 Azim, *The Colonial Rise of the Novel*, 12.

11 'Darkie' is the term used by David Brookshaw to translate 'caneco' and 'monhé'. *Voices Made Night*, trans. David Brookshaw (Oxford: Heineman, 1990), 37.

12 See, for example, Bernardo Guimarães, *A Escrava Isaura* (Mem-Martins: Europa-América, 1978). For a discussion of the figure of the mulatta in North-American abolitionist literature, see also Barbara Christian, 'Shadows Uplifted', in *Feminist Criticism and Social Change: Sex, Class and Race in Literature and Culture*, ed. Judith Newton and Deborah Rosenfelt (New York and London: Methuen, 1985), 181–215.

13 Afrânio Coutinho, *A Filosofia de Machado de Assis* (Rio de Janeiro: Vecchi, 1940) (my translation).

14 Manuel Ferreira, 'Da dor de ser negro ao orgulho de ser preto', *Colóquio Letras*, 39 (September 1977), 25–26 (my translation).

15 Robert J. C. Young, *Colonial Desire: Hybridity in Theory, Culture and Race* (London and New York: Routledge, 1995), 3.

16 Young, *Colonial Desire*, 3.

17 Gayatri Chakravorti Spivak in interview with Sneja Gunew, in *Gayatri Chakravorty Spivak, the Postcolonial Critic: Interviews, Strategies, Dialogues*, ed. Sarah Harasym (New York and London: Routledge, 1990), 59.

18 Knox, quoted in Young, *Colonial Desire*, 15.

19 'Vicemorto' in the original is translated by Brookshaw as 'in surrogate death'. *Voices Made Night*, 35.

20 Brookshaw's translation. *Voices Made Night*, 29. In the original, 'não obstante, porém, todavia, contudo'. *Vozes Anoitecidas*, 68.

21 Bhabha, 'Remembering Fanon', 122.

22 Homi Bhabha, 'The Commitment to Theory', *New Formations*, 5 (1988), 13.

23 Brookshaw's translation. *Voices Made Night*, 35. In the original, 'recuperar o nome de Goa para uso português'. *Vozes Anoitecidas*, 75.

24 See, for example, José Craveirinha, Preface to the Portuguese edition, *Vozes Anoitecidas*, 10.

25 Mia Couto, 'O último aviso do corvo falador', *Vozes Anoitecidas*, 31–44.

Index

acculturation, 149–53
Achugar, Hugo, 96 n.3, 171–72
Adán, Martín, 82, 84, 86, 100 n.35, 108, 109
Alonso, Carlos J., 35–36
Amaral, Aracy, 52
Americanism, 119, 123, 131, 132
Angola, 5, 9, 10–11, 12, 152, 209
Arciniegas, Germán, 14, 24 n.4, 26 n.19,
Arguedas, José María, 109
Azim, Firdous, 196

Bakhtin, 70, 109, 204, 209
barbarism, 54–60, 63–66, 72–75; as antonym of civilisation, 17–18, 51–53, 134–36; as antonym of imagination, 17, 51–52, 55–57, 74
baroque, Caribbean, 179–80, 182, 190 n.26
Baudrillard, 196, 208
Belluzzo, Ana María, 62
Benítez Rojo, Antonio, 26 n.21, 159
Bergson, Henri, 85, 87
Bhabha, Homi, 7, 15, 21, 72, 119, 161, 171, 172, 173–75, 186, 207; on cultural translation, 63–64; on Fanon, 183; as theorist of colonial subjectivity, 22, 196–97, 204; *The Location of Culture*, 63–64, 173, 175
Borges, Jorge Luis, 67–68
Brazil, viii, 12, 18, 41, 59, 60, 61, 71, 185
Breton, André, 170
Burton, Richard, D. E., 184–85

Cabral, Amílcar, viii, 5, 9, 10, 13, 15, 20, 138 n.10, 158
Caliban, dialectic of, 14, 135–36
Cândido, Antonio, 41–42
Carpentier, Alejo, 15, 20–21, 153; and Fanon, 20–21, 169–85; *La música en Cuba*, 153–54; *El reino de este mundo*, 174; *El siglo de las luces*, 20, 21, 169–86
Caso, Antonio, 122
Césaire, Aimé, viii, 8, 13, 14, 15, 21, 124, 138 n.9, 170, 182; author of a new humanism, 128; identified with Negritude, 14, 130; quoted by Leopoldo Zea, 127; *Cahier d'un retour au pays natal*, 170; *Discours sur le colonialisme*, 125, 135
Chabal, Patrick, viii, 10–13
Chanady, Amaryll, 25 n.17
Chiampi, Irlemar, 61–62
Chile, 41

Clifford, James, 30, 32, 35, 37
Colombia, 18, 53, 57–58, 62
colonialism, vii, 2, 5, 52–53, 74, 79, 119, 121, 130, 185; the American experience of, 2, 4; British in India and Africa, 1, 172; distinguished from imperialism, 123; diversity of African experience of, 10–12; European, 126, 141; French, psychological impact of, 172; internal, 42; of the mind, 11, 18, 52, 60, 63, 64, 68; Portuguese, 193, 209
Cornejo Polar, Antonio, 18, 80, 92–94, 95, 104
Coronil, Fernando, 159–60
Coutinho, Afrânio, 60–61, 202
Couto, Mia, 16, 21–23, 191–212; approach to myth in narrative, 192–95; linguistic aspects of works, 208–10; 'O dia em que explodiu Mabata bata', 193–94; 'De como se vazou a vida Ascolino do Perpétuo Socorro', 196–208; 'O último aviso do corvo falador', 209–10; *Vozes Anoitecidas*, 192
Cuba, 4, 5, 15, 60, 125, 141–61, 185
Cuban Revolution, ix, 4–5, 12, 16, 19, 44, 124–26

Darío, Rubén, 108
de Andrade, Mário, 18, 53, 68, 70, 73–74; *Macunaíma*, 70–74
de Campos, Haroldo, 2, 14, 16, 66, 70
decolonization, viii, 2, 5, 12, 53, 129; Latin America in global context of, 19, 119, 126; of the mind, ix, 13; of the Third World, ix; messages of, conveyed through translation, 53
Derrida, Jacques, 63, 174
de Souza, Eneida Maria, 70
Dussel, Enrique, 6, 7, 8, 119, 127

Eguren, José María, 108
emancipation, of the mind, 122
Espinosa, Germán, 57

Fanon, Frantz, viii, 4, 8, 9, 15, 21, 64, 119, 172; compared with Carpentier, 21, 169–85; compared with Ortiz, 20; connections with Leopoldo Zea, 125, 127–29; on remembrance writing, 143; *Peau noir, masques blancs*, 5, 20, 158, 170, 171, 175, 176, 182–83, 184, 185; *The Wretched of the Earth/Les damnés de la terre*, 127, 128, 184
Fernández Retamar, Roberto, viii, 4, 5, 14, 17, 52, 54–55, 125, 135, 137–38 n.9, 138 n.10
Ferreira, Manuel, 203
Ferro, Roberto, 69
Foucault, Michel, 173, 174
Franco, Jean, viii, 97, 148
FRELIMO, 191
Fuentes, Carlos, 15, 17, 26 n.22, 55–56, 58, 170

Galeano, Eduardo, 2, 15, 19, 23–24 n.3, 54
García Canclini, Néstor, 18, 97 n.5, 105, 153, 158, 167 n.38, 171
García Márquez, 123, 170

Genocchio, Ben, 160
Glissant, Edouard, viii, 4, 119
González, Aníbal, 67–68
González Echevarría, Roberto, 169, 187 n.5
González Prada, Manuel, 109, 110
Guatemala, 186

Hernández, José: *Martín Fierro*, 55
Herskovits, Melville: *Acculturation: The Study of Cultural Contact*, 149
heterogeneity, concept of, 104, 106
Hulme, Peter, viii, 24 n.6; 'Including America', 3–6
humanism, 131, 132, 136–37, 175, 177; revised concept of, 15, 127–29, 130; Western traditional tenets of, 180
hybridity, 14, 25 n.16 & n.17, 160, 196, 203, 207; linguistic, 204–05
hybridization, Caribbean theory of, 21, 179–82; in Cuba, 151, 161; processes of in Latin America, 160, 181; as strategy for resisting the force of hegemonic cultures, 172, 179, 181

imperialism, 6, 123, 125, 126, 135, 155, 161; binary logic of, 9; cultural, 11; legacy of Portuguese, 197; US global, 53, 142
indigenismo, ix, 14, 18, 19, 60, 80, 91–92, 94, 110; compared with Negritude, 129–34; literary, 104, 108–09, 114

James, C. L. R., 4, 6, 173
Jitrik, Noé, 69–70
Juárez, Benito, 132

Kadir, Djelal, 16
Keats, John, 65–67
Key Concepts in Post-colonial Studies, 20, 25 n.17, 167 n.41
Klor de Alva, Jorge, vii, 1–2, 3, 4, 13, 23 n.1, 133–34
Kohut, Karl, 17, 52, 56–60, 74
Kusch, Rodolfo, 6

Lamming, George, 4
Larsen, Neal, 40, 96 n.1
Latin American Subaltern Studies Group, 39–40, 49 n.18
Lenin, V. I., 123, 142, 161 n.2
Liberation, Philosophy of, 15, 126–28
Lisboa, João Francisco, 69
Lombroso, Cesare, 144, 146, 163 n.13
Loomba, Ania, 2, 5

Machado, Gerardo, 142, 155
Malinowski, Bronislaw, 50 n.23, 144, 146, 147–48, 149, 153; Preface to *Contrapunteo cubano del tabaco y del azúcar* (Ortiz), 144, 149–50, 156, 163 n.19 & n.20
'Manifest Destiny', 122, 151
Mannoni, Octave, 175
Mariátegui, José Carlos, 2, 7, 8, 16, 18, 79–102, 104, 108, 132, 171; on *indigenismo*, 91–95; on nationalism, 90–95; reflections on myth, 85, 87–90;

as reformulator of Marxism, 43–44; and surrealism, 83–84, 86, 87; 'Arte, revolución y decadencia', 89; 'El hombre y el mito', 88–89; 'Nacionalismo y vanguardismo en la literatura y en el arte', 90, 91; 'El proceso de la literatura', 80, 90, 92, 94; *Siete ensayos de la realidad peruana*, 80, 92, 95,
Martí, José, 2, 19, 61–62, 107–08, 123, 136, 171
marxism, reformulated in Latin America, 43–44; relation of Mariátegui to, 80–82, 84–85, 87
McGuirk, Bernard, 68
Melis, Antonio, 80, 84–86, 87
Memmi, Albert, 59, 128–29
Menchú, Rigoberta, 186
mestizaje, ix, 14, 25 n.16, 52, 157, 181; category different from *métissage*, 14; as ideology, 18, 19, 92, 131, 133–34
Mexico, 2, 15, 37, 38, 125, 133, 186
Mignolo, Walter, viii, 3, 119; 'La razón postcolonial: herencias coloniales y teorías postcoloniales', 6–9
Mintz, Sydney, 154, 156–57
Modernism(s), European, 160; Latin American, 17, 52–53, 62, 64, 107
modernismo, 107, 108, 110, 153
modernity (Western), 7, 79, 105–06, 127, 159, 173; alternative models and experiences of, 104, 110; critiqued by Vallejo, 112; cultural, 181; dominant paradigms of, 14–15; Latin American relations with, 31, 35–36, 38; singular temporality of, 107, 113
Moreno-Durán, Rafael Humberto, 17, 52, 55–57
Morse, Richard, 135–36
Mozambique, 9, 10–11, 152, 191–93, 197, 198–200, 202, 207, 208–09
mulatto, 202–03, 207

Negritude, viii, 12, 14, 19; and *indigenismo*, 129–34
neocolonialism, 141, 142
Neruda, Pablo, 123
Neto, Agostinho, 9

Ortega, Julio, 112
Ortiz, Fernando, 13, 14, 16, 20, 44, 50 n.23, 141–61; compared to Fanon and Cabral, 20; *La africanía de la música folklórica de Cuba*, 145–46, 166 n.37; 'Los cabildos afrocubanos', 147; *Contrapunteo cubano del tabaco y del azúcar*, 144, 148, 151–52, 154, 159, 160, 164 n.21, 168 n.49; *Entre cubanos: psicología tropical*, 155; *Hampa afrocubana: los negros brujos (apuntes para un estudio de etnología criminal)*, 144, 145, 146, 147; *Los negros brujos*, see *Hampa afrocubana: los negros brujos (apuntes para un estudio de etnología criminal)*; 'Las supervivencias africanas en Cuba', 146
Osborne, Peter, 110

Palmié, Stephan, 157, 163 n.18
Pan-Africanism, 13
Pan-Americanism, 13
Pau Brasil Manifesto, 60–61
Pérez Firmat, Gustavo, 28, 159, 160, 167 n.45
Peru, 2, 15, 18, 19, 43, 87, 89, 90, 93, 94, 104–06, 108–11
postcolonial, characterization and definition of, 2, 4–5, 7–8, 30, 36, 38, 41, 45, 75, 141 ; discourses, 8–9, 29–30
Poveda, José María, 155
Pratt, Mary Louise, viii, 158

Rama, Angel, 53, 60, 158
RENAMO, 191, 194
Ribeiro, Darcy, 2, 24 n.3
Richard, Nelly, viii, 32–33, 38, 42–43
Rodó, José Enrique, 2, 14, 61–62, 122, 171
Rowe, William, 88

Said, Edward, 8, 13, 15, 32, 47, 171, 172–73, 186, 189 n.17; on travelling theory, 34–35; *Culture and Imperialism*, viii; *Orientalism*, 172, 175
Salas y Ferré, Manuel, 144, 146, 155
Salazar Bondy, Augusto, 127
Sánchez, Luis Alberto, 91
Santiago, Silviano, 71, 75
Sarlo, Beatriz, 62
Sarmiento, Domingo Faustino, 6, 51, 54–55, 58, 73, 131–32, 171
Sartre, Jean-Paul, 122, 126
Schwarz, Roberto, viii, 33, 43, 71

Sédar Senghor, Leopold, viii, 5, 10, 14, 24–25 n.11, 124, 127, 128, 130
Sorel, Georges, 85, 86, 87
Spencer, Herbert, 144, 147
Spivak, Gayatri, 7, 8, 22, 48 n.6, 171, 186, 204
subaltern, 40, 112, 131, 132, 143, 151, 156
syncretism(s), 14, 26 n.21, 149, 151–52, 203

Terán, Oscar, 86, 87
Thénon, Susana, 68
Third World, ix, 12, 31, 35, 137, 170–71, 175
transculturation, 14, 16–17, 20, 21, 28, 31, 37, 44–45, 143, 146, 148–60
translation, as cultural phenomenon, 53, 63–70; and the expression of postcolonial subjectivities, 64, 68–69; intralingual, 67–70; and parody, 69–71; political significance of, 18

Unamuno, Miguel de, 155
universal, in tension with the local, 15, 36–37, 176; set up in opposition to nationalism, 39

Valencia, Guillermo, 18, 53, 64–67
Vallejo, César, 16, 19, 103–17; 'Telúrica y magnética', 114–15; *Trilce*, 19, 106, 111–13
Vasconcelos, José, 14, 19, 123, 132; *La raza cósmica*, 133

Vaz de Caminha, Pero, 59, 68, 71; 'Carta pras Icamiabas', 71–74

Whitman, Walt, 107, 113

Young, Robert, ix, 166 n.36, 187 n.5, 203, 204

Zea, Leopoldo, 5, 7, 8, 9, 16, 19, 119–39; and Fanon, 127–29; *América latina y el mundo*, 124–26; *Dependencia y liberación en la cultura latinoamericana*, 126–34; *Discurso desde la marginación y la barbarie*, 134–37; *Filosofar a la altura del hombre*, 120–21; *La filosofía como compromiso*, 122; 'La filosofía como compromiso', 122, 126; 'La filosofía latinoamericana como filosofía de liberación', 127–28; 'Norteamérica en la conciencia hispanoamericana', 121; *El positivismo en México*, 121